Language Skills
for Journalists

$1295

Language Skills for Journalists

Second Edition

R. Thomas Berner
School of Journalism
The Pennsylvania State University

Houghton Mifflin Company   Boston
Dallas   Geneva, Illinois
Hopewell, New Jersey   Palo Alto

Acknowledgments

The author gratefully acknowledges the following sources for their permission to use copyrighted material.

CHAPTER 2 **Pages 28–29:** Bill Welch, "Drama on Eve of Holiday," *Centre Daily Times,* 29 August 1969. Reprinted by permission.
CHAPTER 3 **Page 70:** "These parts . . . adjectives." © 1969, Houghton Mifflin Company. Reprinted by permission from *The American Heritage Dictionary of the English Language.* **Page 75:** Red Smith, "Guess What's Happening to Baseball," *New York Times,* 22 November 1976. © 1976 by The New York Times Company. Reprinted by permission.
CHAPTER 5 **Page 123:** "Notes on People," *New York Times,* 4 December 1976. © 1976 by The New York Times Company. Reprinted by permission.
CHAPTER 7 **Pages 182–183:** Definitions of *bee, copulate, neighborhood.* © 1969, Houghton Mifflin Company. Reprinted by permission from *The American Heritage Dictionary of the English Language.* **Page 183:** Charles E. Little, "Atlanta Renewal Gives Poor to Communities," *Smithsonian* magazine, July 1976. Copyright 1976 Smithsonian Institution, from *Smithsonian* magazine. **Page 184:** Jean Stafford, "At This Point in Time, TV Is Murdering the English Language," *New York Times,* 15 September 1974. © 1974 by The New York Times Company. Reprinted by permission. **Pages 185–186:** H. L. Mencken, *The American Language, Fourth Edition.* (New York: Alfred A. Knopf, Inc.) Copyright 1946. **Page 190:** Emily Dickinson, poem #1651, from *The Poems of Emily Dickinson.* (Cambridge, Mass.: The Belknap Press of Harvard University Press.) Reprinted by permission of the publishers and the Trustees of Amherst College from *The Poems of Emily Dickinson,* edited by Thomas H. Johnson. Copyright 1951, © 1955, 1979, 1983 by the President and Fellows of Harvard College. **Page 198:** William Borders, "Intensive Campaign Draws Many to Vasectomy," *New York Times,* 22 November 1976. © 1976 by The New York Times Company. Reprinted by permission. **Page 198:** William K. Stevens, "General Motors Cuts Size of Cars," *New York Times,* 22 November 1976. © 1976 by The New York Times Company. Reprinted by permission.

Cover Photo: James Scherer
On the cover is the latest in remote bureau systems from Atex, Inc., the leading manufacturer of text processing publishing systems. The Atex 500 workstation is a stand-alone system for reporters and editors to use for text entry and editing. This workstation offers much of the functionality of the sophisticated Atex systems in use at some of the largest newspapers and magazines around the world.

Printed in the U.S.A.

ISBN: 0-395-34098-5

Library of Congress Catalog Card Number: 83-82323

BCDEFGHIJ-H-8987654

This book is dedicated to Karen, Tracey and Amy, who appreciate my efforts.

Contents

Chapter 5
Modification   115

Chapter 6
Punctuation   145

Preface

Life is nothing more than a first edition, and we get no opportunity to improve on it with a second. Textbooks, on the other hand, don't necessarily imitate life, and the wise author eagerly embraces the opportunity to revise a first edition. This revision provides an opportunity to incorporate suggestions and advice given by journalism education colleagues from many different institutions.

New to This Edition

Two new features in this second edition of *Language Skills for Journalists* are self-diagnostic tests and review exercises. The self-diagnostic tests appear at frequent intervals throughout chapters. They test students on material they've read, allowing students to accumulate knowledge in a way that also helps them retain what they've learned. Because the self-diagnostic tests appear frequently, they allow users to establish a comfortable learning pace. In Chapter 2, for example, lessons on subjects and verbs and traditional sentence patterns are reinforced through self-diagnostic tests that appear near the beginning of the chapter. Several pages later, students are tested on subordinate clauses and then on identifying types of sentences. Four more self-diagnostic tests dot the remainder of Chapter 2. Other chapters are similarly organized.

Review exercises appear at the back of the book, and consist of twelve separate exercises, ten sentences in each. They are designed to evaluate cumulatively students' knowledge of grammar and writing skills treated in the book. The sentences are cross-referenced to the text so that students can identify and correct errors by reviewing points of grammar. The exercises offer such variety that a student may be tested on the principles of modification, subject-verb agreement and parallel construction all within one sentence. We have used these cross-referenced exercises at Penn State since shortly after the first edition of *Language Skills for Journalists* was published, and the student response has been favorable. Since we use the book as a supplement in a beginning newswriting and reporting class, we believe that the review exercises fit in with the book's supplemental role and allow us to focus the course on our main purpose—teaching beginning newswriting and reporting.

A number of changes have been implemented to make the book easier to use as a reference. The book has been re-designed with more prominent and more frequent headings. For example, twenty-six subheads help the student find specific help in the section on the comma. The glossary, new to this edition, is basic, simple and functional. Not only are terms defined, but examples of usage are also given. The spelling chapter has been replaced by a list of frequently misspelled words. The appendix "Other Language Tips," written before the current alphabetized news agency stylebook was published, has been dropped.

A Practical Book

This is a practical book for journalists and journalism students. It provides ways of dealing with common language problems by presenting a multitude of examples from journalistic writing and by providing many exercises for practice. My purpose in writing this book is to help make students sensitive to how the English language operates so that they can use it more effectively. In short, this book is for people who think about language and love to use it to its maximum effectiveness.

My approach is both functional and traditional. I prefer that the students using the text learn the function of our language rather than some ancient rule. I have tried to illustrate not only rules themselves but the reasons why they exist. If students learn why something is done, they will learn more quickly and retain the knowledge.

While many examples adhere to news agency style, I have discovered that style sometimes depends on whether the writing is done on a typewriter or a video display terminal. A VDT, for example, allows journalists to italicize book titles, which was not always the case before the more versatile electronic newsroom. I italicize book titles in the text—which is book style—but not in the examples—which is news agency style. I've tried to make every example adhere to style as recommended by the Associated Press and United Press International. The differences in style and, in some cases, usage can make excellent teaching points. They are, I like to think, points of creative tension. They force students to think and to make judgments, and no editor should complain about that result.

Students should be encouraged at the beginning to take the language usage test in the back of the book. That way, they will have an idea of their strengths and be able to define goals for using this book.

Grammar and the Journalist

Grammar is not a sexy topic. "Investigative journalism" sounds exciting; "grammar" doesn't. But grammar describes the writing and the speaking characteristics of a people. And journalism students should realize that if they want their stories read or listened to, they must adhere to their readers' and listeners' conventions of grammar.

I tell my students that the subject isn't as formidable as they believe. After all, I point out, you have been learning grammar since you were a child. As you learned to speak, you imitated your parents and other people close to you. You formed sentences you had never heard anyone speak—and they were, for the most part, grammatically correct, yet nobody told you a subject is followed by a verb is followed by an object, and so on. This book provides the bridge between the student's learning to date and the accepted patterns of usage that will carry the student into the future. This book provides routes to effective language skills.

Acknowledgments

Many of the examples in this book come from newspapers, magazines and the newscasts of radio and television stations. Many of their editors permitted me to reprint work, and I appreciate that. Also helpful were the colleagues who provided me with examples or served as sounding boards for ideas. Two colleagues I would especially like to acknowledge are John N. Rippey and H. Eugene Goodwin. The three of us have wrestled with devising sensible language skills tests for our students, and I have borrowed from our joint efforts in order to create the language usage test. These two colleagues also offered useful suggestions for the glossary.

Also helpful were the journalism instructors who commented on this edition's manuscript and guided me in making useful changes. Manuscript review, although sometimes painful for an author, remains a constructive way of helping to produce textbooks that benefit their users. My deepest appreciation goes to Samuel J. Archibald, University of Colorado at Boulder; Thomas A. Bowers, The University of North Carolina at Chapel Hill; Sharon S. Brock, The Ohio State University; Merritt Christensen, University of Wisconsin-Eau Claire; Wilbur L. Doctor, University of Rhode Island; Pat Flynn, University of Southern Mississippi; Mary Connelly Graff, Temple University; Larry J. Horney, Ball State University; Paul Jess, The University of Kansas; Carol Lindell-Hoyt, Lewis & Clark College; Thomas B. Littlewood, University of Illinois at Champaign-Urbana; Howard L. Seeman, Humboldt State University; Michael Sewell, Texas Wesleyan College; Bruce M. Swain, The University of Georgia; and Herschel M. Wilson, Humboldt State University. I cannot say enough about the six English teachers who helped shape my attitude toward the language during the years I was in junior high and high school. Rarely can a person boast of having had six good English teachers. I hope my children are half as lucky.

My students in news writing, reporting and editing also helped me revise this book. Two other young people who have contributed on a regular basis are my daughters, Tracey and Amy, whom I have the pleasure of closely observing as their language skills grow.

Finally, I want to thank Gerry Lynn Hamilton, a colleague who edited the first edition and thereby reduced my workload for the second. No writer is above the pencil, and it is a pleasure when one knows a good editor is reading his copy.

To everyone, I hope you find this edition of *Language Skills for Journalists* a practical and useful book. If you have comments or suggestions, please write to me % Marketing Services, Houghton Mifflin Company, One Beacon Street, Boston, MA 02108.

R.T.B.

Language Skills
for Journalists

Chapter 1

Writing

How to Write Better

No book can provide an easy formula a person can follow to become a good writer. Good writing is difficult; it is a labor of love. Most good writers say writing is the hardest thing they do. Some good writers hate to write because it is so difficult. Fortunately, the rewards make it worthwhile. Still, words do not just fall upon a piece of paper in their clearest and most logical sequence. The writer must arrange them that way. The writer must be able to take two positions at the same time—that of the reporter of the event and that of the reader or listener of the report. Ultimately the reader or listener must be satisfied. Good writing makes reading effortless. Reader-focused writing is the best. For the broadcast journalist, good writing is good talking, and the result is good listening.

Good writing is clear, concise and interesting. Some journalists add accurate to that list; fiction writers would probably substitute believable for accurate. Clear writing demands a clear mind. Think before you write. Organize in your mind what you want to say. That doesn't mean a word-by-word organization. It means you should be sure of the direction you want your story to go, and it means you must be the driver at all times. If you become a back-seat driver, your direction will suffer.

Organization and Word Choice

To write well, you must organize your thoughts, put them into the right compartments and build the compartments one after the other. Organization is a state of mind and a state of function. Usually, journalists write without benefit of formal organizational tools. They don't have time for extensive outlines, and even rough ones seem a waste of precious seconds when a deadline is fast approaching. Still, good journalists do not go into a story barren of thought. As the event they are covering unfolds, they are thinking of how to write about it. Good writers know that writing is more than putting words on a page. They know that good writing is a process of observing, digesting, thinking, explaining, and that the quality of one step affects the next.

1

The journalist has no choice but to think about writing the story as it is happening. Time is crucial to any editor, whose responsibility to get the paper out or the newscast on the air transcends any feelings that may be hurt in the process. Ideally, journalists should rewrite what they have written, but this is usually an impossibility. Nevertheless, it can be adjusted for by thinking thoroughly before writing. Good writing, for the most part, is rewriting; but journalists seldom have the time or energy to rewrite. That is why every thought they put into a story before beginning to write is important.

One useful way of organizing a story is according to the way it happens. However, because of journalistic writing's compact, direct nature, which is necessary for conveying the most information in the least amount of time, newswriting does not always follow that structure. The inverted presentation of information is the standard way of writing news stories today. Critics call it, with much disdain, *formula writing.* However, the detractors do not realize that all writing, be it fiction, magazine or television, has a formula. The formula is to tell the story in the most efficient and understandable way.

Organizing a story well is not the only method used to gain clarity. How you organize each sentence in the story is just as important. If you are having problems writing good sentences, the following advice applies particularly to you.

Keep your sentences short. Use active verbs. Use plain words. Avoid clever phrases. Short sentences convey your thoughts best. Short sentences cannot become bogged down with too many thoughts. The average length of good sentences is 20 words. All sentences are kept simple. The results can be very boring.

If you are having problems, start with the core of expression—the short sentence—and build from there to complex and compound sentences and combinations of both.

Use plain words and active verbs in short sentences. If your average sentence length is 20 words, you will see that you cannot put too many thoughts or ideas into one sentence. Because of that, short sentences carry your thoughts best. But short sentences also tend to be simple sentences (subject-verb-object) and can be very boring—sometimes better for putting someone to sleep than getting an idea across.

What I have just done, for the most part, is reworked a paragraph of short and simple sentences into a paragraph of complex sentences of varying structure and length. A writer finds it easier to build from the simple sentence to the complex (and compound and compound-complex) than to edit such sentences down into simpler ones. You can write short and simple sentences, then edit or revise them into suitable complex, compound and compound-complex sentences. Of course, you should retain some simple sentences. A mix of sentence types is the most effective.

You will enrich your writing by keeping your prose uncomplicated. Americans love their writing that way; they adore anyone who can make clear to them something complex. When the late Leon Jaworski, the special prosecutor of the Watergate scandal, wanted a lawyer to write the investigating team's report, he picked George Frampton, "a brilliant young lawyer with an analytical mind and *the ability to write clearly* [italics added]."

Plain words make for clear writing. As Benjamin Franklin wrote in the *Pennsylvania Gazette:* "To write *clearly,* not only the most expressive, but the plainest words should be chosen [Franklin's italics]." Use words your readers will understand; don't use pretentious or learned words when simple and plain ones will do the job.

Why would anyone obey a sign in a park that says: "Plucking or mutilating of flowers and plants is forbidden under law"? It's pretentious. Good writers are not pretentious. Avoid *utilize; use* is fine. *Capitulate* may make a potential enemy think twice, but if your present enemy has *surrendered,* your potential enemy will get the message. *Contusions* and *lacerations* are *bruises* and *cuts* everywhere but in hospitals. *Fractures* are *breaks,* be it of rocks or bones or broken homes (*fractured* homes!). And if you and your steady *terminate* your relationship, tell your friends you *ended* it, or better still, just say, "We broke up." Perhaps you'll say it happened because your steady became *corpulent,* which is a big way of saying *fat.* Some may doubt the *veracity* of your explanation; others will doubt its *truth.* They'll say you're *mendacious,* and if you are, then you've been *lying.* Perhaps the way you stated your position was not *lucid* to everyone; try again and make it *clear.* And if you *concur* with what I've said, just nod your head or say, "I agree."

Abstractions also diminish clarity. Do not write about improving *student-teacher ratio* when you want to say *reducing class size. Nourishment* may conjure up thoughts of a steak dinner, which would be misleading if the word you want is *apple,* which is more concrete than *fruit, food* or *nourishment.* According to Jack Cappon, the general news editor of the Associated Press, *presidency* is an abstraction; the president's name isn't. "A broader housing policy is an abstraction," Cappon writes. "Building 700 apartments for slum dwellers is not. . . . A health problem can be anything from an ingrown toenail to terminal cancer." Other abstractions on Cappon's list include: *confrontation, negative impact, sweeping changes, procedures, unduly alarmed.* Two other abstractions are *wide* as in *wide experience* and *vast* as in *vast majority.* Vague as those phrases are, they are doubly dangerous when used in broadcasting. Patient readers can study the printed word; listeners get only one chance—and if they hear a word wrong, they don't get a chance to hear it again.

The advice of a retired journalism professor, Charles H. Brown, applies here:

> The essential problem of news writing for any medium—the newspaper, the news magazine, radio, or television—lies in making the information instantly comprehensible to large numbers of people. It is not to delight with clever phrases, to charm with the mellifluous flow of language, or to transport beyond the real world to an imagined one: the art of news communication is the art of clear writing. Whatever other values the writing may have, it is bad writing from the viewpoint of the news communicator if it is not immediately clear.

Learning from Other Writers

Learning to write well involves, in part, imitating others who write well. I don't mean borrowing the phrases and words of other writers the way I did as a beginning sportswriter for a very small daily newspaper. My guidance until then had come from high school English teachers who did not teach newswriting. So I turned to a large daily newspaper to learn newswriting. One of that paper's sportswriters always referred to a basketball player I also wrote about as a "carrot-topped senior" (meaning he had red hair). I leaped on the phrase. I used it every time I could and even a few times when I shouldn't have. The lesson I missed was how sportswriters use descriptive phrases as a substitute for a person's name to avoid repetition. Instead I stole someone else's phrase (and it was trite to begin with) and made it my own. That is not imitating another's writing.

Read a lot of newspapers. I am amazed at the number of journalism students who have never seriously read newspapers until they entered journalism school and then have a hard time getting into the habit. But do not limit yourself to newspapers. Read other literature as well. See how the masters of our language used it to its best effect. Do not overlook the Bible. Its simplicity makes it one of the best written works in our culture. Its writers used no razzle-dazzle to explain the Creation

> And God said, Let there be light: and there was light. (Genesis 1:3)

or the flood that put Noah in his ark

> And the rain was upon the earth forty days and forty nights. (Genesis 7:12)

When John described the weeping of Jesus, he did not assault us with overwrought language, such as, "Tears poured quickly from the face of the Master; his face wet with the gush of his tears." Instead, John wrote:

> Jesus wept. (John 11:35)

When David kills the giant Goliath, readers of the Bible are treated to straight (that is, unemotional) reporting.

> And David put his hand in his bag, and took thence a stone, and slang it, and smote the Philistine in his forehead, that the stone sunk into his forehead; and he fell upon his face to the earth. (I Samuel 17:49)

A beginning writer may want to know who some of the good writers are. Any list would be personal and incomplete. Here is such a list, the names of writers I read not because of subject matter alone but also because I like the way they use the language or the way they construct an argument: E. B. White, George F. Will, Jessica Mitford, John McPhee, Jonathan Schell, David S. Broder, Frances Fitz-Gerald, Lewis Thomas, Norman Mailer, Tom Wolfe, Barbara W. Tuchman, Geoffrey Wolff, Tracy Kidder, Joseph P. Lash and Jack Kerouac.

The Critic

Having a good critic is another important part of learning to write well. Of course, criticism requires the writer to develop a thick skin, but writers benefit from good criticism. The best critic is a disinterested, dispassionate and uninvolved person— an editor. But when an editor isn't available, use your rommate or a friend. After all, you are trying to communicate with anyone who reads. Let your friend tell you if what you have written makes sense. Don't let your critic read it and say, ''It's fine.'' Ask your critic what you've said in your story. If you are a good writer and your critic is a conscientious reader, he or she will be able to tell you. Spouses and parents are good critics, too. Your family and relatives know good writing. They may not know how to write well, but they certainly know what they like and understand. Good critics don't need a portfolio of college degrees. If you feel they do, your writing probably reflects your mistaken attitude, which readers will grasp just before they stop reading.

Self-criticism is as important as having a good critic. Self-criticism is the most ego-smashing thing you will ever do. Nothing destroys you more (or so you'll feel) than to tear apart your own work and redo it. But you cannot fall in love with what you write. Love your writing as you would your child, but correct it when it's wrong no matter how painful that may be. Don't be afraid to whip sentences into shape when wholesale revision is the only cure. Don't be bashful about changing a word or two—or even discarding some. Do it with as much honesty as you can muster. It is better that you put your work into the best possible shape; only you and your ego know about it and feel the pain. When an editor needs to make frequent revisions, it reveals a careless or uncaring writer, one the editor will quickly lose interest in.

Learning to write well is like learning to type well; it requires practice, practice, practice. Write and revise, and write some more. When writing, compose on a typewriter or video display terminal, which will give you the advantage of practicing two skills at once. As a journalist you will go to a typewriter or video display terminal better prepared for the pressure of deadlines if you have practiced extensively. If you have disciplined yourself, you can handle deadlines.

Economy in Good Writing

Journalism students have difficulty appreciating the idea of tight writing. Yet it is probably the concept most widely agreed upon among good writers and teachers of writing. They may not agree on using an adjective as a noun or whether a comma should be used in a compound sentence, but almost all teachers of writing and all writers agree that tight writing is essential.

Tight writing means using no more words than necessary to give a sentence a precise meaning. Tight writing keeps the reader reading. Loose, uneconomical writing loses the reader to a television program or household chores because he or she feels the wordiness of an article steals time from something more important.

According to Philip Knightley in *The First Casualty,* a study of war correspondents, tight writing started for economical reasons. In the telegraph's infancy more than a century ago, the rate for news stories was $5 a word. ''Sending a summary of a battle by telegraph meant adopting a new style: crisp, concise, and packed with facts,'' Knightley writes. Additionally, tightly written stories give editors room for more stories in their newspapers or broadcasts. Economy of expression takes on even more importance in the video newspaper, with its limitations of a small screen and a restless audience.

To fully appreciate tight writing, every journalist should work for a highway department. If you want to see clear messages simply stated, examine the signs highway engineers erect. The people who write these messages cannot waste words—they are limited to a relatively small space intended to be read quickly and understood immediately by any motorist. My favorite sign stands at an intersection where only a right turn is permitted. The person who wrote the message did not say NO LEFT TURN, for that would have meant a motorist could drive through the intersection, a movement equally dangerous in this instance. Instead, the sign writer produced: RIGHT TURN ONLY. Those three words convey this message: It is dangerous to turn left or drive through this intersection at all times of day and night. Violation of this sign's message may result in a bad accident or an arrest.

The second part of that sign's message is not an actual part of it. Rather, you know that to ignore a legally posted sign on a highway can result in your being arrested, fined and maybe even jailed. Your knowledge is conventional information, information about customs that every member of a society learns. And it is with conventional information that tight writing begins.

Conventional Information

One of our society's conventions is using an ambulance to transport accident victims or seriously ill persons to a hospital. Why then report that an ambulance took an injured person to a hospital? That's something ambulances do. When something other than an ambulance is used, a journalist might report it. (Exception: some news media routinely mention the name of the ambulance company, particularly if it is a volunteer group, in the interest of good will.)

Furthermore, if an ambulance is involved, why bother with *taken to the hospital* at all? In place of *taken* a journalist could use *admitted* (if that is the case) or *treated*.

Ellenberg was treated for head injuries at Cadbury Hospital.

That sentence tells the reader Ellenberg wasn't admitted, just treated. Those who disagree can always add *and released*.

Ellenberg was treated for head injuries at Cadbury Hospital and
released.

Journalists should provide new information for readers and listeners, not information they already know. Isaac Bashevis Singer, who won the Nobel Prize for literature, once told a journalist: "Journalism doesn't do any damage to a fiction writer. You inform people. A writer who does not inform, who tells people what they already know, is not a writer." A story filled with what people already know will not burden readers after one or two paragraphs because they will have stopped reading. How much would you read of a fire story that described fire trucks or of a football story that detailed the size of the field? We already know that information, or we don't care, or the information is not important to the news. We want to know about the fire and the football game. The fire and the game are what is worth reporting.

Needless Detail

Some journalists waste the reader's or listener's time by giving more detail than needed or by giving, in essence, the same details twice. Look for that in this sentence:

> Police said the juvenile was taken to Cadbury jail, where she was detained to await the arrival of her parents.

Doesn't this say the same thing?

> Police said the juvenile was detained at Cadbury jail to await the arrival of her parents.

The second example says the same thing as the first—only in fewer words. If the juvenile was detained at the jail, she had to have been taken there. A crime story produced this wordy example:

> The intruder forced the resident into the basement, where she was locked inside.

No doubt the resident did not volunteer. Try this:

> The intruder locked the resident in the basement.

The following examples—from accident and drug-smuggling stories—have to be rewritten to remove the needless detail.

> Williams and Jones noticed the car along Route 322 near the Route 45 intersection. *Finding the car empty,* they *looked around and* found the victim in a ditch 60 feet away.
> Williams and Jones noticed the empty car along Route 322 near the Route 45 intersection. They found the victim in a ditch 60 feet away.

> Barnhart said gastric juices would destroy the swallowed condom and the cocaine *would spread through* Polsby's *body and* kill him.
> Barnhart said gastric juices would destroy the swallowed condom and the cocaine would kill Polsby.

Some journalists pump stories full of needless information and detail only one or two readers might be interested in.

> Described this week in *U.S. Patent No. 3,978,908,* the process greatly reduces fire and pollution hazards.

Giving the patent number adds nothing to the story.

> The process, patented this week, greatly reduces fire and pollution hazards.

The reader also is not familiar with the number of every law and the number of every section in every law or policy.

> The board excluded *section 6-9-10,* which deals with the number of students allowed on a bus. The section says there may be no more than five standees.

Section 6-9-10 may be important to the school bus coordinator, but it's not something the reader or listener knows or needs to know.

> The board excluded a section that limits to five the number of standees on a bus.

You can also get trapped into blow-by-blow reporting when it isn't needed.

> Gov. Dick Thornburgh has sent a letter to the Canadian government thanking that country for offering him unspecified aid during the Three Mile Island plant crisis last year.

The reader is not interested in how the governor conveyed his appreciation. A better version:

> Gov. Dick Thornburgh has thanked the Canadian government for offering unspecified aid during the Three Mile Island nuclear plant crisis last year.

As a matter of interest, the second paragraph of this story began: "In a letter . . ." Why say it twice?

Stating the Obvious

Some journalists state the obvious over and over, giving them another place to tighten their writing. After saying that the following story is about a meeting of the Dallas Sports Advisory Board and that the board is voting on schedule changes, the writer doesn't need to repeat the name of the school.

> The board also agreed on a recommendation to add two girls' cross-country meets *to the Dallas High School schedule.*

Clearly the Dallas board does not make decisions for another board. And if the Oklahoma legislature passes a law to reduce speeding, obviously the law applies only in Oklahoma; the Oklahoma legislature has no authority in other states. The logic applies to any rule-making body.

> A public hearing will precede the meeting *and testimony will be heard* on vacating October and Erie alleys.

Public hearings are convened to hear testimony just as power lines are built to transport energy.

The utility wants to construct a *new* 230-kilovolt *power* line *to transport energy* from a substation in Fernville to its plant in Clive.

Can you imagine a utility wanting to construct an *old* line? And *230-kilovolt* says *power*. Similarly:

The fire was confined to a shed, *where the fire started*.

The pilot was bound for Dubuque *before the crash*.

Since it was a fatal crash, the italicized phrase states the obvious and is extraneous to the story.

Weak Phrasing

A phrase that unnecessarily permeates too much writing today is "there is." Too often a writer uses the phrase when a better sentence could be constructed without it. The most common abuse appears at the beginning of a sentence, creating an indefinite—*i.e.,* non-news—introduction.

There will be a budget increase of $39,059 next year, the city manager announced.

Such a limp beginning can be excised in the interest of economical and strong writing.

The budget will increase $39,059 next year, the city manager announced.

The phrase also appears within sentences and usually deserves the same treatment it receives at the beginning: elimination.

A Conrail spokesman, who asked not to be identified, said there is nothing other than routine business on the agenda.

Strongly put:

A Conrail spokesman said the agenda contains nothing other than routine business.

The advantage in both rewrites is that the sentences gain strong and precise verbs, which make the messages clearer.

Finally, this section ends with a qualifier: My experience with "there is" sentences has been that I write a lot of them but remove most when I edit. Every time I see "there is" in a sentence, a red flag appears in my mind and I attempt to change the sentence to eliminate the offending phrase. I have also found that about 10 percent of the "there is" sentences I write do not get better by eliminating the phrase. Sometimes a writer has to accept the lesser of two evils.

Prepositional Pile-up

Prepositional pile-up, which turns sentences into incomprehensible monsters, is another place to tighten writing. The prepositions that lead off the phrases are italicized in the following example.

> An increase *of* more than $39,000 *in* the budget *of* the joint sewer
> authority *for* sewage treatment *in* Clive and Ryan townships was
> proposed last night.

That 26-word sentence loses about 25 percent of its fat when some of the prepositional phrases are converted into frontal modifiers.

> A $39,000 budget increase to treat sewage for the Clive and Ryan
> township joint sewer authority was proposed last night.

One of the prepositional phrases ("for sewage treatment") became a verb phrase ("to treat sewage").

The rewritten sentence saves six words. A six-word saving may not sound like a lot until you figure how many times in a 700-word story you can eliminate unnecessary words. Then multiply the saving by the number of stories in a newspaper or newscast. The saving could result in additional stories getting in print or on the air. To the print journalist, the eliminated words accumulate into inches; for the broadcaster, seconds and minutes.

However, don't be misled into believing that every prepositional phrase can be turned into an adjective. Consider how much you put before the modified noun, and if it's a long string of words, then you've created a monster. You could convert "Thomas Williams, a member of the board, said" into "board member Thomas Williams said"—a form broadcasters prefer—and not do damage to clarity. But if the information is lengthy, such as "Thomas Williams, a member of the Tishomingo Area School Board, said," you would be better off not converting that to "Tishomingo Area School Board member Thomas Williams said." The reader swallows little doses easily and chokes on anything bigger.

Sometimes the prepositional phrase belongs before the noun it modifies simply because it contains crucial information. Unintended deception results when journalists write like this:

> City council proposed a tax increase of 5.5 mills . . .

The amount of the tax increase has been hidden in a limply stated sentence. Better to say:

> City Council proposed a 5.5-mill tax increase . . .

Verb-Noun Constructions

Weak verb-noun constructions can easily be turned into strong verbs. Why write *the commission gave approval* when *the commission approved* says the same thing more forcefully? What's the loss in meaning when you write *City Council will study the proposal* instead of *City Council will make a study of the proposal?* And while many organizations *hold a meeting*, they can also transact the same business when they *meet*. To tell the members of the organization they're going to meet, don't *get in contact with them* just *contact them*. And if you're going to tell them what the first order of business will be, don't say the meeting will *get under way* with a speech when *begin* or *start* reduces the number of words. Other typical examples: *received medical attention* equals *was treated*, *voted in favor of* equals *approved*, *take the place of* equals *replace*.

Redundancy

A phrase or sentence is considered redundant when it contains extra, unnecessary, superfluous or repetitive words. For example: a restaurant once advertised that it offered "daily luncheon specials *every day*," a store boasted of values "too numerous *in number* to mention," and a journalist wrote that an issue "had been debated *back and forth*." The examples contain redundant phrases (in italics).

Think of the many redundant phrases pushed upon readers. Careless writers tell people *to closely scrutinize the consensus of opinion*, the wordy stepchild of *to scrutinize the consensus*—all other words are redundant because they are inherent in the words used. Knowing precise meanings would have helped the writer of the following:

Smoke rising high over the building billowed over a large traffic jam below.

Billowing smoke naturally rises. The non-redundant version of the preceding:

Smoke billowed over a large traffic jam.

Because we know that heat can scorch, the following sentence from a fire story contains a redundant prepositional phrase (italicized):

The fire chief had no damage estimate for the shed or for the main building, which was scorched *by the heat*.

Here are some sentences to study for redundant or extraneous words (the offending words are italicized):

A *huge* throng *of people* gathered at *twelve* noon on Easter *Sunday* to debate the *controversial* issue.

During that time *span*, a *passing* motorist saw a *flaming* inferno he knew had been started by *young* juveniles.

The widow *woman who lives* down the street is pleasant.

In the event that our *invited* guests don't come, we will *bring to an* end our friendship with *all of* them. (Begin the sentence with *if*.)

The three will appeal to Superior Court *for a decision in their favor*.

The judge ruled that students have the *legal* right to vote in the district where they go to college.

Police are not allowed to release the record of a suspect's *prior* convictions.

The treatment plant *currently* discharges its effluent into Lost Creek.

Thomas F. Williams died of cancer in his native Wales, *where he was born.*

City Council plans to install *pedestrian* sidewalks in the alley.

Obviously some of what could be deleted from the preceding examples is not redundant, just unnecessary. Some examples, of course, would not be redundant given a different context. Talking or writing about a person's conviction in court *today* leaves you in a position of describing the person's other convictions as *prior.* Similarly, *fiscal budget* has the trappings of redundancy because most budgets are fiscal. But writing about a person's fiscal budget and the way that person budgets time might require a writer to make the distinction clear by using *fiscal budget.*

Millions of redundant phrases exist and society will no doubt create more. You will have to be alert at all times. Here are some you can avoid:

Redundancy	Solution
remand back	remand
soothing tranquilizer	tranquilizer
is in need of	needs
could hold practice	could practice
other matters recommended	also recommended
she went on to say	she said
two separate buildings	two buildings
make an addition to	add
compromise solution	compromise
general public	public
completely destroyed	destroyed
legal contract	contract
cooperate together	cooperate
free gift	gift
narrow down	narrow
reason why	reason
previous experience	experience
minor quibble	quibble

Throwaways

Entire sentences are often unnecessary to news stories. Such sentences are throwaways or brick walls—sentences that stop the reader because they don't advance the story toward its conclusion. It is considered a fault of journalistic writing that such a premium is placed on advancing a story that sometimes necessary background is excluded. But good journalists are afraid to tamper with the restless reader's interest by offering even one sentence that apparently leads nowhere. Most often throwaway sentences show up as scene-setters in which the writer provides an unnecessary context. Such sentences are so static they should be bottled and sold as a cure for insomnia.

In the following, the first sentence—taken from the middle of a story—is a throwaway:

> A preliminary report on the survey was delivered by John S. Warren, regional planning director, at a meeting of the commission last night at the municipal building. [Yawn] The report recommends that housing for the elderly not be implemented on a wide scale because little need exists. [At last, the news!]

The first sentence is not really background in the sense that it provides information the reader needs to understand the story; it is part of the present story and could be said more forecefully, without putting the reader to sleep.

> A preliminary report on the survey, given last night by John S. Warren, regional planning director, recommends that housing for the elderly not be widely implemented because little need exists.

Among other things eliminated were some conventional data—that the information was given at a meeting and where the meeting occurred. If necessary, they can be mentioned later in the story. The sentence is better still this way:

> Little need for more housing for the elderly exists, Regional Planning Director John S. Warren said last night.

The fact that Warren is quoting a survey could be put in the next sentence or paragraph.

> Basing his remarks on a survey by the regional planning staff, Warren said . . .

Here are the lead and second paragraphs of a story:

> An official of the American Heart Association said today that 61 percent of the deaths in Cadbury last year were caused by heart-related diseases.
> The announcement was made by Dr. Marian F. Williams, president of the Cadbury Chapter of the Heart Association, who released the 1975 statistics giving the origins of the heart-related deaths. The statistics are:

> | | |
> |---|---|
> | heart attack | 257 deaths |
> | stroke | 67 |
> | rheumatic heart | 10 |

    hardening of arteries   6
    other causes   21

The second paragraph does nothing to advance the story. Here is a rewrite of the second paragraph:

> Dr. Marian F. Williams, president of the association's Cadbury chapter,
> said that 257 of the 378 deaths were caused by heart attacks. The
> second biggest killer was strokes, 67, followed by rheumatic heart,
> 10 . . .

The restructuring ties the announcement and the highest statistic to immediately give the reader some news.

Don't assume, though, that all throwaway sentences are bad. Sometimes one is necessary to provide background that cannot be subordinated harmoniously to a main clause. Then a throwaway sentence should be used because in such cases clarity is the goal and if the reader is put off by an unclear story, the journalist has failed anyway.

In the example below, a lead is followed by a paragraph that is not a throwaway; it does move the story along because it gives background the reader should have.

> Hopewell County last night became the third municipality in the six-
> county region to adopt the comprehensive plan.
>   The plan to guide growth in the region during the next 20 years has
> also been adopted by Pickett and Hunterdon counties. The region's
> remaining counties have not held a public hearing on the plan.

The second paragraph is a neat summary that explains the lead and puts Hopewell County's action in context.

In broadcasting, throwaways are not as obnoxious. Broadcast journalists rely less on subordinating background because the results are lengthy and complex. Instead, they present the newscast in a string of simple and short sentences that will not baffle listeners. Two 10-word sentences sound better than one 20-word sentence.

Elliptic Writing

Although you may not realize it, you probably already write and speak elliptically. You do not write or say, "I am shorter than she is short," when "I am shorter than she" is clear. It is common to drop the second (even third and fourth) of parallel elements because the first element is carried over. That is elliptic writing.

> He runs to school and he walks to work.

Elliptically written, the sentence reads better without the second *he*.

> He runs to school and walks to work.

At its wordiest the following sentence could be written:

> She likes physics and *she likes* chemistry.

Such a construction takes the directness out of the sentence.

> She likes physics and chemistry.

In elliptic writing all parallel elements are not repeated. In the following sentence the italicized words are understood and did not appear in the original:

> Johnstown was cut off from the world, its railroads *were* washed away and *its* bridges *were* destroyed.

The original:

> Johnstown was cut off from the world, its railroads washed away and bridges destroyed.

Sometimes prepositions and articles are discardable:

> The chairman of CBS Inc. said today that within the last decade the idea *of press freedom* and *the* practice of press freedom have been endangered around the world.

The sentence reads better without the italicized matter.

> The chairman of CBS Inc. said today that within the last decade the idea and practice of press freedom have been endangered around the world.

There is a danger in elliptic writing, best shown in the following sign on the Ohio Turnpike:

DRIVE SLOWER WHEN WET

The first missing element is the subject of the sentence. Because the sentence is direct address, the subject *you* is understood. Also understood is the verb *are* in the second half of the sentence. But what makes the verb understood is the elliptic subject of the second half of the sentence. That subject is carried over from the first half of the sign. What the sign really says:

(YOU) DRIVE SLOWER WHEN (YOU ARE) WET

But what the sign means is:

(YOU) DRIVE SLOWER WHEN (THE HIGHWAY IS) WET

While such a construction may be perfectly clear to the driver of an automobile, it would not be in print or on the air. The caution, then, is that you make sure what you are omitting has a preceding parallel element.

Don't be lulled into believing that all elliptic writing is clear or desirable. In the following, the writer dropped the preposition *by,* whose absence changed the meaning of the sentence:

> Evidence of the controversy was exhibited *by* last month's petition from residents protesting the continued development of the tract and the presence of several residents at last night's meeting.

Do you know where the second *by* belongs? The prepositional phrases piled one atop the other make the meaning of the sentence unclear. Prepositional phrases adhere to the closest noun (or verb, if that's what they're modifying), which means you reach an area in the sentence that seems to say:

> . . . the continued development *of the tract and the presence* . . .

At first reading I thought *tract* and *presence* belonged to *of* and that the full phrase modified *development.* In other words, what was being developed was *the tract and the presence.* Only after three readings did I realize what was meant.

> Evidence of the controversy was exhibited *by* last month's petition from residents protesting the continued development of the tract and *by* the presence of several residents at last night's meeting.

The writer, in attempting to be compact, was inexact. Two sentences might have solved the problem—two sentences totaling 33 words instead of the 28-word mess that resulted.

> Evidence of the controversy surfaced last month in a petition from residents protesting the continued development of the tract. The evidence reappeared last night with the presence of several residents at the meeting.

Omission of Pronouns and Verbs

The pronouns (such as *who, that, which, where*) used to introduce clauses and sometimes the verbs that follow can be dropped as long as the intended meaning remains intact. Such writing is common to complex sentences (sentences containing main and subordinate clauses).

> Joseph R. Jones, *who is* 75, today predicted he would live another 75 years.
> Joseph R. Jones, 75, today predicted he would live another 75 years. (A broadcaster would say: Seventy-five-year-old Joseph Jones predicted today he would live another seventy-five years.)

> Firemen responded to an early morning blaze *that occurred* in a shed at Smith Labs.
> Firemen responded to an early morning blaze in a shed at Smith Labs.

Any house *that is built* on a hill will provide a good view for its
residents.
Any house on a hill will provide a good view for its residents.

You can't always drop *that*. It sometimes serves as a buffer without which a
collision of words would result, giving a different meaning.

He said that last night we would study.

He said last night we would study.

The difference is between when the studying will be done (first example) and when
the speaker made the statement (second example). The second example does not say
when the studying will be done. Similarly, the omission of *that* in the following
changes the meaning:

Paley said that at a recent general conference of UNESCO a press-
restricting proposal was discussed.

Paley said at a recent general conference of UNESCO a press-restricting
proposal was discussed.

The verb *feel* creates unintended meanings when *that* is dropped.

He *felt the girl* was a good student.

He felt *that* the girl was a good student.

You might argue that the reader would understand in the first example nobody is
touching the girl. That is true; but it might require a second reading, which is not
good, or it might raise a smile in an otherwise serious story or broadcast. A second
reading might also be needed in this:

Joseph Thompson and other conservatives *warn Gov. Kellner's plan* for
instant voter registration could spell doom for conservatives.

So that the plan isn't being warned, *that* is needed.

Joseph Thompson and other conservatives warn that Gov. Kellner's plan
for instant voter registration could spell doom for conservatives.

Writing to the Point

Writing to the point has virtue beyond saving words. It also produces sentences that
communicate clearly. Several years ago the Federal Trade Commission was debating how to phrase a stronger health warning on cigarette packs, the feeling being
that "Warning: Cigarettes may be hazardous to your health" was understated.
Someone suggested: "Warning: Cigarette smoking is dangerous to health and may
cause death from cancer, coronary heart disease, chronic bronchitis, pulmonary
emphysema and other diseases." The receiver of such a message might conclude

that cigarettes have a "safe" side. But Rudolf Flesch, a readability expert, made the point clearly and briefly: "Danger: Tests prove cigarettes can kill you." No doubting that message.

Those who write to the point use fewer words. A student turned in this sentence:

> The transcripts for the trial, which lasted 9½ months, contained 28,314 pages.

She got this back:

> The transcripts for the 9½-month trial contained 28,314 pages.

Likewise, this sentence

> At the time the strike went into effect, there was no agreement in sight.

became

> When the strike started, no agreement was in sight.

Another good effort reduced the total number of words in two sentences by 50 percent and eliminated one sentence.

> Up until that time, it was the longest murder trial ever recorded in American history, lasting a total of 9½ months. Also, the Manson case was at the time the most expensive criminal trial.

> Until then, the Manson murder trial was the longest (9½ months) and most expensive in American history.

To write to the point, subordinate information that otherwise is given—without good reason—a sentence all to itself. Here is an example:

> Police reported a hot plate was stolen from G-4, Thomson Hall, March 17. *The hot plate* was valued at $64.

Get to the point.

> Police reported a hot plate *valued at $64* was stolen from G-4, Thomson Hall, March 17.

There's too much here

> In describing her reasons for running, Mrs. Florio cited her own experience with school board matters gained by attending board meetings.

but not here

> In explaining why she's running, Mrs. Florio cited the experience she gained attending board meetings.

The shortened version does not say what the experience is. But the sentence comes from an interview with a candidate for the school board. It is doubtful such a candidate would discuss her experience in making apple pie or that apple pie would be the topic of such an interview.

Dropping the Infinitive

Occasionally someone will use an infinitive where one isn't needed.

> Won't unionization help *to reduce* the bureaucracy and red tape?

There's nothing wrong with:

> Won't unionization *help reduce* the bureaucracy and red tape?

The Writer's Duty

The value of clear, tight writing can never be overstressed. No prodding in the struggle to write clearly is redundant. We live in an age of expanding information, of more messages coming at us in more ways—newspapers, magazines, television, bumper stickers, posters, video newspaper, home computers. Bombarded, we want our messages brief. Video messages especially need to be brief because impatient "readers" do not turn to the screen to labor but to learn quickly. The writer who can accommodate our desire for brevity will be forever employable in many media.

The message of the information age, then, is this: Remove the unnecessary. A good editor will do that, given the time. But the place to write tightly is not at the copy desk; it is at the video display terminal or typewriter as you write or edit your own writing. The important thing is not to tax the copy editor's patience or waste the reader's time with extra words. Both will tire of you quickly, and whereas the copy editor may go on deleting extra words, the reader is likely to look for something else to do.

Self-Diagnostic Test 1.1

To determine how well you understand the major principles of tight writing, edit the following sentences to make them tighter. The answers appear in the back of the book. Review what you miss.

1. The body of the hunter was found by a clump of trees about 200 yards from a tool shed on the Smith farm by T. R. Thompson of Cadbury Gardens.

2. There were about a dozen people in the church when the fire started.

3. Another weakness Mrs. Williams discussed is a recently passed state mandate requiring a program for gifted students.

4. This is a professional course that is aimed at improving the skills and knowledge that are needed for effective news work.

5. There was a brief flash of controversy last week when Knepper condemned the mayor.

6. Tom Drew then spoke to the Council and said that he owns five pool tables in his place of business.

7. Sen. Jones said in a speech last night that Russia's army is getting stronger every day.

8. Required mandatory conservation measures must be followed.

9. There were 67 deaths due to strokes.

10. City Council voted in favor of taxing pool tables.

11. Another school bus was immediately dispatched to take the children to school.

12. The new store will be more than five times the size of the present store when completed.

13. During the trial the jury was sequestered and kept from publicity.

14. The district will also hire para-professionals to aid teachers. Para-professionals are paid $2,800 yearly. Superintendent of Schools Thomas F. Williams said these steps will help eliminate classroom crowding and will cost approximately $60,000.

Exercise 1.1

A. Edit the following story and turn it in to your instructor for evaluation.

Name _____

Cadbury University submitted a proposal to Governor Hilton S. Knapp in Capitol City today that would eliminate Cadbury's special tuition benefit to faculty and staff by the year 1984.

Cadbury employees are the recipients of a 75 percent discount in tuition payments for any course they or their dependents study in. Any employee's dependent who qualifies for the 75 percent tuition discount would pay $87.50 under the present tuition of $350 a term for a full-time student.

The discount of 75 percent has been a political thorn in Cadbury's side since the legislature earlier this year proposed the abolition of the benefit immediately.

Cadbury contends that the abolition of the benefit immediately would be unfair to employees who were hired with the full and complete understanding that they would receive a reduction of 75 percent for all dependents, including children.

Cadbury's proposal, as submitted to Gov. Knapp, would be equitable to all of its present employees, a Cadbury spokesman said, because it would ensure that those recently hired would still have an opportunity to avail themselves of the tuition reduction according to their contracts while those hired in 1984 would be hired with the full understanding that their dependents would have to pay full tuition.

The Cadbury spokesman warned that there would be problems with ending the benefit. He said that in the future persons hired to work for Cadbury University would have to be offered a higher-than-average salary to compensate for the lack of the tuition benefit. Without an increase in salary, the spokesman said, Cadbury salaries would not be competitive with other universities and colleges that offer tuition reduction benefits to their employees.

The spokesman said that the proposal to the governor to end the special tuition benefit by 1984 is a compromise Cadbury had to put into effect because the legislature wants to make sure the benefit ends next year.

B. Edit the following sentences so they are tighter and turn them in to your instructor for evaluation.

Name _____

1. Police said that the death appears to have been from natural causes.

2. Gov. Charles said that the thing that concerns him is the rate of inflation.

3. There was discussion at earlier board meetings about the possibility of the school district borrowing up to $240,000 at low-interest rates.

4. The suspect is alleged to have pointed his weapon at the victim several times.

5. The board voted to meet with the doctor to discuss the possibility of the physician visiting the prison three times weekly for the purpose of giving physicals to new inmates.

6. The fire chief said the fire started in the engine and spread throughout the car, destroying it.

7. The accident victim was taken to the Cadbury Hospital in the Goodwill Ambulance and admitted.

8. He managed to race out the door of a Washington grocery store where he had been stopped, beginning a journey that took him away from the United States and to Buenos Aires.

9. Elderly citizens highly in need of low-income housing earn less than $5,000 a year, the survey found.

10. Williams grabbed hold of a 2–0 pitch and lofted it in a high arc over the right-center field wall for his second home run.

11. The course was divided into a number of phases.

12. Police said the passenger received an injury of the foot that was not serious.

13. The honor includes a cash award of $100.

14. The corporation made significant contributions to the alumni fund.

15. For the session last night, Thomas F. Williams, vice president of council, presided and will continue for the remainder of the year. To fill the post of vice president, John Klein was appointed to the position.

16. Sauers was taken to Cadbury Hospital by the American Hose Co. Ambulance where he was treated for minor injuries and released.

17. State police said the arrest was the result of a lengthy investigation.

18. With the passage of time, it became more complicated to resume the project.

19. He is a friend of the Smiths, who are frequent visitors here.

20. When they hold a meeting, they discuss everything.

21. At a meeting of City Council last night, 15 citizens voiced objections to council's plans for a new street in University Heights.

22. When asked if Manson ever would be released, Bugliosi said that distinct possibility exists.

23. The dog catcher said that the matter would be handled in a routine fashion.

24. The actual facts of the case will never be known to the general public.

Chapter 2

Sentences and Paragraphs

The Sentence

The thread of every story is the sentence. No writer has room for a false stitch in sewing a story together. Sentences must proceed logically one after the other until the story is finished.

It is far easier to tell what sentences do than to tell what they are. In *Understanding English,* Paul Roberts says that definitions of sentences number more than 200, that the short definitions "are either untrue or impractical or both," and that "English sentences are too complicated to be encapsulated in a definition." Roberts titled the chapter he devotes to sentences "Something That Ends with a Period."

Traditional and Non-traditional Sentence Patterns

Traditional sentences contain at the minimum a subject and verb, often thought of as the actor and the action. *She smiles* is an example. Sentences also have a subject-verb-object (or object of action) pattern. That is the way people talk, which makes it the ideal pattern for broadcast and print journalists.

        s   v   o
The boy struck the ball

Another pattern is subject/linking verb/complement, in which the complement modifies or describes the subject.

     s lv   c
She is smart.

A sentence is a logical pattern reflecting the order in which people usually think. People do not separate one idea into sentences. A person who watched a Little League baseball game would not report a player's success at bat by saying:

The boy.
Struck.
The ball.

The reporter would instead put together all the related elements of the player's success into one sentence.

> The boy struck the ball.

If the reporter wanted to explain more, perhaps what happened to the ball, he or she would tell that in the same sentence, because what happened to the ball is the result of the boy striking it.

> The boy struck the ball, which bounced over the pitcher's head and into center field.

The reporter would not say the preceding in two sentences. He or she would not say:

> The boy struck the ball.
> *Which bounced over the pitcher's head and into center field.*

That is not logical. Yet that is the way some novices write. They fail to perceive the logic of an action or thought. They disjoint logic by separating major and subordinate ideas into separate sentences. Often one of the elements cannot stand by itself because it is a *dependent clause*—a clause that depends on a main clause to give it meaning. The disjointure is a *sentence fragment* (italicized in the preceding example). Editors and professors scorn sentence fragments; good writers avoid them.

Another sentence fragment typical of novices:

> Because the person with a college education will understand dimensions others may miss.

Because is a conjunction that shows a relationship, and that relationship is best shown within one sentence. What follows *because* in the preceding example relates to a prior thought. The thoughts should be joined.

> A college education gives a person a fuller life because the person with
> a college education will understand dimensions others may miss.

Bad fragments typically have nothing to stand on, nothing to relate to. Writing a sentence fragment is akin to taking a newborn child away from its parent and expecting the child to survive on its own. Such an expectation is illogical; survival is impossible. Do not disjoint the logic of a sentence. Do not use sentence fragments.

Despite what you have just read, you may have seen sentence fragments in newspapers or heard them on news broadcasts. Your eyes and ears are fine. You may have read or heard sentence fragments in a question-and-answer structure in which the answer was not the traditional sentence structure of subject-verb-object. For example:

> So which gift package did the housewife who has everything pick? *The*
> *one with the appliances she doesn't need.*

Other examples exist, but most come from the typewriters of book writers and reviewers, columnists, and magazine and feature writers, not from the video display terminals and typewriters of everyday journalists who write hard news. Regardless, the exceptions are worth mentioning so when the time to use them arrives, you will know you aren't violating any strict law of grammar. As you study these, note that they have some logic to them, that they are not like the disjointed fragments scorned earlier. The first comes from *The Camera Never Blinks* by Dan Rather of CBS News. (All italics are added.) To the question of how to start preparing for journalism, Rather wrote:

> And the answer is so simple. *With reading, with books, with words.* Education starts there. So does good writing.

Here is another, this one from a sports column by Bill Lyon of *The Philadelphia Inquirer:*

> But you check him out and he doesn't breathe through gills. His feet aren't webbed. *No dorsal fin between his shoulder blades.*

Despite the absence of a subject and verb (in that case, *There is*) the reader carries the thought to completion without any labor. The reader does the same thing in the following, written by Peter Gwynne in *Smithsonian* magazine:

> *Plutonium. The stuff of bombs. Intensely radioactive for hundreds of thousands of years.* For many Americans, the very word invokes a dread akin to botulism or anthrax or worse.

That is the opening paragraph of Gwynne's article. Notice how he builds up the length of each sentence—one word, four words, eight words—before he uses traditional sentence structure. Good writers recognize that people do not always think in full sentences and the writers use fragments to show that.

A very short fragment at the end of a sentence or paragraph serves well for emphasis or humor, as these examples show:

> Some of the Volunteers will sit in the stands come autumn. *Involuntarily.*

> George Ade was a famous man from a few days after *Fables in Slang* was published until around 1920. *Rich, too.*

> Back in December Penn State was a floundering wrestling team, one that was given little chance of beating the likes of Navy and Lehigh. *Especially Lehigh.*

However, using sentence fragments as special effects can be overdone to the point of creating a defect. The fragment is effective because it is used sparingly. Very sparingly. Now back to basics.

From the traditional patterns explained at the start of this chapter flow an infinite number of variations called simple, compound, complex and compound-complex, all important more in function than label.

Self-Diagnostic Test 2.1

To determine how well you understand traditional and non-traditional sentences, underline the traditional sentences in the following, which is a sidebar to an accident story. The answers appear in the back of the book.

Lights.

Red blinkers. White spotlights. Neon. On-off, on-off, on-off twin yellow caution lights look down on an ant heap of sweating men clambering across the shattered carcass of a truck—wedged fast in the corner of the house.

One dead. Five injured.

The living are gone. Bandaged. Rushed to hospital asepsis.

One remains. In a tangle of broken metal, glass, plaster, brick and wood. Wedged fast in the truck in the corner of the house.

Children's bare feet pad across the ridged asphalt of the highway where wheel rims gouged a path.

The crowd.

A boy and girl embrace in the roadway, in the glare of spotlights, examining the shafts and tubes of the exposed underside of the truck—the skeleton of some unfamiliar sea beast.

A quiet crowd.

Policemen. "Put out your cigarettes."

Black-booted firemen stand in a slick of diesel fuel and light cigarettes.

Fuel trickles from a ruptured tank, vanishes, reappears in a shimmer on the curb, running in silent counterpoint to the nearby stream, splashing into the light, beneath the bridge, and gone.

Thick odor of diesel fuel.

Knots of men—dark slickers of firemen, white rescue squad coveralls, gray police tunics—form and dissolve.

Firemen in shorts, sneakers and hard hats.

Ropes. Cables. Wires.

Men with pikes gingerly pick away the sagging block facing of the house. Masonry tumbles onto the truck cab, billowing dust, exposing wide-plank inner siding.

Dials. Gauges. A fireman stands for hours beside the truck, hose ready, while a second monitors water pressure.

Lights.

Flashlights. Headlights. Flash bulbs.

A wheel turns slowly, spilling shattered blocks onto the sidewalk. "Stand back."

An uncut pizza rests on a table in the corner room.

The wreckers arrive. Two, three, the fourth seems half as high as the house. Conference. Debate.

Newcomers edge around the fire trucks, staring. How? Who?

A father carries his sleepy daughter—long blonde hair and sweat-shirt—piggyback through the crowd.

The crowd thins. Going home. To rest. For a final day of work before a long weekend.

Labor Day.

Lights.

Exercise 2.1

A. Underline the subject(s) and verb(s) in these sentences and turn the exercise in to your instructor for evaluation.

Name _____

1. The article explores an area of journalism and advertising not previously explored.

2. Rye and corn replaced sugar and peaches as the staples on the family's table.

3. Walking slowly on a warm day keeps him cool.

4. The kidnappers called Williams between six and nine times Monday.

5. Cadbury residents last night asked City Council to hold the line on taxes.

6. Tomorrow will be a partly cloudy to mostly cloudy day.

7. So tonight the network tries again with five comedies—four of them new.

8. Tyler's current series is in its ninth and final season.

9. About one-fourth of all the turtles in the world live in North America.

10. Scientists emphasize research.

11. Exhibits of historic and contemporary photographs and a lecture series will highlight History of Photography Week.

12. The destroyer pulled out of the harbor and headed toward Africa.

B. Label each of the following as a traditional sentence or a fragment and turn your answers in to your instructor for evaluation.

Name _____

1. Not a show of defiance, but more a release of emotions during a rare win.

2. Flowers for display in competition at the fair.

3. Williams prepared to resume the radio commentary he had interrupted to seek the nomination.

4. Because both sides were required to secure counsel from someone other than their solicitor.

5. Where we find a clear spot is where we'll camp for the night.

6. The indictments are expected to come under a broad charge of conspiracy to defraud consumers.

7. A place where local veterinarians can refer animals with special problems.

8. The case, in part, originated with the construction of Cadbury Junior High School.

9. Which lacks traditional room construction.

10. Ran 15 miles.

11. Five years ago Dallas Barnes and Robert Delinger were on opposite sides of the law.

12. The hunter and the hunted.

13. The man who jumps in first.

14. Anyone who knows how to fix cars is welcome to work on mine.

The Simple Sentence

The best sentence is the simple sentence. It sticks to one idea or action.

> The boy struck the ball.

That doesn't mean, though, that a simple sentence is necessarily short. Through connectives and a variety of modifiers, a simple sentence can become quite long. First, a connective, which creates a compound object:

> The boy struck the ball *and* the rock.

And now a prepositional phrase:

> The boy struck the ball and the rock *at the same time*.

And another:

> The boy *in the blue trousers* struck the ball and the rock at the same time.

And with some modification in front of the subject (in this case, an adjective):

> The *tall* boy in the blue trousers struck the ball and the rock at the same time.

The sentence can be made longer still with a *compound predicate* (the verb and all its complements and modifiers), a pattern not to be confused with a compound sentence.

> The tall boy in the blue trousers *struck the ball and the rock at the same time and fell*.

In an early version of this sentence the connective *and* was used to create a compound object, *the ball and the rock*. Now *and* has also been used to create a compound predicate. A five-word sentence has become one of 19 words. But despite its length, it's still a simple sentence. Here is a simple sentence of 30 words, its length reached through the addition of two participial phrases.

> The clean air bill also covers other air pollution sources, generally giving industrial areas more time to meet standards while offering added protection for areas that now have clean air.

Here's the breakdown:

Basic Sentence	The clean air bill also covers other air pollution sources,
First Phrase	generally giving industrial areas more time to meet standards
Connective	while
Second Phrase	offering added protection for areas that now have clean air.

The preceding is atypical of broadcast journalism because of its length and complexity. A broadcast journalist would convert it to two sentences.

> The clean air bill also covers other air pollution sources. Generally, the bill gives industrial areas more time to meet standards while it offers added protection for areas that now have clean air.

Such an approach is easier on the ear; the listener can grasp the information more readily.

The Compound Sentence

The compound sentence relates at least two ideas or actions of equal importance. A compound sentence consists of two closely related sentences that might also be written as separate sentences—that is, both ending in a period. Compound sentences are joined with connectives (often called *coordinating conjunctions*) such as *and, but, or, nor, while, yet.* Another connective is the semicolon (;).

> It wasn't the subfreezing playing conditions or a matter of being outplayed; the game was decided by puck luck.

The use of compound sentences avoids tedious writing. When correctly structured, they take the place of two simple *but related* sentences.

> The president is waiting for the bill, but the House has not yet acted on it.

With some revision that sentence could have been written as two sentences.

> The president is waiting for the bill. The House has not yet acted on it.

But to write that as two simple sentences would make for tedious reading.

Compound sentences are mishandled when they are edited into two simple sentences, their relationship broken by a period. For example:

> The Rolling Stones' operations director and a woman are missing west of Nassau. A multinational air and sea hunt has been launched.

The sentences are related, not like cousins but like twins, and should not be separated.

> The Rolling Stones' operations director and a woman are missing west of Nassau, and a multinational air and sea hunt has been launched.

As before, the length of a sentence has nothing to do with what type of sentence it is. Compound sentences can be short.

> John hit the ball and Marty caught it.

> He likes to swim in the ocean; she likes to swim in a pool.

or long

> The substance of the Panamanian talks was not made public, but Panama's minister for canals took part in them.

even too long

> Hundreds of off-duty policemen, protesting work schedules and delayed pay raises, picketed Monday at nearly all of the city's 52 station houses while representatives of the Fraternal Order of Police sought, once again without success, to persuade the mayor to agree to their demands for better working conditions.

The best thing to do with an awkwardly long compound sentence is separate it into shorter sentences.

> Hundreds of off-duty policemen, protesting work schedules and delayed pay raises, picketed Monday at nearly all of the city's 52 station houses. At the same time, representatives of the Fraternal Order of Police sought, once again without success, to persuade the mayor to agree to their demands for better working conditions.

Sentences with compound predicates may look like compound sentences, but they are not. Here is an example of each:

Compound Subject	*John and Marty* ran to the cabin.
Compound Predicate	The revolution *was called "Helter Skelter" and was considered started with the first slayings.*

The Complex Sentence

Not every idea or action in a sentence is as important as another. A secondary idea or action is subordinate to the main idea or action. The important idea or action appears in the independent or main clause, independent because it needs no help in conveying an idea. For example:

> The tall boy in the blue trousers struck the ball and the rock at the same time.

That is an independent clause. By itself it has meaning. But the idea or action in a subordinate clause does not have meaning by itself; subordinate clauses depend on main clauses for their meaning. Standing alone they are the much scorned fragments mentioned earlier.

Creating a Subordinate Clause   To subordinate a clause or clauses, use *that, which, who, because, after, where, although, though, when, if.* (Remember, though, that through elliptic writing the pronouns that lead off subordinate clauses are sometimes discarded. The sentence, however, is still labeled complex.) Here is a complex sentence:

> *When the first pitch was thrown,* the tall boy in the blue trousers struck the ball and the rock at the same time.

The subordinate clause is italicized. It makes no sense by itself. Here are other examples of complex sentences:

> John Smith, *who is 61,* makes a good living predicting the outcome of political campaigns.

> *If his well connected Republican staff members were called upon to lead the investigation,* they would undoubtedly end up looking into the activities of fellow Republicans and other members of the establishment.

> One of the most frequent complex sentences in journalism begins with an attribution tag.

> He said *Williams could do the job.*

Such a structure defies the conventional definition that a subordinate clause cannot stand by itself because it has no meaning. In journalism, however, the distinction is that the unattributed sentence is the opinion of the writer, and writer's opinions are not allowed in news stories. The preceding complex sentence could also be written:

> Williams could do the job, he said.

Clauses and Relationships   The failure to use complex sentences is the failure to perceive complex relationships.

> Ford criticized Carter for not mentioning the Humphrey-Hawkins bill.

The bill would provide jobs for all Americans who want them. Carter
once endorsed the bill.

Three simple sentences do not convey the essence of Ford's criticism. The first
simple sentence says nothing; left out is the crucial explanation of what the bill
would do and the significance of Carter's silence. The following two simple sentences suggest that Ford's criticism, what the bill would do and Carter's prior
endorsement are separate ideas. They are not. There is a very important relationship
that must be stated—and a complex sentence is the proper vehicle.

Ford criticized Carter for not mentioning the Humphrey-Hawkins bill,
which would provide jobs for all Americans who want them and which
Carter once endorsed.

Incorrect Subordination   One of the pitfalls of subordination is subordinating the
wrong thing or something incongruous with the main clause. The wrong thing:

An 81-year-old Minnesota man was hunting *when he died of a heart
attack early today*.

The key point of that sentence is italicized. The news has been subordinated to a less
important piece of information. There should be no subordination; the sentence
should read:

An 81-year-old Minnesota man died of a heart attack while hunting
early today.

Now the key point is in place; it is no longer hidden.
Incongruous:

The judge rejected the neighbors' request for $2,500 in damages
*although he estimated that a horse drops an average of 24 pounds of
manure daily*.

The italicized portion of that sentence has nothing to do with the sentence's main
point—the judge rejecting the claim. If you remember that a sentence is a logical
pattern, that everything in it is logically related, you won't subordinate incorrectly.

Length   Complex sentences do not have to be long.

When I am hungry, I eat.

If I were you, I'd leave.

In fact, complex sentences can be made very long by compounding the subordinate
clauses, which was done in the Ford-Carter sentence. Here are the opening two
sentences from a column by David S. Broder of *The Washington Post*. In addition to
noting the differences in length, also note the compound predicate and the effect
Broder achieves by following a very long sentence with a very short one.

If you are James Reston of *The New York Times* and you're moved to celebrate Queen Elizabeth II's silver jubilee, you hop the Concorde to London in the morning, chat with the Chancellor of the Exchequer and the Leader of the Opposition in the afternoon and file an utterly definitive column on the state of her Majesty's realm in plenty of time for a nap before theatre and a late supper with the *Times'* London bureau chief, Johnny Apple, at his mansion in Belgravia. If you are not James Reston, however, you have a problem.

Advisory   It is important to remember that a subordinate clause (or clauses) needs a main clause in order to function clearly. The following sentence, based on one from a newspaper, is an example of a missing main clause:

Thomas F. Williams, the son of David and Mary Williams, 100 Schuylkill Ave., Henshaw, who graduated from Louisiana State in May with a BS degree in agronomy, who had been serving as president of Alpha Gamma Rho fraternity.

Without a main clause, there's nothing to make that sentence go.

Self-Diagnostic Test 2.2

To determine how well you understand main and subordinate clauses, identify both types in the following sentences. The answers appear in the back of the book.

1. Monahan, who says he would have had more trouble in the West if Williams had chosen O'Hara instead of Sen. Shaw as his running mate, scheduled a speech today in San Francisco.

2. Despite crowds that established records for high attendance with each passing year, the county event is quieter and more serious.

3. Several universities, because they annually have good football or basketball teams, lead the nation in the number of people applying for admission.

4. Harrison had stated earlier that he wished to serve only one term if elected.

5. And now the middle-aged high-school dropout, a maintenance employee at a small college, was reminiscing about the golden moment two months earlier when he surprised everyone by passing the entrance examinations at the school where he worked.

6. If for any reason the customers wish to discontinue direct deposit or

wish to redirect their check to a different financial institution, it is a simple procedure to make that change.

7. Dr. Stanton urged the graduates to be alert in defending their liberties, which he said "are as precious as life itself."

8. The United States announced today it will exchange diplomats with Cuba for the first time in 16 years.

9. Although formal relations may be a long way off, the diplomats will be in charge of a full range of activities between the two countries.

10. When demand for electricity is high during the 24-hour period, the water will be discharged from the reservoir into Cato Dam and will turn turbines to generate power.

The Compound-Complex Sentence

A compound-complex sentence contains at least two related ideas or actions and at least one subordinate idea or action. Here is an example from *The Washington Post*:

Main Clause	Gas would be piped ashore from the sites,
Subordinate Clause	which are between 47 and 92 miles off the coast,
Connective	and
Main Clause	pipelines would carry the gas from the coast to the country's most lucrative industrial and residential markets.

Note that the subordinate clause adds amplifying information to the first main clause. In this case, the subordinate clause could be dropped without doing harm to the main clause. However, that particular subordinate clause is an example of giving detail at the right moment. Here is one more compound-complex sentence:

He says the election could be closer because the incumbent is closing the gap, but he says it's going to be Janice Reilly just the same.

Like any other sentence of great length or complexity, the compound-complex sentence does not function well in broadcasting.

Exercise 2.2

A. Collect from newspaper stories, columns and editorials examples of simple, compound, complex and compound-complex sentences.

B. Identify the following sentences as simple, compound, complex or compound-complex and turn them in to your instructor for evaluation.

Name _____

1. Warren, who was not present at the 25-minute hearing, was convicted May 20 by a jury of trying to impede a federal grand jury probe of an influence-peddling scheme involving the sale of admissions to state-operated medical and veterinary schools.

2. The legislature passed the law July 2 and it took effect early this month.

3. The measure, which passed in the last legislative session and must be approved again this year, would have the attorney general run for office every four years during the presidential election.

4. The Republican commissioner, whose successor will be named by county Judge F. Thomas Williams, told the two Democratic commissioners that another reassessment of property values would be a "hard apple to bite," but that the time has come to conduct the reappraisal.

5. A similar arrangement was made between the American and Egyptian governments prior to their resumption of diplomatic relations in 1974.

6. Thirty-one other states have some form of postcard registration.

7. When Dallas made retirement mandatory at 65, those already working for the Sanitation Department were exempted.

8. Monahan was in California; Williams in Colorado.

9. One proposal that has surfaced recently is to use the water of Cato Dam to generate electricity.

10. Eight of the indicted guards and civilian employees were charged with other criminal acts as well, including the sale of confidential inmate records, the fencing of stolen property, the arranging of auto-insurance frauds and brutality against one inmate.

11. On her way from the airport Monday, the movie star was mobbed

by an enthusiastic crush of children, and the prime minister stopped
their car briefly.

12. This book is interesting, but that book is better.

13. Tractor-drawn wagons, with guides, will leave from the horticulture
and agronomy farm headquarters every 45 minutes to one hour.

14. Barnhart said that the best way to remove the cocaine would be
surgery because gastric juices would eventually eat through the
condom.

15. The Yankees are a good baseball team, but the Cincinnati Reds are
the best, which is why they won the World Series in 1976.

16. The weather shrank the number of guests at an outdoor dinner party
at the governor's home from more than 400 to fewer than 30 and
forced them inside.

17. The Nevada Assembly Friday defeated the Equal Rights
Amendment by a vote of 24–15.

18. Though Gibson has said he has some ideas about ways to negotiate
a settlement, aides say he plans mostly to listen rather than try out
his own conceptions.

19. British diplomats will work out of the Swiss embassy while Russian
officials will be in the Bulgarian embassy.

20. Knapp has strongly opposed the amendment, but he cannot legally
veto a constitutional amendment.

21. "This was highly prejudicial to the defendant, and he is at least
entitled to a new trial," Linn said.

22. In the coming week, incoming students will meet the president of
the university, the dean of all the colleges and the head of every
department to hear their ideas and suggestions on college life.

Positioning for Clarity

A writer can structure a sentence—say, a complex one—in one pattern (subject-
verb-object-subordinate clause) and that sentence would serve its purpose. But the
writer could move the sentence from one paragraph to another, and depending on

the new sentences around the moved sentence, its pattern might no longer work to full advantage.

A clause at the end of a sentence may, when shifted to the beginning, provide transition to a new subject or give context to the new subject. A qualifying phrase that just hangs on to a sentence needs to be moved to a position that removes a misleading implication. An attribution tag, repeated throughout a story, no longer need appear at the beginning of a sentence. Bury it, but if possible keep it away from the end of a sentence, for sentence beginnings and endings provide good positions for important information. Transitional markers, too, should not come too early or too late to dim their effectiveness.

Subordinate Clauses   Subordinate clauses can appear in various parts of sentences: the middle of a main clause, before a main clause, at the end of a main clause.

The tax bill, *which is long and complex,* will be voted on tomorrow.

The president, *who is eager for a rest,* will begin his vacation next week.

You could edit both of those clauses in the interest of tight writing. Broadcast journalists especially would do that in order to keep the subject and its verb together. In broadcasting, writers do not insert long or confusing phrases between subjects and their verbs.

The long, complex tax bill will be voted on tomorrow.

The president, eager for a rest, will begin his vacation next week.

The second sentence could also be written:

Eager for a rest, the president will begin his vacation next week.

Even though the modifying clauses were edited and moved from behind the word they modify to in front, they were still kept as close as possible to what they modify. But you would not shift the clause in the first sentence so the sentence would read:

The tax bill will be voted on tomorrow, which is long and complex.

The subordinate clause now modifies *tomorrow.*

Qualification   There are many sentence patterns in which the modification can appear at the beginning, middle or end of a sentence and the reader will understand what it modifies. But you should avoid such a loose approach to sentence structure. The writer of the following did not:

I have never been sick a day in my life, excluding my childhood years.

What is wrong is that the qualification of the main clause is not given first as a warning or tip-off to the reader. The sentence violates truth in writing. The example sets up the reader to believe one thing, then qualifies it. It's like this sign in a clothing store:

½ OFF

ALL LEISURE SUITS

(except some national brands)

Placing the modifying phrase first immediately gives the reader the qualifications or modifications of the main clause. There is no misleading the reader in this:

Excluding my childhood years, I have never been sick a day in my life.

Sometimes the related clause must appear first; otherwise, what it explains is not clear.

Nations have responded negatively to the president's statements on human rights because of increased nationalism.

The question is, were the statements made because of increased nationalism? No— and the proper stress makes that clear.

Because of increased nationalism, nations have responded negatively to the president's statements on human rights.

Remember, though, that because the beginning of a sentence is a good place for vital information, it ought not be wasted on trivia. Unless you are concerned with transition, don't place a time element at the start of a sentence, especially a lead such as this:

At last night's Cadbury City Council meeting, city manager Tony Sarno presented a draft of a construction contract.

Attribution Tag   Journalists must also consider the placement of attribution tags. In some instances, print journalists place the attribution tag at the end of a sentence because they want to give the news first, then follow it with the source of the news. They believe the news is more important or of more interest than the source.

The United States will enter into a unique trade agreement with Russia, *a State Department spokesman announced today.*

Some editors prefer the source first so the reader knows immediately who is speaking. Broadcasters demand the source first because it represents the natural speaking pattern. People, when they speak, don't put attribution tags at the end of their sentences.

A State Department spokesman announced today that the United States will enter into a unique trade agreement with Russia.

No one can lay down a rule that covers every situation. Once newspaper or magazine journalists have quoted someone with full identification, they will shift later attribution tags to the middle or end of a sentence, again because of the feeling that what is being said is of more importance or interest than who said it. Suppose a story began with the source, as in the case of the trade agreement announcement. The second paragraph, a direct quotation, might be written like this:

> "The agreement will allow the two countries to exchange goods heretofore banned in both countries," Assistant Secretary of State Thomas F. Williams said.

Attribution consistently used at the beginning of a sentence can get clumsy.

> *Monahan said* that, if necessary, the government should have the right to enforce mandatory conservation methods.

Also, such a structure uses a strong position (the beginning) for the attribution tag. Bury the attribution tag and a better sentence results.

> If necessary, *Monahan said,* the government should have the right to enforce mandatory conservation methods.

Bury it haphazardly, though, and ambiguity reigns.

> The presidential searchers are looking, Dixon said, intensely for someone who has shown scholarly ability and has had extensive administrative experience.

Phrases for Context   Just as important as qualifying phrases are subordinate clauses that provide a context for a direct quotation. When they follow the direct quotation, they force the reader to back up to see what the direct quotation means.

> "That kind of hits us where it hurts," Councilman Josh Labinski said when told the cost-plus fee would be used for housing outside the city.

A better sentence would not make the reader back up; it keeps the reader moving along.

> When told the cost-plus fee would be used for housing outside the city, Councilman Josh Labinski said: "That kind of hits us where it hurts."

Now you have a context for the direct quotation; now it means something. But the sentence's structure suffers because it violates the journalistic practice of not beginning a sentence with a dependent clause. Broadcasters do not allow sentences written for the ear to open with dependent clauses. Newspaper editors, communicating in a different medium, prefer that sentences open with the main thought followed by any subordinate thought. The advice is good. But like any other advice or rule, you should ignore it when logic says otherwise. Many of this book's sentences begin with dependent clauses because of my feeling that giving qualification first enhances overall sentence clarity.

Here are four sentences, each one structured a different way. Which sentence is the best?

Dr. Lewis Thomas said last night that man must consider the influence of all life on the separate parts of life *if he is to survive.*

Dr. Lewis Thomas said last night that man—*if he is to survive*—must consider the influence of all life on the separate parts of life.

Dr. Lewis Thomas said last night that *if man is to survive,* he must consider the influence of all life on the separate parts of life.

If man is to survive, Dr. Lewis Thomas said last night, he must consider the influence of all life on the separate parts of life.

The fourth sentence functions well. The qualification or context is first, the attribution tag is buried, and the main clause follows. The commendable feature of the second sentence is that it sets off the qualification with dashes, which give emphasis. However, some might see that sentence as choppy because of the abruptness. They, no doubt, would pick the third or fourth sentence.

Transition One stress that should come at the beginning of a sentence is the signal that tells the reader that what is to follow contradicts or clashes with what he or she has just read. The transition marker *however* is sometimes placed at the end of a sentence to the detriment of meaning.

The planning commission proposed a four-lane link between the two bypasses. Planner James Dugan said that building the link would cost an extra $20 million, *however.*

However—the tip-off that what is to follow is not in accord with what has just been said—belongs at the start of the second sentence or near the start.

The planning commission proposed a four-lane link between the two bypasses. *However,* planner James Dugan said that building the link would cost an extra $20 million.

The planning commission proposed a four-lane link between the two bypasses. Planner James Dugan said, *however,* that building the link would cost an extra $20 million.

Some writers would never put *however* at the beginning because they feel it hangs there too limply to be effective. William Zinsser suggests placing *however* as early as is reasonable (a natural break in the sentence, as in the second of the two preceding examples) so that "its abruptness then becomes a virtue." It's up to your ear or your editor.

Comparison Here, for side-by-side comparison are sentences structured differently for different stress.

The House, when it reconvenes, will pass the tax-reform bill. After that is done, the congressmen will review legislation on food stamps. Even though both proposals are good ideas, opposition exists in the two parties' caucuses. The local congressman opposes the tax-reform bill because it does not actually reform the tax laws.

When the House reconvenes, it will pass the tax-reform bill. The congressmen will review legislation on food stamps after that is done. Opposition exists in the two parties' caucuses even though both proposals are good ideas. Because the tax-reform bill does not actually reform the tax laws, the local congressman opposes it.

It is not a question of which one is better. What you should observe is the difference in stress—and remember the importance of that difference when writing.

Self-Diagnostic Test 2.3

To determine how well you understand the major points made in this section, do the following exercise. Rearrange the order of each sentence so that it appears in a logical pattern. The answers appear in the back of the book. Review what you miss.

1. "I am fine. Just a few scratches. Nothing serious," said Congressmen Evan Evans after being injured in a plane crash at the Flagstaff airport last night.

2. [A lead] If America goes back to organic farming, 50 million people would starve to death, the president of the Federation of Farmers said yesterday.

3. The president praised American farmers for being so productive that they create a surplus the government is able to ship to less fortunate nations even though the number of farmers is decreasing.

4. The old saying goes, "If you want to dance, you have to pay the piper." That is the belief of many, including the state's legislators, when it comes to financing education.

5. The mayor also objected to a section of the ordinance that would ban the parking of recreation vehicles in front-yard driveways, labeling it "regulatory overkill."

Sentence Variety

When writers construct sentences, they must give thought not only to main and subordinate clauses and emphatic order, but also to variety. Variety in sentences—both in structure and length—makes for good writing. To write all sentences in the same structure makes for tedious writing. To write all sentences in the same structure makes for tedious reading. To vary sentence structure and length is good.

The lack of structural variety in the last three sentences is poor—especially when you want to keep the reader reading. You already know that subordination of a minor idea is one form of sentence structuring, one way of creating variety. Inverting normal word order is another.

Problems   The problem with inverting the natural order of a sentence is that it distorts the conventional pattern on which people rely, and, when used repeatedly, disorients them. The standard inversion is putting the verb before its subject—in other words, starting a sentence with its verb. The disorientation begins immediately, for what good is a verb if the reader doesn't know its subject? What value is action without an actor? News sense, then, ought to guide journalists. What should the reader/listener know first? Here is an example of a sentence in which illogic prevailed over news sense.

Contained in the bag was a .32-caliber revolver.

Written in the normal pattern, the sentence is stronger because an active verb replaces a linking verb (*was*). The sentence is also tighter.

The bag contained a .32-caliber revolver.

Here is another example, this one a headline found in a 1946 edition of a magazine.

FROM DECK TO DESK MOVES MEMBER

Decades later persists the problem. Some writers invert the order of the attributive verb and its subject and cause confusion.

"My life was for them," cried Amos Jones Wednesday after the
bodies . . .

Is *Wednesday* the speaker's last name or the time element? The time element. But that would be more obvious if the attribution had not been inverted.

"My life was for them," Amos Jones cried Wednesday after the
bodies . . .

Another flawed inversion occurs with linking verbs when writers place the predicate in the subject position.

Experimenting with temporary malls on some downtown streets and
making South Hall Avenue near City Hall a two-way street are among
the recommendations that will be made to City Council on Friday night.

The inverted order fails because it forces the reader to proceed too deeply into the sentence before finding out what the sentence is about. Until seeing the word *recommendations,* the reader has no idea what the sentence is about.

Exceptions   Sometimes inversion is the lesser of two problems.

> The residency of the State Ballet at the main campus during the summer, the Invitational Film Festival for film critics in November, a photographic exhibit by the National Endowment for the Arts, and the purchase of video cassette equipment for the Graduate Center will be funded by the money allocated for the support of cultural activities.

Part of the problem with the sentence is the passive voice, which is discussed later. The sentence could be rewritten in the active voice or it could be inverted. Inverted it would read:

> To be funded by the money allocated for the support of cultural activities will be the residency of the State Ballet at the main campus during the summer, the Invitational Film Festival for film critics in November, a photographic exhibit by the National Endowment for the Arts, and the purchase of video cassette equipment for the Graduate Center.

Sometimes inversion serves as transition.

> City Council postponed action on a proposal to plant trees in the city's parking lots. *Also postponed was* action on a plan to install street lights in Celtic Circle.

The italicized portion of that sentence gets the reader from one unrelated topic to another by linking them through the postponed action. Too much of that, though, spoils a story.

Change in Stress   Consider also that you can sometimes invert sentences to change the stress. This is not a change in word order; functionally, the order is the same—noun-modifier-verb-modifier-object—or whatever the case may be. In leading into this discussion on sentence variety I wrote:

> Inverting normal word order is another [way].

But I could have written:

> Another way is inverting normal word order.

Short sentences, lend themselves better than long ones to such changes. The reader or listener won't lose the thought or miss the stress in a seven-word sentence. In a longer sentence let clarity dictate.

Positive vs. Negative   Another device for achieving variety is to change a negatively phrased sentence into a positively phrased one. Usually, you merely need a different verb.

> The gymnastics team's coach asked for a new gymnasium because the gymnastics team *has no* adequate facilities.

To get onto the positive track, you might write:

> The gymnastics team's coach asked for a new gymnasium because the gymnastics team *lacks* adequate facilities.

In converting the negative sentence to a positive one, I also replaced a meaningless verb (*has*) with a meaningful one (*lacks*).

Sentence Length

After World War II the wire services asked readability experts to examine their stories in an effort to improve them. Briefly, the experts determined that, on the average, short sentences (17 to 20 words) of short or common words built around active verbs are the best. What resulted was the popular idea that all sentences could be no more than 20 words. Many people ignored the word *average*.

From *The Bulletin* in Bend, Ore., comes a good example—a story with sentences averaging 18.6 words. The writer, Dave Swan, achieved that by writing only 10 of 37 sentences longer than 20 words. Here are four unrelated paragraphs to show some of Swan's pace:

> Henry "Hank" Bostleman, 532 NW Riverside, Bend, has been blowing glass for 25 years. He is now 70.
>
> Bostleman is a neon sign blower. He works for the Carlson Co., 1605 NE Forbes Road.
>
> "I really enjoy having something to do," he said. "A lot of people my age don't have enough to keep them busy."
>
> "The new modern equipment has quite a few refinements on it," he said. "But I've used this for years and it still works. In fact, I just had a sign come back in for repair that has been working for over 17 years. I think that's pretty good!"

What should not escape you—whether you are in print or broadcast journalism—is that some of the most effective sentences are direct quotations. People don't talk in long sentences. A sentence is too long if it can't be spoken in one deep breath. If your sentences make people gasp for air between the beginning and end, they are too long. Stop run-on sentences, such as this one:

> And yet, at this writing, there are only nine days left before the fiscal year runs out and the state is still without the essential financing to make it run efficiently and without the complete waste of funds which might result if there's no budget and revenue plan before July 1 and institutions will have to borrow money at high interest rates in order to keep going.

The run-on sentence stumbles because by saying so much it ultimately says nothing.

The reverse of the run-on is a string of short sentences—say, 10 words and under. A story built on such short sentences will read like a parody of journalistic writing. A good journalist can let fly with a length of words that have flow, rhythm and stamina and that count toward a meaning rather than a quota.

Cutting the Length   Naturally, when writing against a deadline, you cannot measure the length of your sentences. The secret is learning to write sentences of the right length before deadlines become a part of your life. Compute the average length of your sentences. If the average is high, find ways to reduce it.

Look at what you write; do you go on and on without putting in periods while at the same time ignoring commas, semicolons and other devices that might make reading your sentences easier or do you spot natural breaks in your long sentences and stop the sentences before they get out of hand? The preceding sentence is 53 words long. To make it read comfortably, change it to three sentences.

> Look at what you write. Do you go on and on without putting in periods while at the same time ignoring commas, semicolons and other devices that might make reading your sentences easier? Or do you spot natural breaks in your long sentences and stop the sentences before they get out of hand?

The paragraph has been reduced to an average of slightly more than 17 words a sentence by inserting punctuation marks that indicate full stops—periods and question marks—rather than punctuation marks that merely slow the reader down—commas and semicolons. This sentence should become two:

> The agency said Moscow had also bolstered its military presence in Cuba by sending increasing numbers of military advisers and constructing bases and using the island "as a bridgehead for contention with the United States, and for infiltration in the Western Hemisphere, especially the Caribbean."

That sentence contains 45 words for the reader to grasp in one breath. A period after *bases* and some editing would have made the preceding marginally digestible.

Plodding   *Sentences* trying to say too much at once creates long sentences, as evidenced by these examples from a student's paper:

> Bugliosi, a former deputy district attorney for the Los Angeles County District Attorney's office, made the statement in response to a question from the audience after his speech on the Tate-LaBianca murders for which he successfully prosecuted Charles Manson and four members of his family.
>
> Although he had been called in 1967 to prepare a search warrant for Sirhan's car, Bugliosi said he had no further involvement with the case until late 1975 when one of the bystanders accidentally shot during the RFK assassination petitioned to have the murder weapon test-fired again.
>
> More importantly, a number of individuals who were present at the hotel where Kennedy was shot in the hours and days after the killing,

among them hotel employees, Los Angeles police officers and a former FBI agent, say that bullets were found there which were never mentioned in the state's case.

My advice to the student: Provide more bam-bam-bam and less plod-plod-plod. Here's a rewrite. It begins one paragraph later than the original because the first paragraph in the original is a throwaway:

> Bugliosi, who in 1967 prepared a search warrant for Sirhan's car, said he became involved in the case again when a bystander at Kennedy's assassination asked to have the murder weapon test-fired again. The request was made in late 1975.
>
> More importantly, Bugliosi said, some of the witnesses and investigators contend bullets were found at the scene of the assassination but never mentioned in Sirhan's trial. Among those making that claim are a former FBI agent, some Los Angeles police officers and some hotel employees, Bugliosi said.

The rewrite's longest sentence is 33 words. The original's shortest is 45 (the throwaway sentence). And while some of the rewrite's brevity was reached by eliminating extraneous or redundant information, the main work of shortening the sentences came by not cramming too much between periods. Note that the date of the request rates a sentence to itself, as does the explanation of who said there were unmentioned bullets.

Natural Breaks   Transitional areas in sentences provide ideal places for windy writers to insert periods. Make sure, however, that you're not putting a period in an unnatural spot. Don't, for the sake of brevity, punctuate this sentence

> He drank 15 gin and tonics and 17 glasses of beer at the fraternity house party and then passed out.

like this

> He drank 15 gin and tonics. And 17 glasses of beer at the fraternity house party and then passed out.

when what you could do is

> He drank 15 gin and tonics and 17 glasses of beer at the fraternity house party. And then he passed out.

Not . . . but   Be careful when dealing with *not . . . but* constructions, which cannot be separated between two sentences.

> What you need is not a profound knowledge of the terminology of the English language's grammar, but a sensitivity to how the language operates.

To replace the comma (which some writers would not use anyway) with a period would foul the meaning of the sentence by creating two very fuzzy fragments.

Pace   While working on reducing the length of your sentences, also try to vary their length. It is not enough to vary structure; you've got to work on your pace too. If you stick to one main thought a sentence, you will vary your sentence length naturally. Here are sentences of virtually unvaried length:

> He said a president should lead this country and that right now there is a lack of leadership.
> "Never has a president vetoed so many bills since the Civil War," O'Neill said.
> Ford defended himself, saying the vetoes have saved millions of dollars in deficits.
> Of the 56 bills Ford has vetoed, Congress has sustained 42 vetoes, he said.
> Earlier this year Ford vetoed a $3.7 billion appropriations bill for public works jobs.
> He said the extra billions were not enough to make jobs where the jobs really are needed.

The length of those sentences is 18, 14, 13, 14, 14 and 17 words, which is hardly variety. This is readily apparent when you look at the sentences. Each is virtually the same length; each ends around the same place in a line. Sight alone indicates there is a problem. As an exercise, rewrite those six sentences with a more varied structure. The secret: tighten and subordinate.

Self-Diagnostic Test 2.4

To determine how well you understand the major points in this section, do the following exercise. Reduce the length of these sentences by inserting periods where they fit naturally. Slight editing may be necessary. The answers appear in the back of the book. Review what you miss.

1. Under the student regulations, in effect in a student government election for the first time, the cost of all on-campus campaigning for all student candidates is paid entirely from the student activities fund and no personal contributions are permitted, except for a limited amount channeled through committees recognized by the Undergraduate Student Government.

2. Last April the commissioners held a meeting with hospital officials to discuss a list of possible Elmbank uses, and, with a few exceptions, the hospital officials approved the list before agreeing to further negotiations.

3. A Soviet spokesman initially reported that the jet had been seized by five gunmen but later said that three were involved—one carrying a Somalian passport, the second carrying an Ethiopian passport and the third carrying a Moroccan travel permit.

4. Clifford has come under mounting pressure from students, lawyers, and more recently, alumni of the school, to appoint an impartial group to investigate allegations of a cover-up at the school where faculty members have testified that more than half of last year's engineering class of 250 students could have been involved in collaborating on a take-home test last April.

5. Notices will be sent to about 150 school superintendents—the first superintendents to leave their positions since the state's financial crisis forced reductions in the public school system but in some instances the superintendents will be pushed to lower-paying positions than they had; in others, they will be let go altogether.

6. The society said the highest number of species reported by a group in this country was 221 turned in at Des Moines, Iowa; 62 other groups in communities from Virginia to Washington listed 125 or more species.

Exercise 2.3

A. Compare the average sentence length of news stories in various newspapers. Study, too, the length of sentences in one newspaper, breaking down your study by sections in the paper, such as Page One, lifestyle (or whatever it's called), editorial, sports, business.

B. In news stories with long sentences, rewrite the sentences so they are shorter and easier to read—either for print or on the air.

Some Sentence Faults

A sentence can fall down—or at least trip—any number of ways. Some of these get through treatment in the chapters ahead. For now, though, the discussion centers on structure, non sequiturs, parallel construction and false series—four of the many problems that can ruin a sentence.

Structure   Mistakes made in structuring sentences are easy to avoid provided the writer keeps a clear mind at all times. Discipline yourself to think clearly as you write—no matter what the pressure. If you must stop while you're constructing a sentence to see where you've been, then do so. Sometimes you'll discover that the end and the beginning don't match and you'll begin anew.

Read the following and think about what you might have changed to make the sentence clear:

> The charges were brought by Cambridge police in connection with an incident in which a pedestrian was hit by a vehicle on South Mahanoy Street Saturday night and then left the scene of the accident.

First, realize that the sentence says "a pedestrian was hit . . . and then left the scene of the accident" when what really happened was that the car left the scene. You could change the connective *and* to the pronoun *which* to at least make it clear that the car did the leaving.

When the writer neared the end of the sentence, he had forgotten the beginning. Go to the beginning. The first problem appears in the first four words—the passive voice (*were brought*) of the main clause's verb. Avoid passive voice wherever possible; it's a backward way of saying things. Switching to the active

> Cambridge police *brought* the charges . . .

I drop two words (*were, by*). Further pruning

> . . . after a car hit a pedestrian . . .

leaves eight more words by the wayside.

> . . . and left the scene on South Mahanoy Street Saturday night.

Four more words dropped; in addition, I placed the car's actions (*hit* and *left*) closer together. By separating them too much, the writer sent the reader backward looking for the verb's subject when the reader should have been going forward. By changing to active voice, I produced a better sentence.

> Cambridge police brought the charges after a car hit a pedestrian and left the scene on South Mahanoy Street Saturday night.

Errors in sentences are mostly a byproduct of length. The longer the sentence the more opportunity there is for error. The writer of this sentence tried to cram so much into 28 words that he shifted the subject and never made it clear when he turned to the sentence's original subject:

> She was admitted to the psychiatric ward of a hospital, where her family was permitted to visit her and was to be transferred to a district hospital today.

The subject of *to be transferred* should be *she,* but as the sentence is constructed, it's *family.* Two sentences would correct the error.

She was admitted to the psychiatric ward of a hospital, where her
family was permitted to visit her. She was to be transferred to a district
hospital today.

Here is a shorter sentence that is still constructed poorly enough to be confusing:

The statements by both candidates were in answer to questions from the
Arms Control Association, a private disarmament study group, and
published Monday.

The last three words confused me because it is not clear what the subject of
published is. The writer has two options—a rewrite or two sentences.

Published Monday, the statements by both candidates were in answer to
questions from the Arms Control Association, a private disarmament
study group.

The statements by both candidates were in answer to questions from the
Arms Control Association, a private disarmament study group. The
statements were published Monday.

Misplacement of a time element can sometimes confuse a reader.

William Monahan's opposition *seized yesterday* on his admission . . .

That is not what Saul Bellow meant when he wrote his novel *Seize the Day*.
Transpose the verb and the time element.

William Monahan's opposition yesterday seized on his admission . . .

Non Sequiturs   A non sequitur is an incongruous phrase within a sentence, a phrase
that does not logically fit with the main thought. Editors frequently advise reporters
not to let background material stand alone in a story but to blend it with current
material. The thinking is that background material standing alone is like the throwaway
sentence discussed in Chapter 1, that it does not advance the news thread of the
story. Thus journalists often scatter background throughout a story, usually in
subordinate clauses. However, when the subordinate clause does not logically belong
with the main clause, the writer has created a non sequitur.

Spanos, who is married to the former Sue Harvey of Clemson, said his
major league debut wasn't as bad as he thought it would be.

The writer was not wrong to want to mention Spanos' wife, since she was a local
resident and some readers of the newspaper in which that sentence appeared might
know her. The writer was wrong to link Spanos' debut in major league baseball with
his wife.

The writer charged with getting some life into a story can easily create non
sequiturs. The editor orders that the staff do more than just report comments. "Give

me some color,'' the editor demands. One of the newsroom minions covers an otherwise dull meeting and in looking for detail to enliven the story notices that one of the participants jiggles keys in his pocket. Now this could be a sign of nervousness or an indication of the speaker's deceit. The reporter, unfortunately, handles the action this way:

> "Everything in this proposal is according to your guidelines,'' Dillon said, jiggling keys in his pocket.

For the sake of some color, the reporter has created a non sequitur. Good writers maintain vigilance against non sequiturs, for the writers know how such slips can confound readers and cause undesired laughter. Rather than link a major league debut and a baseball player's spouse, a good writer will place the unrelated information in separate paragraphs. Likewise, if certain details have nothing to do with the action, the good writer ignores them.

Violating Parallel Construction   Consider how disconcerting it is to walk on an uneven surface that throws off your balance. Parallel construction abuse does much the same thing to people reading stories. Obviously you cannot write stories containing nothing but 20-word sentences. So, as you vary your sentences among simple, compound, complex and compound-complex, you must be aware of parallel construction. Problems with this construction often develop when you list items in a series, be they nouns, verbs or entire clauses. Remember to maintain the same form or function for all coordinate elements within a sentence. The following does not violate parallel construction:

> He likes *books, birds* and his *car.*

Parallel construction is not a matter of singular and plural number, but of consistent form or function. Thus, the use of prepositional phrases in a series would not limit the writer to the preposition that begins the series.

> He can sleep *at* night, *during* the day and *in* the evening.

Verbals in a series are maintained in parallel construction.

> The wildest onslaught of tornadoes and violent storms this year erupted in the midlands Wednesday, *killing* at least four persons, *injuring* scores and *leaving* hundreds homeless.

Here is a sentence in which the first verbal needs a parallel:

> He ordered them *to keep* their farm reasonably free from manure and *the removal* of the manure piled next to the Williams' property.

The second italicized phrase should function the same way as the first.

> He ordered them *to keep* their farm reasonably free from manure and *to remove* the manure piled next to the Williams' property.

Where possible, nouns should have parallel construction with nouns, and adjectives with adjectives. This sentence is flawed.

Police have no idea if the death was accidental or a suicide.

To repair the series, change the adjective *accidental* to a noun.

Police have no idea if the death was an accident or a suicide.

The following sentence does not violate parallel construction, although the parallel functions are not repeated in their entirety:

Taiwan wanted *to compete* as the Republic of China, *fly* its flag and *play* its anthem.

That sentence has been shortened through elliptic writing. Written out fully, it would be:

Taiwan *wanted to compete* as the Republic of China, *wanted to fly* its flag and *wanted to play* its anthem.

Most editors would prefer the first sentence because it is shorter and less demanding on the reader.

Dr. Robert L. Butler, a professor of biology at Penn State, found the following barbarism in an advertisement by an engineer:

My system is practical to use in breeding fish, biological laboratories, and for use in fish farming, the industry of the future, for a good source of protein, very much needed throughout the entire world to help eliminate starvation and for better health.

Among other things, the advertised system breeds not only fish but also biological laboratories. Parallel construction was violated because the writer attempted to put too many unrelated ideas into the sentence—a fault Butler has appropriately named *shack building*.

Clauses in a series should be parallel, as they are here:

He said that was the way to repair it, that there was no other way, and that it was the way he wanted the work done.

"We should be vigilant for those who want too much power concentrated in one place, who want to silence an unpopular minority, who want to jail a reporter or throttle a television station, who want to deny teachers the freedom to teach and students the freedom to learn," Dr. Stanton said.

Here is a sentence that needs parallel clauses:

The receivers tell firemen *where there is a fire* and its location.

The sentence is not as awkward when parallel construction is followed.

> The receivers tell firemen *when there is a fire* and *where it is located*.

If you think as you write and edit closely when you're finished, you won't violate parallel construction.
Sometimes correcting the problem is not a matter of form but of reconstruction.

> The party leader said he *was* upset by the vote and will go to New
> Mexico in an attempt to change it.

> The addition *will provide* the 92 students with four teachers and *follows*
> the recent hiring of a teacher for the fifth and sixth grades.

Some editors might argue that while those two sentences violate parallel construction, there is good reason. But those who don't like the sentences can right the violation by subordinating.

> The party leader, who said he was upset by the vote, will go to New
> Mexico in an attempt to change it.

> The addition, which will provide the 92 students with four teachers,
> follows the recent hiring of a teacher for the fifth and sixth grades.

Sometimes a writer has a good reason to violate parallel construction, especially when time is involved.

> The other six *were killed* and their murders *remain* unsolved.

A change in the tense of either verb would change the meaning. You can't subordinate because the sentence is compound, unlike some of the previous examples that merely had compound predicates. In those, the subject remained the same. That doesn't mean compound sentences should not be parallel. It does mean there are exceptions. The logic of time should dictate in those cases, not the convention of parallel construction.

False Series   Similar to parallel construction abuse is what Theodore M. Bernstein calls "series out of control" and what H.W. Fowler calls "bastard enumeration." From a student paper comes this example:

> "Peanuts" appears in 700 newspapers in the United States, 71
> newspapers abroad, and is translated into a dozen languages.

Insert another *and* and the problem is corrected.

> "Peanuts" appears in 700 newspapers in the United States *and* 71
> newspapers abroad and is translated into a dozen languages.

The problem can also arise with a surplus verb.

Premier Shahpur Bakhtiar today pledged to disband the dreaded secret police, cut off oil to Israel and South Africa, release political prisoners and *introduced* a new war minister.

The cure:

Premier Shahpur Bakhtiar today pledged to disband the dreaded secret police, cut off oil to Israel and South Africa, and release political prisoners. He also introduced a new war minister.

Self-Diagnostic Test 2.5

To determine how well you understand the major points made in this section, do the following exercise. Identify the sentence faults as structure, non sequitur, parallel construction or false series. The answers appear in the back of the book. Review what you miss.

1. Other responses included talking with the child, a verbal reprimand, isolating the child or removing privileges.

2. The doctor said attempts to revive Presley, who appeared in 31 films—including "Love Me Tender," "GI Blues," and "Jailhouse Rock"—continued because of a slight chance that life still existed in his body.

3. He is a determined racquetball player, collector of baseball cards and jogs four miles a day.

4. Williams suggested closing the loopholes for the rich and rejection of salary increases for government officials.

5. Two front gates at the Carbonite Filter Corp., Delano, were damaged Friday when a car crashed into them in an effort to break into the grounds.

6. The recommendations included the possibility of hiring an additional teacher for the junior high and the transfer of a part-time teacher from the elementary school to the junior high.

Exercise 2.4

Make the following sentences parallel and turn your answers in to your instructor for evaluation.

Name _____

1. In other business yesterday, City Council approved plans for reconstruction and landscaping the McAllister Street parking lot.

2. To walk, running and flying are my favorite forms of exercise.

3. To find the business, take the first turn to your right, you'll cross the street and walk one block.

4. Proof that he was human came when he walked in here and talks about his pain.

5. If for any reason customers wish to discontinue this plan or want their checks redirected to another bank, they may do so.

6. The association recommended that the board consider adding two basketball games to the schedule, which increases it to 22 games, and to extend the girls' cross-country schedule to include two meets with Smethport.

7. Williams said he was proud of his role in authorizing the break-ins and feels he had an obligation to authorize them.

8. It would also abolish the service's board of governors, make the agency's chief subject to confirmation, providing an extra $2.3 billion in subsidies, and bar any rate increases or substantial cutbacks in service until next year.

9. As part of its study, the commission traveled through the state holding public hearings, took testimony from parents, teachers and administrators, and observing school activities.

Transition

Not even an apprentice bricklayer would think of building a house without using cement to keep the bricks together. Similarly, no journalist should put together a story whose sentences are not cemented together. The cement is the transition from one sentence to the next. Commonly used transition words are *meanwhile, but, still, nevertheless, for example, however, also, for, and, on the other hand, next, similarly, again, consequently, as a result, in other words.*

But before continuing, look over the preceding paragraph to see how I linked one sentence to the next. What I did was repeat words or variations of words so that the idea was continued. I first used the word *similarly,* which told the reader an analogy was coming. To make sure the analogy was there I not only used a similar idea, I also repeated two of the words in the idea—*cement(ed)* and *together.* In sentence three I repeated the word *cement* and then used for the first time the word *transition,* which I then repeated in sentence four. That's transition—clearly linking past ideas to the present and future. You do it in sentences all the time, using the connectives mentioned in the first paragraph in addition to others.

Linking   Within sentences the two most common transition words are *and* and *but.*

> Councilman Rosenthal said the proposal was faulty *and* she announced plans to modify it.

In that sentence two related actions were linked by *and.*

> Government officials said the hijackers ordered the plane to turn west to Hawaii, *but* the pilot told them he did not have enough fuel *and* he continued on to Los Angeles.

That sentence shows a contrast between two actions. *But* means, among other things, *on the contrary* or *however.* Its purpose is to tip readers that what they are about to read will disagree, contradict or modify what they have just read.

But should not be thought of in terms of internal sentence transition only. As noted earlier, when sentences get too long, a period before *but* is a good place to start shortening them. Whether you use *but* to carry from one part of a sentence to another or from one sentence to another depends largely on readability. Your guide is how much you want to make the reader swallow before you give a break. In this example the writer chose to make two sentences:

> Britain demanded the meeting and proposed that it be held today. But Lebanon proposed a delay until Wednesday afternoon, and Britain agreed.

Because both sentences have two actions (*demanded, proposed; proposed, agreed*), the writer was on safer ground not tying them together in one sentence. It would have been too much to understand.

(Be careful with *but* and its synonyms. Because it sets up a contrast, *but* is not a substitute for *and,* which joins related ideas. Failing to appreciate *but,* one sloppy journalist wrote: "Father Kenney has been a quiet, unassuming priest, but loved and respected by Catholics and non-Catholics alike." There is no contrast; *and* is correct.)

Here are three consecutively written paragraphs that lack transition:

> Lee exhibited her "Children Before Dogs" T-shirt, created for her most widely known campaign, to "Scoop the Poop" in New York City.
>
> Toxicariasis, a disease transmitted primarily by contact with dog feces, especially affects children who often play where dogs are "curbed."

> Lee said she likes dogs but predicted a day when dogs will be banned because owners do not adequately control or care for them.

One possible transition from the first to the second paragraph might have been:

> The campaign is aimed at fighting toxicariasis, a disease transmitted primarily by contact with dog feces. The disease especially affects children.

The key to that transition is to repeat the word *campaign*.

Subject Change   When the subject changes, advise the reader and transition will result. A City Council story with a lead item on a major pedestrian question might signal a change to a new subject this way:

> *In street-paving matters,* the council rapidly approved a series of projects . . .

Beginning the sentence with the new topic advises the reader immediately of a change.

Placement   Transitional words are not necessarily placed at the beginning of a sentence. They do, however, come early enough to bridge the action.

> The change in academic standards was cited by the accrediting team as proof the department was no longer performing its mission well. Members of the department and the dean of the college, *on the other hand,* said standards were not the only thing that should be used to measure quality.

Repetition   Repeating words is a valid transitional device.

> ''The flow of international news has been impeded rather than advanced,'' Paley said, citing censorship and *attempts* at censorship throughout the world. One *attempt* occurred when UNESCO's . . .

Relationships   An additional method of transition similar to changing the subject is showing the relationship of one item in a story to another. A City Council story containing news about a debate on the budget might show a change to a related subject this way:

> *In another fiscal matter,* the Council . . .

That approach tells the reader the subject is still money.

Improvement   Sometimes transition is not a matter of existing or not existing, but rather is a matter of degree. The following example shows a transition that is not bad. But it could be made better.

On the committee are Curtis Boyer of Pickett County, Barry O'Hara of Clive County and Joseph Holt of Orange County. Boyer said a new line could be built parallel to the old one.

The degree of improvement comes in moving *Boyer* to the end of the series of committee members.

On the committee are Barry O'Hara of Clive County, Joseph Holt of Orange County and Curtis Boyer of Pickett County. Boyer said a new line could be built parallel to the old one.

Continuity   Transition can exist on the continuity of the action alone.

High moral standards are required for Fortville police officers, according to Chief Bernice T. Showman.
    Showman said last night she insists on those standards so that respect for the police is maintained.
    "Police officers have to be just a little bit better than anyone else in society so that they won't be looked down upon," she said.

To get from the lead to the second paragraph, the writer repeated the police chief's surname. To carry the story to the third paragraph, the writer used a direct quotation that explains the second paragraph.
    You will discover as you edit that you can remove some transitional devices without doing harm to the story. Often the story's action carries the reader all by itself. Similarly, a question-and-answer format works on the strength of the questions alone. Curiosity on the reader's part supplies the transition. However, questions made up by a journalist within a normally written news story are a cheap device and show a lack of imagination. For example:

Will Kaplan and his associates get out of prison when they become eligible for parole in April next year?

If the reporter doesn't know, why did he write the story?

Contrast   Two characteristics that are opposites can actually make a transition easier. One paragraph ends:

So her physical health is looking slightly better.

And the next begins:

Financially, though, her situation is far from healthy.

Paragraphs   Paragraph breaks can serve as transitional devices. At the end of a city council story a journalist might want to add a list of unrelated actions. To take the reader from the main action to the list, the journalist might write:

> *In other action,* the council:

Or the journalist could shorten that to:

> The council *also:*

In a complex story, paragraphs are often necessary to get the reader from one topic to another. For instance, journalists covering a political debate might focus on the two main opponents. When the time comes to report on the others, the journalist might use this transitional device:

> Also on the platform for the debates were Patrick Neuman, a Democrat, and Mary Agee, a Republican, who are opponents in the local legislative district contest.

The story would then continue by reporting what Neuman and Agee said. Unfortunately, the transitional sentence is virtually a throwaway, which some editors would accept only reluctantly. Here's a better example:

> Lee pointed out that the discoverer of swine flu told her he wouldn't let anyone take the immunization shot since numerous cases of paralysis have resulted from it.
> Lee, executive director of the "Children Before Dogs" organization, also talked on the diseases children contract from the worms in dog feces.
> The larvae of the worm get into the child when he kisses the family pet or plays on the carpeting, she said.

What makes the transitional paragraph in the Lee excerpt superior to the one in the political story is that it is not a throwaway sentence. It presents something more concrete than just identification of two people as political opponents.

Be careful your transition does not commit you to something you might have no control over later. Keeping in mind that make-up editors sometimes have to cut stories to fit a hole and that they usually do so by chopping from the story's end, paragraph by paragraph, consider this transition near the end of a student's story:

> "The flow of international news has been impeded rather than advanced in the past decade," Paley said.
> He cited *three examples* of attempts to censor events in certain countries as efforts to restrict the free press.
> *One example* is . . .

Of course, the student also cited examples two and three. But if the story had been cut and example three was among the missing, imagine how stupid the newspaper would look. To avoid a problem, dump the *three examples* paragraph entirely.

> "The flow of international news has been impeded rather than advanced in the past decade," Paley said.
> *For example,* in India . . .

Now if any examples are cut, the reader will be none the wiser.

Foreshadowing Much the way a fiction writer might hint at what lies ahead in a novel, a journalist writing a multitopic story can also give readers a peek and then use that peek as a springboard to the new subject at the appropriate time. Foreshadowing, in journalistic terms, involves a story that contains information on at least two major items. But since it is not wise to cram the story's lead with too much information, the secondary item is placed in the second paragraph. For demonstration, here is a school board story.

> The Allendale School Board last night raised taxes to help pay for the purchase of microcomputers that will be used in a new course on computer literacy.
>
> The board also agreed to expand the teaching of foreign languages into the seventh grade. Now, foreign language instruction begins in the ninth grade.
>
> The tax increase will cost the average home owner $17 more a year, the board's treasurer said.
>
> [The writer uses six more paragraphs to explain the tax increase and then moves on to the subject of foreign languages.]
>
> *In expanding foreign language instruction,* the board agreed that not only could students learn a foreign language in seventh grade but that they wanted to.

The writer linked the second paragraph to the change in topic by choosing similar words. The foreshadowing occurred in the second paragraph; its promise was kept later. Thanks to the transition, the reader knew immediately when the topic changed and what it was.

Time Time elements can serve as transitions and can be critical to clarity. When the time changes, the reader should be told immediately. If you change the time but don't tell the reader, you will create confusion. Here are two paragraphs in which the time changes, and the time element serves well as a transition:

> *Earlier this year* Feldman warned that the agency would halt virtually all development unless the legislature agreed to set strict auto emission standards.
>
> Lawmakers ignored the threat and defeated the measure twice. *Yesterday,* the Environmental Review Committee also voted, 9–3, to reject the anti-emissions proposal.

Contrived Transitions Whichever transitional device you use, make sure it is real. Don't force it, the way a television newscaster once did.

> [Film of local fire is shown. Film ends; anchorman speaks:] "While there were no injuries in that fire, the death toll in an earthquake in Guatemala has risen to 3,000."

Linking a local fire of little consequence to a tragic earthquake is absurd. Such contrivances, because of their obvious incongruity, make poor transitions.

Paragraphs

Those who have the perseverance to define a paragraph agree that unity plays a key role. Completeness, order and coherence are other sure signs that a writer has a paragraph in hand.

A paragraph should not drift away from the main thought. Because of the different ideas in these two sentences, the following should be two paragraphs:

> The Clive-Cadbury series goes back to 1900 and the record is fairly
> even at 14–13–2, with Clive leading as it always has. Quarterback
> Dave Dillon leads the Cadbury offense in both passing and rushing.

Because the second sentence has nothing to do with the first, it should be placed in a separate paragraph.

Theme-writing rules aside, three general rules for newspaper paragraphs stand out.

The first is: Usually write very short paragraphs because they will put more white space (also called air) into the gray-appearing story and make it easier on the eye—that is, more legible in print. Newspaper columns are getting wider, but the increase is hardly enough to justify increasing the length of paragraphs. Column widths range from 9½ picas (six picas equal one inch) to 14 and 15 picas. But a check of several nationally known newspapers revealed that the width of the column of type had no apparent effect on the number of sentences in a paragraph. Most of the paragraphs were short no matter what the column width.

The second rule is: Don't bury "quotes" (direct quotations) at the end of paragraphs. If there is a quote a journalist wants to use, he or she should display it. That is why a copy editor would break the following into two paragraphs after the first sentence:

> Malta's newspaper criticized a reported British plan to use the offer of
> assistance to win concessions in talks on the future of naval bases on
> the island. "It appears that some British diplomats have been on the
> lookout for opportunities to use aid as a public relations gesture," one
> newspaper said in an editorial. "This may do for panty-hose makers,
> but it is hardly becoming of a nation like Great Britain."

However, getting a quote out front in a paragraph can lead to confusion when the person being quoted is also being mentioned for the first time. When changing speakers or characters, tell the reader immediately. That did not happen here:

> The Phillies have lost 11 of their last 12, scoring a total of 13 runs in
> their last nine games. Pirate pitcher Jim Rooker went the distance on a
> nine-hitter Wednesday night.

> "I don't know, I really don't know," Phillies Manager Danny
> Ozark said in his team's hushed locker room. "But I think we're going
> to snap out of it. We should, and I feel we will win."

At first reading it appears the writer is quoting Jim Rooker because Rooker is the last person mentioned before the quote. In such a situation, start the new paragraph with attribution so the reader knows immediately who is speaking. Perhaps this is even better:

> In his team's hushed locker room, Phillies Manager Danny Ozark said:
> "I don't know . . ."

In any case, don't make readers scramble back and forth in a story to find out what they want to know. Always keep the story clear.

The third rule is: Good, logically organized paragraphs—like good, logically organized sentences—help make good stories. Some novice writer might create a paragraph of two unrelated sentences, realize the mistake and then convert the two unrelated sentences into two unrelated paragraphs. Unfortunately, the writer has not solved the problem—merely highlighted it. If in fact the two sentences should relate, the writer can unite them more closely. If the second changes subject, perhaps a transition will solve the problem. Perhaps, too, one of the offending sentences needs to be moved elsewhere in the story or deleted.

Point of View

Point of view in journalism means two things: the opinion of the writer or the position/perspective from which he or she reports a story. It is the second—the literary application—that will be discussed here. Journalists, for the most part, should assume a neutral point of view. They should not identify with anyone— neither the people they are reporting on nor the people they are reporting for. Of course, this doesn't mean reporters don't care about these people; it means they don't mix identities with them. If, for example, a speaker says: "We must do our best to improve conditions in this country," a journalist might paraphrase the quotation as:

> The people must do their best to improve conditions in the United
> States, Romano said.

When paraphrasing quotations, shift the pronouns, *I, you, we, our* to third person pronouns or nouns (such as the speaker's name or, as in the preceding example, *the people*). Badly paraphrased, a speaker's statement can damage the writer's credibility, as in this example:

> Most people operate at only about 10 percent of *our* sexual potential, an
> associate professor of biology said last night.

The correct pronoun is *their*.

The use of *we* outside direct quotations in news stories leads to confusion when the reader turns to the editorial page and reads an editorial that says: "We believe the president . . ." In that clause, it is the *editorial we;* it belongs only on the editorial page. The confusion is compounded by opinion page headline writers who insist that *we* in a headline is not the same as *we* in an editorial or column. Thus: HOW WE GOT IN TROUBLE IN VIETNAM. Had that writer been thinking, he or she would have substituted *U.S.* for *we*. Another headline writer failed the same test by writing on a Sunday opinion essay: WE HAVE GOOD REASON TO HATE THE BRITS. We? The newspaper? Americans? No. Argentines. The column, published in a U.S. newspaper, was written by an Argentine-American during the war between Britain and Argentina over the Falkland Islands.

Despite the plea for a neutral point of view, newspapers must face the reality of where they exist. A New York newspaper reporting the visit of someone to that city would write:

King Tut of Egypt *came* to New York today from Washington, D.C.,
where he had been visiting for three days.

When you're in New York, you can't *go* there. But if you're in Washington and you're writing about the same event for a Washington newspaper, your point of view shifts.

King Tut of Egypt *went* to New York from Washington, where he had
been visiting for three days.

Some newspapers are more provincial about point of view than others. The story is told of a day when Great Britain was covered by a thick fog. Ships dared not sail from the island to Europe and vice versa. Who was cut off from whom? Reportedly, one London newspaper headlined its story:

CONTINENT FOGGED IN

This provincialism extends to newspapers circulated in a very wide area. Often a major newspaper's headline on a story distant from its base will include words such as upstate and downstate. UPSTATE MAN WINS HONORS may be fine for the people *downstate,* but what about the people who live in the vicinity of the story? Will they pass over it because they believe *upstate* means upstate from them? Better to use the points of a compass or the name of a town than to confuse the reader.

Editors of newspapers that are sold in more than one community are acutely aware of how a slip in point of view might be taken by readers of one community after the editor has spent a lifetime telling all communities that none is favored above another. One Pennsylvania newspaper covers an entire county that includes a university. When someone at the university dies, its public information office writes an obituary that invariably includes the words, "He *came* to the university in . . ." From that writer's point of view, *came* is correct. But from the point of view of the newspaper's audience, which includes people not connected with the university, the point of view has to be changed. After all, readers do not necessarily identify with the university and their livelihood does not necessarily derive from the university. Hence, the newspaper edits that phrase to say: "He *went* to the university in . . ."

However, if someone born in another county becomes a resident of the newspaper's county and dies there, the paper writes: "He *came* to Centre County . . ." If the person is a native of the county but dies elsewhere, the paper writes: "He *went* to Miami in . . ." Clearly, the paper has a county point of view. Thus, when one reporter whose beat covered only one community wrote: "The Lanse Fire Co. expects delivery of its new truck *here* Tuesday," the editor ordered *here* cut from the story. To the editor, *here* meant the entire county, which wasn't what the writer of the story meant.

In the same vein, a wire service story datelined Pittsburgh included this phrase: "Before *coming* to Arkansas in 1973 . . ." The correct word for that Pittsburgh story is *going*. If you remember come *here*, go *there*, you shouldn't have problems.

Time magazine, on a cover for its United States edition, blurbed a story this way: A POPE COMES TO BRITAIN, which was incorrect. The readers were in the United States so the pope was *going* to Britain, not *coming* to Britain. The blurb would have been correct only on the cover of *Time*'s British edition.

One of the most serious betrayals of point of view involves chauvinism, the tendency to report the news filtered through the reporter's prejudices. In sentence after sentence evidence shows up suggesting that the world is male and that women are inferior. This sentence demonstrates the problem:

> Three terrorists, one of them a woman, shot and killed Rafael del Cogliano, 38, a commissioner . . .

What were the other two? The man who wrote the sentence revealed his chauvinism by pointing out the gender of only the female terrorist. The underlying message to readers is: "Hey, folks, here's a gal who totes a machine gun." In the interest of even-handed writing and a neutral point of view, the sentence should say:

> Three terrorists—two men and a woman—shot . . .

The bias extends into race, national origin and many other matters. But the point remains the same. Do not stereotype someone by sex or age or race. Write about people's human qualities rather than characteristics more typical of, for example, gender. Not all men are muscular brutes, not all women are housewives; men can be gentle and women fierce. Treat everyone the same.

The principle behind point of view requires journalists to remember not how their words read or sound to them but how the reader/listener will interpret the words. Remembering the audience's point of view is extremely critical in journalism because failure to do so can create ambiguity or indicate to the reader/listener an unintended bias that could interfere with the main point of the news. If you keep your audience in mind at all times, you probably won't have problems with point of view.

Chapter 3

Functional Grammar

Parts of Speech—Then and Now

At one time traditional grammarians taught eight parts of speech—no more, no less. Those teachers said English contained nouns, pronouns, verbs, adjectives, adverbs, prepositions, conjunctions, interjections. Students were required to memorize the definitions of those parts of speech. "What is a noun?" the teacher would ask. And the students would reply: "A noun is the name of a person, place or thing."

The belief was that you could not use a noun in any other function except a noun function. Dictionaries determined what nouns (and other parts of speech) were. Such blind faith, though, creates problems. One dictionary says *football* is a noun, as in "He threw the football" and "The football is next to the bench." Very clearly *football* is used as a noun in those sentences. But what is it in this sentence?

The football field isn't large enough for three teams.

A very strict teacher might say the sentence is incorrect because *football* is a noun and nouns do not function as adjectives. Adjectives modify nouns; they do not serve as nouns themselves. But *football* does modify something—*field*. The teacher might win the debate by saying that *football field* is perceived as one concept; that both words are nouns. True. But the dictionary also says *field* is a verb ("Iowa *fields* good football teams") and an adjective ("He is a *field* hand at the Smith farm"). It should be apparent, then, that it is impossible to define a part of speech without seeing how it is used. That's functional grammar.

Grammar today is classified according to the way it is studied: traditional, structural or transformational. Other descriptions include generative, which some no doubt would call degenerative. But no matter what it's called, our grammar is still the study of the conventions of contemporary language usage and not the study of some rules set down in the eighteenth century and adhered to blindly ever since. We must concern ourselves with how words and phrases function today and label them accordingly.

Generally speaking, the parts of speech can be divided into four very broad categories: nouns (including pronouns), verbs, connectives and modifiers. No matter what you want to say about, for example, a clause (relative, dependent, independent), your primary concern is how it modifies a noun or a verb or another clause. When you talk about the number and tense of a verb in a clause, you do it in the context of how that clause modifies another part of a sentence. Journalists care about making their sentences and punctuation conventional only because they want their stories to be understood by their readers. Hence, they are concerned with function, not some esoteric study of grammar.

More enlightened dictionaries, while still labeling words as noun, verb, adjective, and so on, qualify themselves. *The American Heritage Dictionary of the English Language,* after advising its readers that its entries are traditionally labeled, says:

> These parts of speech are not to be regarded as perfectly exclusive categories. Many nouns in English, for example, can be used to modify other nouns in the manner of an adjective but nevertheless lack other essential characteristics that would require their classification as adjectives.

The opposite is also true. Today we think nothing of using as nouns what once were only adjectives, such as *the local* when we mean *the local division of an international union,* or *the international* when *the international union* is understood. The sales pitches that interrupt our television viewing are *commercial messages* yet we refer to them as *commercials.* Editors write *editorials,* which are really *editorial opinions.* The verb intensifier *must* also functions as a noun (''This story is an advertising department *must*'') and as an adjective (''The president views the environmental bill as *must* legislation''). The verb *hires* is also used as a noun in some newsrooms (''The last three *hires* at our newspaper came from the same university''). Some people consider that incorrect, although *hires* has had such a usage since the Bible was written. Similarly, *cancels* is listed as a noun in dictionaries of all ages, although its noun usage is common among philatelists only (''The Postal Service will offer a new plan for obtaining first-day *cancels''*). Oil producers and headline writers have turned the adjective *crude* into a noun (TRAIN LOADED WITH *CRUDE* DERAILS) and printers who set type on Linotype machines would understand Jack Kerouac's conversion of a proper noun into a verb (''. . . at that very moment the manuscript of *Road* was being *linotyped* for imminent publication . . .'').

One verb that many will not accept as a noun is *think.* Perhaps the noun usage became popular after A.A. Milne, describing an action of Winnie-the-Pooh, wrote:

> He took his head out of the hole and had another *think* . . . [italics added].

The word *hedge* was once a noun meaning shrubs; today it's also a verb (''He *hedged* on the bet''). The word *dare* at one time was most commonly used as a verb; today, though, we also use it as a noun (''He took the *dare''*). An adverb, *out,* has gained respectability as a noun (''He looked for an *out''),* and *physical,* an adjective, also functions as a noun (''The soldier reported for his *physical* at 9 a.m.''). A lot of words in American English function at least two ways, such as:

attire	gasp	nick
bag	guard	note
bend	halt	outlaw
benefit	honor	parallel
blank	hub	pass
cart	hurl	rake
damage	inch	scheme
deal	insert	scorn
flank	knight	visit
flow	lead	warp
gain	model	whine

In addition to using the same word in two or more ways, we convert nouns into modifiers by changing their form (*Congress, congressional; fish, fishy; disease, diseased*) and adjectives into nouns through a similar process (*sweet, sweetness; pure, purity*). And *en* to an adjective and you have a verb (*black, blacken; white, whiten; red, redden;* although *blue, bluen* doesn't work). Before a noun *en* or *em* creates a verb (*code, encode; power, empower*). Nouns also become verbs by adding *ed* (*chair, chaired; author, authored*), although some editors won't accept those two because they don't fill a need in the language—a test a writer should make a new word pass before using it.

Further conversion of nouns occurs when we prefix them with *de, re,* or *be*. Some people want to *de-sex* the language, although I've never heard of anyone trying to *sex* it. A book reviewer once referred to children kept out of school against their will as being "involuntarily de-schooled." The instructions on a certain kind of light tell the user how to put in a new bulb by advising:

To relamp, pull down on glass.

Imagine the cowboy outfitted with two pistols being described as a "bepistoled terror," an example based on a syndicated columnist's description of a very famous American general. A sports columnist once praised a sportswriter whose books had "bejeweled the game of baseball."

Sometimes when we use the same form of a word to function as a noun, adjective or verb, the result can be confusing. When a colleague asked, "Did you ever see a pelican fish?" I replied, "No. Can a pelican fish fly?" I heard *pelican* as an adjective and *fish* as a noun and thought I was about to learn of some new creature. Luckily, various forms of verbs do function as nouns and adjectives with less confusion than that aroused by the preceding example.

Other Examples of Functional Grammar

Some professors will tell students they've used a word incorrectly by saying, "That's a noun," when the students used a noun to function as a verb. The professors are usually right, but for the wrong reason. The issue is not whether a word is a noun or a verb or an adjective, but whether the word is clear and necessary in a particular function. It is not necessary to say:

The driver *ignitioned* the car.

What's wrong with:

The driver *started* the car.

On the other hand, a new word may be created to encompass a broader concept. Joan Ryan of *The Washington Post* once interviewed Dick Schapp, at the time the editor of *Sport* magazine. Schapp was talking about a story (described as a "scandal-tinged feature") he had written about a well-known football coach. Schapp said about the story:

"It had to be *lawyered"* [italics added].

The first reaction of any stuffy grammarian would have been to scream, "That's not a verb!" And the dictionary would have supported the grammarian. The word is not listed as Schapp used it. But does that matter? Look at the word again. Does it not say the story had to be legally laundered or legally cleaned or the libel had to be removed by a lawyer? I think it does, and I believe its use is legitimate.

Some critics might also object to *summer* as a verb because we already have the perfectly good *vacation*. But "We vacationed in Switzerland" lacks the specificity of *summered*, which denotes a season.

Another creation not found in old or new dictionaries comes from *The Quill*. Referring to a federal judge, the magazine reported:

Kelleher forbade all note-taking except by *credentialed* news reporters, the attorneys involved and the parents of the defendant [italics added].

I have heard it said that proposals passed from one committee to another and then another have been *committeed* to death. Of course, people who don't know what it's like to deal with committees may not appreciate the phrase, so its use is confined to those familiar with the phenomenon. On the other hand, most of us are familiar with a lot of small taxes slowly depleting our wages—a process known as being *nickeled and dimed* into poverty.

As the times change, so do the functions of words. People who collect supermarket discount coupons call their action *couponing*. The usage is not that strained; more than 150 years ago anything bearing coupons was said to be *couponed*.

New functions for old words grow out of a shorthand approach to speaking or writing. When U.S. Senator Daniel Patrick Moynihan began publishing a newsletter, he invited his constituents to comment "about this adventure into *newslettering*," which says "publishing a newsletter" but in fewer words. Moynihan, by the way, reported that William Safire, who writes a column on language for *The New York Times*, told his readers: "If my good friend, the senator, continues to newsletter me, I shall ask my post office to deadletter him."

During the Democratic National Convention of 1976, the party felt it had in Jimmy Carter a candidate who could win the presidency. To make sure all went well, a platform suitable to Carter was adopted. Almost anything Carter didn't like was reworded, diluted or removed. It was the year of party harmony, and the platform was quickly adopted with barely a murmur of protest. Howard K. Smith of ABC News told his audience there had been no fight over the platform because it had been *Carterized* before it was presented. That one word—in the right context—says what took me four sentences to say. What makes the word so good is that it is evocative; it conjures up for the interested viewer all that went into Carter's rise to national prominence.

Novelist John O'Hara created a word in the same vein as *Carterize.* Knowing that most of his readers were familiar with Walter Mitty, the shy man who dreamed of performing heroic deeds, O'Hara wrote in one of his newspaper columns:

> It is, of course, the spot every professional politician sees himself in at one time or another. If you pitch four innings for Gibbsville High School, you cannot fail to *mittyize* yourself as the hero of the World Series, and it's a dream to live on because the chances are so great against its ever coming true [italics added].

What linguistic quibbler would object to *mesmerize,* given its origin with Franz Anton Mesmer, a French hypnotist?

Carterize, mittyize and *mesmerize* suggest that a writer can take a noun and add *ize* to create a verb. Forget it. Imagine memorandums for President Dwight D. Eisenhower being *Eisenhowerized?* It's too much. The *ize* treatment doesn't always work (*doorize*) or it can sound pretentious (*formalize),* which journlists shouldn't. Still, some people won't give up. A journalism professor told his colleagues he was soliciting answers on how "criteria are operationalized in judging papers"; a spokesperson for the Pentagon said the building would have a skeleton staff for the holiday, a staff that had been "skeletized even further" because of bad weather; when zoo keepers have too many animals of one breed, they "euthanize" some, according to one television journalist; a college president who went about the country hiring talented faculty was said to have done it in order to "excellentize" the institution.

If the *ize* treatment doesn't work, the president of the United States doesn't have to worry—a verb will come along. For President Reagan, a fiscal conservative and persistent budget-cutter, the word *Reaganed* was used to describe someone who had lost a job because of budget reductions.

Creating new functions is one thing; straining current usage is another. The feature writer who said that some people at a party had "gate-crashed" ignored the standard usage, "crashed the gate." It is more conventional, and because of that, it doesn't make the reader stop and take note. It doesn't shout, "Hey! Look at me! Aren't I cute?" When usage interrupts reading or sidetracks listening, the writer has done a disservice. That could happen in the following sentence, which is derived from an editorial:

> Can you imagine a disease striking *conventioning* members of the American Legion and nobody else?

There's nothing wrong with saying "members of the American Legion convention." Likewise, the author of a news release that said someone had "concepted" a product need look no farther than "conceived" to find a standard word.

Sports fans probably wouldn't stop reading after seeing this sentence in *The Washington Post:*

> Theismann bounced right up after a wicked hit when he was *blind-sided* and sacked early in the scrimmage [italics added].

To the fan (and the quarterback) *blind-sided* means to be tackled from an approach the football player can't see—the blind side. The verb has also entered the language of politicians. U.S. Sen. Gary Hart once complained to a news magazine about not being dealt with candidly, saying he had been "blind-sided."

Some functional usages need to be explained, as was done in this quotation from a United Press International story:

> "I can't see any excuse for this unless the officials were improperly trained or they were guilty of *homering* [favoring the home team]. . . . I doubt very much if the officials were *homering*." [italics added]

Here are some recent examples of functional grammar. Most of them show new verbs.

> The second major finding indicated by the data in the study was that *The Chicago Tribune, The Los Angeles Times* and *The Washington Post trended* from pro-war to anti-war during the time frame covered . . . (Paper presented at a convention of journalism professors)

> The champion *decisioned* his challenger in a fight most fans figured would last no more than five rounds.

> About 1,800 people were forced to the streets in the bitter cold from the Copley and the Sheraton Boston, many barefoot and *pajamaed*. (United Press International)

> The horse was destroyed, the jockey *ambulanced* to the hospital . . . (Jack Kerouac in *Desolation Angels*)

> He had just discovered sports that year and *monologued* me at length about why baseball was so popular . . . (Wilfrid Sheed in *The Good Word & Other Words*)

> Surely Renato Danese, who *curated* the show for the Bell System, must have wanted something like that. (Owen Edwards in *American Photographer*)

> Councilman Richard Wion countered that it would be illogical to ask the county *to sidewalk* its property and not make a similar request of the Union Cemetery Association. (*Centre Daily Times,* State College, Pa.)

I thought I had another example when I heard a sportscaster, Jim Simpson of NBC, describe a football field with artificial grass as being artificially *turfed*. I found *turfed* in a 1949 dictionary, but not in a 1969 dictionary. Few dictionaries list the word *tenure* as a modifier.

> She is a *tenured* faculty member at UCLA.

If not common to the country at large, it is a very common word among college professors. Less common is this usage:

> The president of the university stopped *tenuring* research faculty in 1970.

That word also is not listed in any dictionary.

Young children, not yet ingrained with the grammatical prejudices of their elders, are fertile with examples of functional usage. Perhaps because she liked to get to the point quickly, a 3-year-old once said

> Watch me *batoning*.

which is shorter than saying

> Watch me twirling my baton.

She also once advised two of her dolls who were wearing cowboy hats to play cowboy by saying:

> You two go *cowboying*.

Equally to the point, a 6-year-old got into the backseat of the family car, her safety first in mind, and demanded:

> I want to be *seat-belted*.

There was no doubting what she meant, even though she had taken a noun and converted it into a verb.

A 3-year-old once told his mother that the wind had stopped by saying, "It has stopped *wind-ing*," a usage that would not work in writing without the hyphen, but would have no problem over the air waves.

Here are some other examples from the files of first-ear observation. A 12-year-old horsewoman uses *pasture* as a verb; an 11-year-old describing slow-moving traffic said it was "snailing along"; an 8-year-old gave her father a kiss while he was snacking on a pretzel, then told him, "You have a pretzelly smell"; caught whispering in her older sister's ear, a 4-year-old said: "We're secreting."

Are those usages correct? They worked for the moment. More interestingly, they exhibit the latitude that speakers of English have. They can create a word for the moment—and never use it again.

The late Red Smith of *The New York Times* once wrote in his sports column:

> They said that if the standard contract did not bind the player to his employer from cradle to grave, players would be *gypsying* across the map in greedy pursuit of the top dollar [italics added].

Some dictionaries list *gypsy* as a verb, but Smith told me he learned his definition as a child.

> To gypsy, to travel from place to place schlepping family, household goods, horses and maybe a dancing bear, has been a part of the language familiar to me since, as a child in Green Bay, Wis., I saw gypsy caravans answering that description—and ran indoors lest they kidnap me and sell me into slavery, as all right-thinking boys knew to be the gypsy custom.

Smith closed his letter:

> As to converting nouns into verbs, we do it often, of course. We sin instead of committing a sin. But I have my own limits. I will not *host* you unless you will *guest* me. If you *author* a textbook, I will not *reader* it.

Syndicated columnist George F. Will has complained about Americans' "perverse national genius" for turning "respectable nouns into disagreeable verbs." The following are some examples of what Will might scorn:

> The player *plated* the winning run in the eighth. (What's wrong with *scored?*)

> The union president accused the manager of trying to *revenge* the bus drivers who were on strike for three weeks. (*punish?*)

> Rizzo, who has *mayored* Philadelphia for almost seven years, sought to change the charter to allow himself to run for a third term in 1979.

> Because we didn't have room for the unexpected guests, they had to be *hoteled.*

> The candidate said she opposes *illegalizing* abortion. (*banning?*)

> The athletic director said the university was *scholarshiping* hundreds of athletes.

> These antique clocks are shipped sturdily *cartoned.* (*packed?*)

> [A tennis player speaking on television] I once *ballboyed* for so and so. (No comment!)

Maybe reactions to some of the examples used in this chapter depend on how sensitive or defensive people are about the language. I prefer to be flexible, perhaps because I do not view functional usage as an ominous and destructive force. For despite its flexibility, the language also has its limitations, as linguist Ronald Langacker explains:

> Since a language is used primarily for communication, a speaker is not free to innovate without limit; his linguistic system must remain similar enough to the systems of the people around him to enable them to understand him.

Furthermore, journalists are usually not creators of new functions for old words. When it comes to new language, journalists most typically repeat what they hear—and then only after they have heard it enough times that it has gained some currency in society. Journalism tends to mirror society, and its practitioners cannot step outside that society's language boundaries without fear of losing readers and listeners. The novice, then, should appreciate the language's flexibility as well as acknowledge its limitations.

Parting advice comes from newspaper columnist James J. Kilpatrick to a convention of the Associated Press Managing Editors:

> Let us stick with the words we have. When your reporters feel the innovative impulse, suggest that they lie down until it goes away.

Self-Diagnostic Test 3.1

To determine how well you understand the major parts of speech, identify the italicized words and phrases according to their function: noun, verb, modifier, connective. The answers appear in the back of the book.

1. The *key* vote on the *proposal came* after only an hour *of debate* in which *Democratic* senators from the city *contended* that the proposal would cut *city* revenues by as much as $65 million a year.

2. At a *news* conference, Morial said the *mayors* would also *ask* the lame-duck *session* of Congress *and* the administration for a *job-creating* program *keyed to repairing the nation's roads and bridges.*

3. Two years ago *Congress ordered* the VA to conduct *scientific* research into Agent Orange's *effects, but* the study has not gotten started because of *difficulties* in designing it.

4. The results showed that Thompson had won an *unprecedented third consecutive* term with 1,816,101 votes to Stevenson's 1,811,027—*a margin of 0.14 percent.*

5. An old *man stabbed* his *critically ill* wife twice in the back *with a kitchen knife* in an unsuccessful *mercy-killing* attempt at a nursing *home,* police said *Sunday.*

6. A *federal judge* yesterday *declared unconstitutional* the *only* law in the nation *that requires teaching the biblical account of creation in public schools.*

Chapter 4

Conventional Grammar

Nouns and Pronouns

Defining what a noun is can be tricky. Adhering to the traditional definition (*name of a person, place or thing*) leaves little room to maneuver words into a necessary function. If we accept *football* as a noun only, how could we economically describe the field on which the game of football is played?

Linguists say that a word is a noun when it can be used in certain areas of a sentence, as the subject of a verb or as the object of a verb or a preposition. If we break down the preceding sentence according to function, with stress on which words are nouns, we would probably agree on every one. Here is the sentence again—with all nouns italicized:

> *Linguists* say that a *word* is a *noun* when it can be used in certain *areas* of a *sentence*, as the *subject* of a *verb* or as the *object* of a *verb* or a *preposition*.

Effect on Verbs

Consider what effect some of the nouns had on other parts of the sentence cited above. For one, the noun serving as the subject of the sentence influenced the verb. *Linguists* is plural (that is, more than one), so the verb must agree with it in number and person. *Person* used to be a confusing label in grammar, especially when applied to verbs. Traditionalists say there are six persons:

Person	Singular	Plural
1	I say	we say
2	you say	you say
3	he, she, it says	they say

But although there are six persons, a writer needs to learn only two verb forms in the present tense. Most verbs in the English language follow the same pattern—add an *s* to form the third person singular, present tense. Disregarding for the moment irregular verbs and other tenses, you need to recognize only two forms: third person singular and all others. The only time you have to worry about a verb ending being influenced by a noun is when the noun is third person singular, present tense. Had *linguist* (meaning only one) been used in the example, the verb would be *says*.

Effect on Pronouns

Another word influenced by a noun in the sentence on linguists is the word *it*. Called a *pronoun (I, you, he, she, it, they,* for example), *it* takes the place of a noun. The noun determines whether a pronoun is singular or plural, of masculine, feminine or neuter gender.

> *Carnegie Building* is old; *it* was built early in this century.

In that sentence the pronoun refers to *Carnegie Building,* which is singular. Thus, so is the pronoun. The noun that influences the pronoun is called its *antecedent.* If the antecedent is plural, so is the pronoun.

> *Leaders* of the hospital union said yesterday *they* would defy a restraining order obtained by the city.

They refers to *leaders.* The pronoun agrees with the noun. The most common pronoun error is not having the pronoun agree with its antecedent.

> The girls' cross-country *team* has had difficulty in finding competition because of *their* winning record.

Their should be replaced by *its* to be correct.

> The girls' cross-country team has had difficulty in finding competition because of *its* winning record.

Similarly:

> T. Roger Smith of Kernville told the *commission* the power company will take advantage of *them*.

The correct pronoun is *it*.

> T. Roger Smith of Kernville told the commission the power company will take advantage of *it*.

However, because *it* is neutral and impersonal, some writers use the word as little as possible. To avoid *it*, change the sentence to:

> T. Roger Smith of Kernville told commission *members* the power company will take advantage of *them*.

A plural noun allows the use of the plural—and more personal—*them*. An incorrect pronoun can be funny, as an advertisement from an X-rated movie attests:

Take *your* lover to see this film . . .
Before *they* take someone else!! [Italics added.]

A long sentence gives rise to pronoun error because the writer often forgets what he or she is referring to.

The combination of renovation costs at Elmbank, a feared lack of control over operations and dwindling confidence in dealing with Willow Community Hospital officials finally prompted the Conejos Medical Services Authority to put Elmbank behind *them* and build a new medical center in Conejos.

Them was meant to refer to *Authority* (5 words back), but because *them* is plural, it really refers to the last plural noun, which is *officials* (12 words back). The wrong pronoun changes the meaning of the sentence. To be correct, *it* should replace *them*.

Sometimes pronouns are used in a sentence other than the one in which the antecedent appears.

Among those rescued was *Mary Storms,* a 22-year-old secretary who had served as a volunteer at the post and married one of the defenders. *She* lost a leg and broke an arm during the bombing. *She* was several months pregnant but lost *her* child. *Her* husband has been killed.

Note, too, that the pronoun agrees with its antecedent in gender (male, he; female, she; neuter, it). In that example all of the pronouns are female because they refer to a woman.

Sometimes pronouns refer to a noun ahead instead of back:

When *they* got to the stream, the *campers* took off their boots.

Unclear Antecedent

Although a pronoun can refer to a noun in another sentence, the situation gets confusing when there is a noun in the same sentence as the pronoun but the noun is not the pronoun's antecedent. Consider this example from *The Gannetteer,* a magazine published for employees of Gannett Co. Inc.

A helicopter put Pribble on board. Because of *his* size, one of the crewmen had to make the flight to the hospital on a runner outside the bubble.

The writer intended the pronoun *his* to refer to *Pribble,* but *his* really refers to *one* in *one of the crewmen,* which caused Gordon V. Metz, the assistant news editor of the San Bernardino (Calif.) *Sun-Telegram,* to comment: "We put the crewman on the runner because of HIS size; we meant Pribble's." There is no sin in repeating a word when it will remove an ambiguous pronoun.

A helicopter put Pribble on board. Because of Pribble's size, one of the crewmen had to make the flight to the hospital on a runner outside the bubble.

Because listeners of radio or television news broadcasts have nothing in front of them to refer to, broadcast journalists use as few pronouns as possible. They favor repeating a word over using a pronoun. Given these two sentences

President Carter said he would announce his proposals on energy conservation later today. *He* said the proposals would make everyone unhappy.

broadcast journalists would write

President Carter said he would announce his proposals on energy conservation later today. *The president* said the proposals would make everyone unhappy.

Also keep in mind that pronouns refer to the nearest noun. Confusion often results when another noun intercedes between an antecedent and its pronoun.

Britain has agreed to sell to Egypt a highly advanced radar air defense *system* to double *its* holdings of ground-to-air missiles.

Such a sentence might make the reader reread to determine if *its* refers to *system* or *Egypt* (or, remotely, *Britain*). *Its* belongs to *Egypt*.

Britain has agreed to sell to Egypt a highly advanced radar air defense system to double Egypt's holdings of ground-to-air missiles.

Missing Antecedent

Make sure the pronouns you use do have antecedents. Nothing can be quite as confusing as a pronoun with no clear antecedent.

Breslin is on the list, he said, because he voted against a federal strip mine bill. Breslin said he did that because he feels *it* is a state, not a federal, function.

What *it* refers to is unclear. Even in the context of the story, the pronoun's antecedent was absent. I'll hazard a guess to make the sentence clear.

Breslin said he did that because he feels regulating strip mines is a state, not a federal, function.

Too many pronouns spoil the flavor of a sentence, especially if there is no antecedent because the writer used a pronoun to begin with.

Acting under Jones' implied orders, *they* killed not because *they* had a fear of what Jones might do to *them* if *they* did not but because *they* had a pre-existing hostility toward society.

The sentence would be clearer if it had started like this:

Acting under Jones' implied orders, *his followers* killed . . .

Overworked Pronouns

Overworking a pronoun—that is, using the same pronoun several times to refer to different nouns—can be confusing.

> According to police, Dennis, 21, got the cocaine into this country by putting *it* into a condom, tying *it* shut, and swallowing *it*.

To make clear there's been a shift in antecedents, repeat the new antecedent.

> According to police, Dennis, 21, got the cocaine into this country by putting it into a condom, tying the condom shut, and swallowing it.

A similar example:

> Such was the case last week when Mr. and Mrs. Thomas F. Needle of Pine Street filed suit against *their* neighbors, Mr. and Mrs. Donald Black, seeking to have *their* horse farm declared a public nuisance.

Dropping the second *their* in favor of using the possessive form of the antecedent makes the sentence clearer.

> Such was the case last week when Mr. and Mrs. Thomas F. Needle of Pine Street filed suit against their neighbors, Mr. and Mrs. Donald Black, seeking to have the Blacks' horse farm declared a public nuisance.

Pronouns in Attribution

Attribution tags, because they can contain an unrelated pronoun, need careful watching, as this example shows.

> Jones, only 5-feet-2, convinced his followers *he* was Christ, he said.

The pronoun in the attribution tag refers to the speaker the reporter is quoting. Maybe the reader will understand the *he* in *he said* does not refer to Jones. Then again, maybe the reader won't.

Pronouns are used frequently in attribution tags because the writer does not want to repeat a person's name to the point of monotony. The caution is: Don't use too many pronoun attribution tags. Return occasionally with the person's name or some other clearly identifiable tag so the reader doesn't forget who's speaking. And if two direct quotations are separated by a paragraph that does not refer to the speaker, use the speaker's name in the paragraphs where he or she is quoted. It is disconcerting to meet a pronoun too far removed from its antecedent.

False Antecedent

Pronouns can make murderers out of murder victims.

> Post-mortem stab wounds in the *victims* show that *they* killed with gusto.

Post-mortem stab wounds in the victims show that *the killers* killed with gusto.

Indefinite Use

Still another problem with pronouns is using them indefinitely when it isn't necessary. Here is an example of a common usage:

It will be cloudy and warm today.

Of course, there's nothing wrong with:

Today will be cloudy and warm.

But some writers refuse to be direct, and they fall back on the indefinite pronoun, which creates vague sentences.

It was figured the pay increases will total $232,131 a year, based on average salaries.

What does *it* refer to? What does *it* mean? What's wrong with

Pay increases will total an estimated $232,131 a year, based on average salaries.

Finally:

It used to be that home fire warning devices were available only as part of extensive and costly fire alarm systems.

The *it* does nothing positive; get rid of it.

Home fire warning devices used to be available only as part of extensive and costly fire alarm systems.

Other Antecedents

Antecedents are not restricted to nouns alone. A phase or clause can be an antecedent, which is the case in the following:

Imagine if *the error is made in the lead*. Here are two leads where *that* happens.

The italicized phrase in the first sentence is the antecedent for the pronoun in the second.

Here are two leads *where the error is made in the lead*.

As long as the result is clear, it is more economical to use a pronoun in the second sentence.

Pronoun Forms

The form pronouns take depends on how and where they are being used in a sentence. Learning the various forms so that you do not write *hisself* for *himself* is a matter of rote.

Personal Pronouns   The personal pronouns used as the subjects of verbs are:

Person	Singular	Plural
1	I	we
2	you	you
3	he, she, it	they

When used as objects, pronouns take these forms:

Person	Singular	Plural
1	me	us
2	you	you
3	him, her, it	them

In their possessive form, pronouns look like this:

Person	Singular	Plural
1	my (mine)	our (ours)
2	your (yours)	your (yours)
3	his (his)	their (theirs
	her (hers)	
	its (its)	

The forms in parentheses are used in elliptic writing when the object referred to is known.

> Is this your book?
> No, it's hers. (No, it is her book.)

The apostrophe is not used to create the possessive form of pronouns. That is a major exception to the convention of making the possessive form by adding *'s*. If you remember that possessive pronouns are possessive to begin with, you won't add *'s*. You don't have to make possessive what already is.

Reflexive Pronouns   Reflexive pronouns are used to emphasize a noun.

> The president *himself* will attend the security meeting.

Reflexive pronouns take these forms:

Person	Singular	Plural
1	myself	ourselves
2	yourself	yourselves
3	himself	themselves
	herself	
	itself	

Relative Pronouns   Relative pronouns (*who, which, that, what*) relate an independent or dependent clause to a main clause.

The student *who* loves writing will write all the time.

The college, *which* already offers 100 majors, is considering adding another one.

This is the house *that* Jack built.

I see *what* you mean.

Use *who* to refer to humans, and *that* and *which* to refer to animals and things.
Only *who* changes form according to pattern. As a subject, it is *who;* as an object, *whom;* in the possessive, *whose.* Some writers have difficulty deciding whether *who* or *whom* is correct. In this sentence, *who* is incorrect.

Who do you believe?

Any time you are unclear if it should be *who* or *whom* in an interrogative sentence, recast it as a declarative sentence to see which function *who* takes.

You do believe who.

In that sentence, *who* functions as an object and the objective form is *whom.* If that recasting does not work, substitute *he/him* or *she/her.*

You do believe she/her.

For this example, the objective form *her* is correct, meaning that *whom* is correct in the earlier sentence.

Demonstrative Pronouns   The last set of pronouns, called *demonstrative,* are *this* and *that* with the plural forms *these* and *those.* Generally, *that* refers to something already mentioned and *this* refers to something coming up. (Distance is another criterion. Something close takes *this;* something farther away takes *that.*) The best example of *this-that* usage comes from former President Richard M. Nixon. When asked a question at a news conference, he often began his response:

Let me say *this* about *that* . . .

This stood for his response to come; *that* for the question already asked.
That is overused or misused when *it* would carry the meaning.

He said that *that* is a good proposal.

Change the second *that* to *it* both to avoid the *that that* construction and because *it*
satisfies the meaning. The remaining *that* can be deleted in the interest of economical writing.

He said it is a good proposal.

Sexism and Pronouns

A form letter acknowledging receipt of a faculty member's letter of recommenda-
tion contained two blanks: one for the student's name and the other for the pronoun
that would agree in gender. Such are the lengths some people will go to avoid using
he/him/his as universal pronouns for men and women.

The issue is simple. Do journalists want to use language that assumes male-
ness? No, they want to be as neutral as possible. *The Associated Press Stylebook*
advises that to avoid pronoun bias a writer should use plural nouns to which the
neutral *they* can be affixed. For example:

Job-oriented training may prepare the *student* for *his* first job.

Job-oriented training may prepare *students* for *their* first job.

Other writers, preferring more precise references to individuals, have adopted a
he/she, him/her approach. Traditionalists consider such a usage awkward and stick
to *he/him* as universal pronouns. Some book authors alternate between examples,
which results in a scorecard approach when the copy editor tries to ensure a bal-
anced number of references between the genders. Other writers have suggested
singular pronouns that are neutral: *s/he, hir, thon*. Like the proverbial snowball in
hell, those creations stand little chance. The news agencies have the best solution:
Recast into the plural.

Self-Diagnostic Test 4.1

To determine how well you understand pronoun-antecedent agreement, underline
the correct form of the pronoun so that it agrees with its antecedent. The answers
appear in the back of the book.

1. Anyone who has ever attempted to wend *his* or *her/their* way

   through football traffic knows how difficult the experience can be.

2. The Spanish press, snarled by a web of restraints on what *it/they* can

publish, faces new problems following the arrest of two journalists
three days ago.

3. Council decided to increase *its/their* budget.

4. The horse by the fence is a trotter. You will never see *him/her/it*
   with a saddle on.

5. Wanamaker's will display *its/their* new fall fashions at a special
   preview Saturday.

6. The board of trustees held *its/their* first public committee meetings
   Thursday and Friday.

7. The school board canceled its June 16 meeting. *It/They* will meet
   June 23 to give the budget final approval.

8. Williams had predicted the shutdown would fail and he blamed the
   news media for promoting *it/them*.

Verbs

Verbs make sentences go; all other parts of speech are secondary to the verb. The
noun alone carries little in a sentence; the verb, everything. The journalist can write
about cars, trucks, city councils and Congress, but what readers or listeners want to
know is: What happened? The verb tells them. Nouns are meaningless without
verbs. *Congress* tells us nothing. *Congress approved* or *Congress didn't approve*
has meaning. Only verbs and their derivatives, verbals, generate action. Look at the
verbs and verbals in this sentence.

> Although reporters have been *imprisoned* in the past, they have almost
> invariably been *charged* with specific violations of rules *imposed* on the
> press.

Here is a verbal acting as a modifier:

> The carefully *worded* statement said that the protest note, delivered last
> Sunday in Rome, does not allege a threat on the aide's life.

Do not mistake *delivered* for a verbal; it is a verb. What you have is elliptic writing
in which the subject and auxiliary verb are understood. Written in full the sentence
would include this construction:

> . . . protest note, *which was* delivered . . .

By deleting the pronoun *which* and the auxiliary *was,* we get a more economical
sentence.

Once you understand the structure of verbs you will understand verbals, which will in turn expand your knowledge of functional grammar. The principal parts of a regular verb are:

Present Tense	Present Participle	Past Tense	Past Participle
treat	treating	treated	treated
wound	wounding	wounded	wounded
impose	imposing	imposed	imposed

The present participle is formed by adding *ing* to the present tense (drop the final *e*, if there is one). The past participle of a regular verb is the same as the past tense.

The present participle, when used as a noun, is called a *gerund* ("*Running* for office is a chore"). When it's used in any other function it is merely called a *participle* ("The *laughing* clown made every child happy"). Regardless of function, the past participle is still called a *participle* ("*Improved* conditions help").

A third verbal is called an *infinitive* ("*To play* well is reason enough *to play*"). Here are some verbals functioning as nouns:

To impose on others is not a good habit.

Imposing on others is a sign of bad manners.

The *wounded* were taken to a hospital.

As modifiers:

The *wounded* soldiers were taken to a hospital.

The *imposing* mountain left us no choice but to detour around it.

The *inspired* soldiers regrouped and fought off the *invading* troops.

Examine your writing for possible verbals buried in uneconomically written sentences, such as:

The soldiers *who were wounded* were taken to a hospital.

By placing *wounded* before the noun, you can reduce the length of the sentence and increase its force.

The wounded soldiers were taken to a hospital.

Don't bury strong words in weak clauses.

Verbs and Agreement

First, let us review how verbs agree with their subjects in number and person. Remember that while there are six persons, there are only two verb forms in the present tense.

Person	Singular	Plural
1	I write	we write
2	you write	you write
3	he, she, it writes	they write

You may believe that even if a verb does not agree with its subject, the meaning of the offending sentence is still clear. That is not true. Note that the meaning of the following sentences is determined by the number of the verb, which is in turn determined by the subject of the sentence (italicized).

Racing *cars* are fun.

Racing cars is fun.

Here are some troublesome constructions.

Compound Subjects   Singular subjects linked by *and* or commas and *and* (which creates a compound subject) usually take a plural verb.

The Senate and the House *debate* different bills at the same time.

According to the party chairman's letter, the date, time and place of the county committee meeting *have* yet to be set.

Each, Every   If each noun is considered as an individual, then a singular form of the verb is used.

Each bill and resolution before Congress *needs* the approval of both houses.

Every boy and girl in the playground *is* where he or she *wants* to be.

The tip-offs are *each* and *every*. They specify the singular.
Singular verbs also follow *everybody, nobody, somebody, anyone, anybody.*

Government officials are careful to avoid creating a feeling that *anyone* but the terrorists *is* responsible for the bombings.

False Compounds   Singular subjects connected by *and* but referring to the same person or thing take a singular verb.

The governor and state party leader *is* thinking about new rules for primary elections.

The Thomas Paine Cottage and museum in New Rochelle *contains* a smaller, square tombstone representing Paine's original burial site.

In the first sentence the governor is also the party leader. In the second the cottage and museum are the same building, not two buildings. The cottage is a structure that houses the museum.

Singular Connectives   *Or, nor* and *but* are connectives that signal the singularity, not the plurality, of your subjects.

> The Senate or the House *finds* fault with every proposal the president has.

> Neither the president nor his secretary *is* accepting telephone calls today.

> Not only the president but his wife as well *likes* to watch television.

Either-or, Neither-nor   In *either-or* and *neither-nor* constructions, the subject nearest to the verb determines the number of the verb.

> Neither the president nor his *advisers were* available for comment.

> Neither the advisers nor the *president was* available for comment.

Some editors would require rewriting because of the awkwardness of the form.

> The president and his advisers were not available for comment.

Rewrite cautiously, though, because emphasis can be changed—as is the case in the sentence above.

False Plurals   Confusion results when the subject appears to be plural because of a modifying phrase attached to it.

> The House in addition to the Senate *is* in session.

> The City Council, along with the Planning Commission, *makes* decisions on zoning.

These constructions again are examples of what some editors might convert to compound subjects. Again the caution is that rewriting might change a desired emphasis. If you stick with these constructions, the way to determine the number of the verb is to drop the modifying phrase so it is clear what the subject of the sentence is.

> The way to keep boys happy is to feed them lots of ice cream.
> The *way is* to feed them lots of ice cream.

> One of our members conducts herself improperly.
> *One conducts* herself improperly.

Although not as common, the reverse construction also causes problems.

> *Members* of the Department of Agriculture's Soil Testing Group *was* at the field today.

Correctly written, it would be:

Members of the Department of Agriculture's Soil Testing Group *were* at the field today.

Collective Nouns   Collective nouns take a singular verb when considered as one unit and a plural verb when considered in their individual parts. Five such nouns are *jury, family, faculty, majority* and *number*.

The majority of the country *supports* the president. (One unit)
The majority of the voters *are* undecided. (Individuals)

The jury *is* out. (One unit)
The jury *were* divided on the verdict. (Individuals)

My family *meets* once a year at Posties Grove. (One unit)
My family *disagree* on whether to hold the reunion on a Saturday or a Sunday. (Individuals)

Some people (myself among them) find plural verbs with singular-sounding nouns to be strange. Thus, wherever the plural is called for, we write:

Members of the jury were divided on the verdict.

That makes the subject clearly plural.

Number   The word *number*, according to H.W. Fowler, usually follows this rule: If it is preceded by the definite article *the*, it takes a singular verb; preceded by the indefinite article *a*, a plural verb.

The number of people who live in the West Ward is high.

In that sentence the stress is on *number* not *people*. But if the stress was on the prepositional phrase, then the verb would be plural.

A number of people who live in the West Ward are Welsh.

To be sure, substitute the word *numerous* for *number of,* and if the sentence makes sense, go with the plural verb.

Numerous people who live in the West Ward are high.

That is nonsense. But:

Numerous people who live in the West Ward are Welsh.

That makes sense.

Numbers   Plural numbers when considered as a unit take singular verbs.

Five million dollars *is* all that *is* needed to finish the project.

Nearly $1 million *was* lost in a similar asparagus strike.

Forty hours of work *keeps* Brewer busy but 50 *isn't* enough for Kellner.

Two years *is* the longest time we can go without that new highway.

He said the wealthiest 1 percent of the population gets 25 percent of the tax benefits and the wealthiest 14 percent *gets* 53 percent of the benefits.

Three percent *is* hardly much of a pay raise.

Note that *percent* takes a plural verb when coupled with a plural noun, as in: 50 percent of the members always attend meetings.

Any, None *Any* and *none* behave differently and can take a plural or a singular verb. If the reference is to a singular noun or pronoun or the writer's intention is to signal just one and no more, *any* and *none* take a singular verb. In fact, that is usually the case. In some circumstances, when the reference is to two or more, then the plural verb is correct.

Complements *It* always takes a singular verb regardless of the verb's *complement* (the word or words that follow a verb to complete a predicate construction).

It *is the mistakes* that bother her.

On the other hand, the verb number that follows *there* is determined by the complement.

There *are* 50 *reasons* why Jewells won't; there *is* one reason why Jewells will.

S-endings Some words that look plural because they end with *s* are really singular and are treated as such. They include: *economics, phonetics, news, mathematics, linguistics, semantics, energetics, pedagogics, aesthetics.* Still others, such as manners, are always plural. A dictionary tells when a plural-looking word takes a singular verb. A dictionary will also tell you which *s*-ending words can go either way, such as *acoustics.*

Acoustics *is* a subject I don't understand unless I'm in a classroom where the acoustics *are* bad.

Some words, such as *politics,* go both ways, although most usages of *politics* take a singular verb, as in this headline:

POLITICS SNARLS STUDDED TIRE BILL

The word receives plural treatment when it means opinions or principles, as in:

His politics are about as messed up as any I've ever seen.

Its plural appearance aside, *Philippines* takes a singular verb. The country's full name is Republic of the Philippines. Thus, this headline, referring to the government, is correct:

PHILIPPINES SEEKS U.S. AID

Singular Disguised as Plural   The following sentences show other plural-sounding and plural-appearing words that are usually treated as singular.

The United Mine Workers represents miners.

Paramount Studios releases seven films a year.

Latin Words   Some Latin words do not form their plurals by adding *s* and therefore their plural forms appear singular. Perhaps the commonest of them is *media*, as in *news media*. Often a journalist (who should know better) will incorrectly write or say:

The news media *is* now a national business of concentrated owners.

Correct:

The news media *are* now a national business of concentrated owners.

The singular form is *medium*. Another incorrect usage:

The larvae of the worm *gets* into the child when the child kisses the family pet.

Larvae is plural and the sentence should read:

The larvae of the worm *get* into the child when the child kisses the family pet.

The singular is *larva*.
Then there is a Latin word that does not follow the preceding pattern—*datum, data*. Although plural, *data* is now being used as either plural or singular.

The data are ready.

The data is ready.

A dictionary will usually settle any doubt about words with unusual plural and singular forms.

Pronoun-Verb Agreement

A pronoun, as you already know, agrees with its antecedent. Likewise, when the same pronoun leads off a clause it is also the subject of the clause's verb and the verb must agree with the pronoun in number. Errors can result because some pronouns have only one form, which can be singular or plural. The writer who forgets about that frequently fails to make the verb agree.

> The provost instructed the vice president for undergraduate studies to initiate a study of the effectiveness of the university's so-called service courses, which *includes* English composition.

The error is in the italicized verb. The antecedent of the pronoun *which* is *courses,* which is plural. Thus, the verb must be plural; it must agree.

> . . . courses, which *include* English . . .

In the following sentence, locate the pronoun's antecedent and then determine if the verb agrees.

> The Association for Intercollegiate Athletics for Women has stiffer rules and regulations, which hamper recruiting procedures.

The pronoun refers to *rules and regulations,* which is plural. Thus, the verb that follows the pronoun must also be plural.

Keep the pronoun's antecedent clearly in mind at all times. Sometimes a word, phrase or clause intervenes between the antecedent and the pronoun. The intervening phrase in the following is italicized.

> He did say that he would look at the list *of names,* which includes the owners of two apartment buildings.

In that sentence, "the list . . . includes," although the plural prepositional phrase will throw off the careless writer, who will use a plural verb. In pronoun-verb combinations, trace the sentence backward to the determining noun and then make the verb in question agree.

There are also sentences in which the noun at the end of a prepositional phrase, not before it, serves as the antecedent of the pronoun. For example:

> Murder is one *of those horrors* that causes otherwise trusting people to lock their doors at night.

If you are confused about what the pronoun refers to, dump the phrase.

> Murder is one that causes otherwise trusting people to lock their doors at night.

That sentence makes no sense because the pronoun's antecedent is missing.

> Murder is one of those horrors that cause otherwise trusting people to lock their doors at night.

As you look at the full sentence again, you can see the pronoun *that* refers to *horrors,* not *one.* Thus, the verb is plural.

Self-Diagnostic Test 4.2

To determine how well you understand verbs and agreement, select the correct verb in the sentences that follow. The answers appear in the back of the book. Review what you miss.

1. Sears *sells/sell* many products, from bedclothes to toggle switches.

2. None of the players *is/are* able to explain the loss.

3. The land in addition to the houses *was/were* sold.

4. Neither the dogs nor their master *hunts/hunt* very well.

5. Each of the members of our microcomputer club *runs/run* four miles daily.

6. The car on the right or the car on the left—I forget which— *runs/run* raggedly.

7. The number of students who took the test for the first time and did poorly *was/were* large.

8. Three *is/are* the maximum number of times a student may take the language test.

9. There *is/are* too many people driving today.

10. The region's proximity to the Atlantic Ocean and the Great Lakes *explains/explain* the moisture and the clouds.

Exercise 4.1

Select the correct verb and turn in the answers to your instructor.

Name _____

1. The president and the pope *is/are* meeting today.

2. A moderate number of deficient students *was/were* well distributed among school facilities in the area.

3. Neither of the two men *has/have* met before.

4. There *is/are* millions of fish in the sea.

5. It *is/are* the problems of grammar that *interests/interest* us.

6. This is one of those sentences that *serves/serve* to show two things—relative pronouns and agreement.

7. There *is/are* less to complain about in the recent assessment than there *was/were* in the previous one.

8. A number of the survivors *was/were* taken to the closest hospital.

9. The cost of the project is $5 million; *it is/they are* going to be hard to raise.

10. News *is/are* what reporters are always seeking.

11. Books *is/are* more popular today than they ever were.

12. Neither the lamb nor the mice *is/are* aware of the rain.

13. Neither the mice nor the lamb *is/are* aware of the rain.

14. Their efforts to hide the facts from the public *is/are* disappointing.

15. Williams said that current academic policy plans and projects of educational policy *was/were* evaluated.

16. A group of Johns Hopkins University scientists *is/are* studying human arteries to see whether arterial patterns can contribute to disease.

17. If you *is/are* one of those students who *wants/want* an extra writing course, this is your chance.

18. He doesn't know that the subject and verb *doesn't/don't* agree.

19. That is just one of the regulations that *upsets/upset* Williams.

20. The board includes seven volunteers, each of whom *has/have* a full-time job.

Verb Tenses

Tense means time. The English language has six major tenses: present, past, future, present perfect, past perfect, future perfect. Most journalistic writing that describes past events relies on the past tense.

Present Tense   Present tense deals with today or with conditions that exist when a news story is written and will continue to exist even if the subscriber doesn't read the paper for 10 hours after the story was written. For example:

> A geographer said yesterday that public schools no longer teach students the effect climate can have on a country's economy.

Some news stories (usually analyses, in-depth articles and features) are written in the historical present, which provides both a sense of immediacy and continuity to a story. Present tense gets the nod in some broadcasting because the viewer or listener sees or hears the news report.

Past Tense   Most newspaper stories are written in the past tense because most news is past; it happened before it was reported.

> Three cars *collided* at Broad and Centre streets today, West Bay police said.

The headline on the preceding would be written in the historical present because one purpose of a headline is to give immediacy to a story. The headline might say:

3 CARS COLLIDE AT INTERSECTION

The past tense of regular verbs is formed by adding *ed* to the first person singular form of the verb: *I walk; I walked.* The form remains consistent in all six persons: *They walked.* If the present tense form ends in *e,* as in *impose,* merely add *d* to form the past tense: You *imposed* quite a burden on me when you asked me to write three stories for today's edition.

Sequence of Tenses   Nothing seems to divide modern-day usage experts as much as sequence of tenses. Basically, the rule that governs the tense of verbs in independent and related dependent clauses states that when a direct quotation is paraphrased, the tense of the verb is changed one degree (e.g., from present to past). In the interest of economical writing, journalists do a lot of paraphrasing. It would seem then that a statement made in the present tense but paraphrased by a journalist should appear in the past tense. For example:

> Williams said, "I don't like the way the bypass is coming. It looks as if it will ruin our environment."

Following the rule of sequence of tenses, that sentence would be paraphrased this way:

> Williams said he *did* not like the way the bypass *was* coming because it *looked* as if it would ruin the area's environment.

Confronted with such a sentence, a reader can honestly ask: Doesn't Williams believe that anymore? In other words, the journalist, by following the sequence of tense rule, has seemingly changed the meaning of what Williams said. Such a paraphrase is called "reported speech." Now examine this sentence:

> Williams does not like the way the bypass is coming, he said, because it looks as if it will ruin the area's environment.

The difference between the paraphrase and the preceding example, called "parenthetical speech," is that the verb in the attribution tag—now situated in the middle of the sentence—no longer governs the tense of the other verbs. In the first example (reported speech), the attribution tag led off the sentence, so the verb *said* governed the tense of all the other verbs, and they had to be changed one degree.

Forget for a moment where the attribution tag appears and consider what is fact. At the time Williams made his statement, he was offering his opinion. The offering of his opinion and his opinion are facts. On the day the statement appears in print, Williams still believes what he said about the bypass. His position is unlikely to change unless the bypass changes. Therefore, logic suggests rather strongly that it doesn't matter where the attribution tag appears in the sentence or whether the sentence is labeled "parenthetical speech" or "reported speech"; Williams' belief has not changed from the time he made his statement until the time the reader sees it in print. Logic calls for the present tense regardless of the structure of the sentence, no matter where the attribution tag appears.

My collection of usage books provides some surprising guidelines (in some cases, rules). The most current book, written by a journalism professor, stands firmly by the sequence of tenses rule as outlined at the beginning of this section. But a grammar book first copyrighted in 1931 (with my edition bearing a 1950 revision date) says: "Observe, however, that there is sometimes a difference in meaning between the past and present tenses in clauses of this type," and then goes on to compare:

He said that he *was* a member of the Communist Party.

He said that he *is* a member of the Communist Party.

"In subordinate clauses like these," the authors state, "the proper sequence must depend upon logic, not upon grammatical tense." That is the lesson of sequence of tenses: Let logic guide you. If use of the past tense changes a person's meaning, ignore the rule of sequence of tenses. A journalist's first allegiance is to accuracy, and changing a meaning is inaccurate.

Historical Present   The tense problem also comes up when journalists are writing about reports and studies. The incorrect tendency is to write:

The study *said* housing for the elderly is not needed for a majority of the city's senior citizens.

But long after the story appears, the study will be saying the same thing. If the study is superseded, then it no longer rates present tense treatment. That belongs to the current study.

Journalists favor the historical present when writing in-depth articles. The logic is that they are quoting long-standing positions on issues, positions not likely to change as soon as the ink is dry on that day's newspaper. However, if you begin an in-depth article in the present tense, do not shift to the past without good reason. If you mix the tenses, you'll confuse the reader because you will have mixed the time. Don't write in one sentence

Jones *says* government is important to all people.

and in another

Jones *said* people are important to government.

The reader will want to know if the past tense of the second statement means Jones no longer believes that. If such is the case, state it clearly.

Misleading Use of Tenses   The past tense of *be* (*was* and *were*) is a popular but erroneously used form, especially in accident stories. Reading such a story, the reader learns that five people were injured. Preceding the list of the names of the injured is:

They *were:*
—Mary Sue Harper, 22, 213 Mountain Ave . . .

By using the past tense the journalist has made the accident a fatal one. If it had been, the journalist wouldn't have written:

Dead *were:*

The past tense of *be* is also sometimes misused in political stories where a vote is reported.

Opposing the senator were five of his colleagues. They *were:*

The first *were* is correct; it indicates a past action. The italicized *were,* alas, sounds as though the five colleagues are dead (perhaps for opposing the senator?).
Journalists are haphazardly aware of the *are-were* problem. In one paragraph of a news story the following appeared:

The residents charged with rioting and destruction of property *were*
[followed by their names]. All except Mr. _____, who *lives* here, *are*
from . . .

A marvelous resurrection if there ever was one.
Journalists also use the past tense in some instances that might suggest the present. In an obituary the journalist might write:

Funeral arrangements *were* incomplete.

That tells the reader that at the time the obituary was written, the funeral arrangements were incomplete, but they might have been completed between the time the story was written and the time it was read later in the day. On the other hand, the survivors of a dead person still exist and should be so treated.

There *are* six survivors.

As in the case of incomplete funeral arrangements, a hospitalized person's condition does not rate the present tense. If a hospital reports a person's condition at

10 a.m. for a story you write at 11 a.m. but will not be read by most people until 5 p.m., the present tense can trip you.

> Hoy *is* in good condition, a hospital spokesman said.

What happens if between 10 a.m. and 5 p.m. Hoy's condition turns critical? Or, worse still, what if he dies? To cover yourself, use the past tense *and* a time element.

> Hoy *was* in good condition at *10 a.m. today,* a hospital spokesman said.

Some journalists might also write:

> Hoy *was* in good condition, a hospital spokesman said at 10 a.m. today.

Unnecessary Shifts of Tense   Compound predicates are trouble spots when the writer, for no apparent reason, changes tense.

> Hassinger said the sign *was* unattractive and *detracts* from the building's appearance.

The writer started in the past tense (*was*), then moved into the present (*detracts*) without good reason. In that sentence, the present tense should have been used because the sign was still standing when the story was written. As far as Hassinger is concerned, the standing sign *is* unattractive and *detracts* from the building's appearance. Had the sign been removed prior to Hassinger's comment, the past tense would have been correct.

> Hassinger said the sign *was* unattractive and detracted from the building's appearance.

Future Tense   The future tense is used to write about events that are going to happen.

> The president *will address* Congress tomorrow night.

In American idiom, the present tense is sometimes substituted for the future.

> Tomorrow *is* Sunday. (Tomorrow *will be* Sunday.)
>
> The Steelers *play* the Packers tomorrow. (The Steelers *will play* the Packers tomorrow.)
>
> Cadbury City Council *meets* tonight to discuss taxes. (Cadbury City Council *will meet* tonight to discuss taxes.)

The major problem with future tense arises when it is misused in the conditional mood, a matter I will explain presently.

Present Perfect Tense   The present perfect tense is used to describe an action that begins in the past and continues to the present or almost to the present. The present perfect is also used to refer to an indefinite time in the near past. The present perfect is identified by the auxiliary verbs *has* and *have,* which are singular and plural respectively, placed before the past participle.

> The Interior Department *has estimated* that the total quantity might be as high as 9.4 trillion cubic feet, about 40 percent as great as the largest discovery on Alaska's North Slope.

While the Interior Department may have made the estimate only once, it is a continuing estimate that will probably be restated if someone asks. The estimate was made in the past but continues through the present.

> The prime minister said the hijackers confessed that their mission was ordered by the militant rebel leader whom the king *has accused* of waging a campaign of subversion against his regime.

When that sentence was written, the king had not retracted his accusation, so it was assumed the accusation was a continuing feeling on the king's part.

Here is another sentence showing action that occurs over an indefinite time:

> In the five years Andrew Eyer *has been conducting* the Famous Symphony Orchestra, it *has increased* in size and quality.

The first verb is written in the progressive form (identified by the *ing* ending). The second verb is present perfect and indicates an indefinite time. When the orchestra increased in size and quality cannot be pinned down to a particular time, hence the present perfect. The use of the present perfect to indicate an indefinite time is frequent in newspapers and broadcasting. Here is a lead on a *Washington Post* story that never gave a definite time for the action.

> The Virginia Highway Department *has approved* a contract for the construction of a $25-million, six-lane elevated highway alongside Arlington County's Crystal City high-rise development to connect Shirley Highway with National Airport.

If approval had come yesterday—or some other definite time—the tense would have been simple past.

> The Virginia Highway Department *yesterday approved* a . . .

In the interest of tight writing, or when the time element isn't important, journalists use the present perfect in leads, which eliminates the need for specifying the time element until, usually, the second paragraph.

> Mexico's banks *have received* a new proposal from U.S. officials on how the country would repay $35 billion in short-term notes.
>
> The plan, which *was disclosed yesterday,* allows the country more time to pay off the notes provided it allows banks to raise the loan's interest rate by one-half point. The banks *made* that request *a week ago.*

Whenever a time element appears in the second paragraph the writer used past tense. But the lead, which has no time element, has a present perfect verb. Also note the use of the present tense every time the proposal is cited.

A different tense creates a different meaning, as shown in this sentence taken from a story about a one-year-old unsolved crime:

> That arson case *has* never been solved.

The sentence suggests the police are still investigating. But the simple past would close the books.

> That arson case *was* never solved.

Instead of present perfect, a journalist might also use the present tense.

> That arson case *remains* unsolved.

If a definite time is given or suggested, scrap the present perfect in favor of simple past.

> Each state representative, this year for the first time, will have a full-time secretary (representatives *have shared* secretaries *in the past)*.

Correctly tensed the sentence in parentheses would read:

> . . . (representatives *shared* secretaries in the past).

Another example:

> Jonathan Culler *has recently received* the Modern Language Association's James Russell Lowell Prize, a $1,000 cash award given for an outstanding literary or linguistic study.

Because *recently* suggests a definite time, write:

> Jonathan Culler recently *received* the . . .

Past Perfect Tense   The past perfect tense denotes an action completed in the past prior to a subsequent completed past action. It is identified by *had* plus the past participle.

> The Cowboys' defense *had* not *permitted* a touchdown in 25 quarters until the Houston Oilers *scored* Monday night.

The first verb is past perfect tense because it indicates action completed before the second verb, which is past tense. Here is another example:

> City Council *had agreed* to bring legal action against the contractor if he did not fix the problem. But by the time council *met* again, the contractor *had fixed* the problem.

The example shows three past actions, with the most recent one (*met*) rating past tense treatment and all other actions rating past perfect. But the past perfect has its flaws when adhered to blindly.

> Police said the rifle used by Needle in last Wednesday's shooting *had been* legally *owned* by Black.

The writer of that sentence used past tense attribution (*said*), which is the most recent past action. The next verb in the sentence (*used*) technically should be an earlier action. But what is not clear is whether the earlier action is a past action— Does Black still own the gun? The sentence suggests he does not. The tense, thus, hinges on that question and not one of past action and prior past action. The problem relates to an earlier discussion on sequence of tenses. And the solution is the same: Don't use the past tense when the situation still exists, that is, when the situation is not past.

> Police said the rifle used by Needle in last Wednesday's shooting *is* legally *owned* by Black.

The error of using the perfect form of the verb with a time element occurs in the past perfect, as it did in the present perfect.

> Earlier *last weekend,* the Coast Guard *had estimated* that up to 500,000 gallons of oil had leaked from the barge.

The past perfect would be correct only if the next paragraph said the Coast Guard changed its estimate.

> But later the Coast Guard estimated the total leakage at twice that amount.

But if the Coast Guard did not later change its estimate, the simple past suffices.

> Earlier last weekend, the Coast Guard *estimated* that up to 500,000 gallons of oil had leaked from the barge.

By changing to past tense, one past perfect (*had leaked*) remains, which is correct. Here is another sentence with the past perfect unnecessarily used because there is a time element with the verb.

> Jackson said negotiations *had started* about *three months ago.*

Put into the past tense:

> Jackson said the negotiations *started* about three months ago.

Future Perfect Tense   Unlike the future tense, which indicates an action that will occur at some time coming up, the future perfect combines the future and the past by indicating the completion of a present, on-going action at a specified time in the future. It is formed by *will have* plus the past participle.

> The president *will have been* in office two years when Congress convenes next month.

> By the time the secretary of state returns from Africa, he *will have made* 15 trips to foreign countries.

> When this book is completed, I *will have used* thousands of sheets of paper.

Simple future tense, on the other hand, conveys a different meaning. It conveys the idea that something is going to happen entirely in the future.

> When this book is completed, I will use thousands of sheets of paper for another book.

Progressive Verbs   Another verb form that sometimes appears in news stories is the *progressive*. It indicates an ongoing condition or a condition continuing over an unspecified time.

Present Progressive

A small group of professors *is resorting* to full-page advertisements in leading newspapers to defend academic freedom.

Past Progressive

Jones *was running* for president until he heard Smith wanted the job.

Future Progressive

The new senator *will be representing* our district during a critical time.

Present Perfect Progressive

Kellner, who *has been recovering* from an arm operation, said she was not aware of the most recent proposal.

Past Perfect Progressive

He *had been writing* poor stories—until someone showed him the mistakes he was making.

Future Perfect Progressive

When the new Congress convenes, he *will have been running* affairs around here for 35 years.

Review   Here is the conjugation of the verb *talk* in all tenses. Note that only in the third person singular of the present and the present perfect tenses is the verb form inconsistent with all other persons and numbers. Knowing that makes the entire process much easier to learn.

	Present	Past	Future	Present Perfect	Past Perfect	Future Perfect
I	talk	talked	will talk	have talked	had talked	will have talked
you	talk	talked	will talk	have talked	had talked	will have talked
he	*talks*	talked	will talk	*has* talked	had talked	will have talked
we	talk	talked	will talk	have talked	had talked	will have talked
you	talk	talked	will talk	have talked	had talked	will have talked
they	talk	talked	will talk	have talked	had talked	will have talked

Verb Moods

Verbs come in three moods—indicative, imperative and subjunctive. Most verbs are indicative; they state a fact or ask a question. The indicative verb is the norm.

The *imperative* expresses a command or an entreaty.

Come here.

Leave the room.

Take this with you, please.

It is the language of cookbooks (''Mix well for 10 minutes'') and textbooks, not of most news writing.

The *subjunctive* expresses, among other things, improbability and condition contrary to fact.

If I *were* you, I'd take the money.

Obviously, I'm not you, so it is a condition contrary to fact.

If this sea *were* empty, we could walk to Europe on dry land.

Obviously, such a condition is improbable.

Rudolf Flesch sees little use for the subjunctive. He says:

> Another grammatical distinction that's dying out is the use of the subjunctive. In fact, for most practical purposes, the English subjunctive has been dead and buried for centuries; but the old-guard grammarians pretend it's still alive in ''condition contrary to fact.''

Flesch dismisses any distinction between *shall/will* and *should/would*. There I draw the line, not because I'm an old-guard grammarian but because I see a distinction worth preserving. First, let us examine condition contrary to fact:

> If I *were* a door, I would be closed all the time.

> If I *was* a door, I would be closed all the time.

Except for the verb, no difference exists between those sentences; the meaning remains the same. It doesn't matter whether I use *were* or *was;* I still can't become a door. The statement still remains a condition contrary to fact, obvious on its face regardless of the verb's mood. But here is an instance where the conditional seems best to preserve a meaning or a status:

> The president proposed a plan that *would* reduce taxes for all but the
> very wealthy.

The mistake often made is the substitution of *will* for *would,* which changes the conditional to the indicative. To use *will* in that sentence would give the president authority beyond the Constitution. He needs a willing Congress and his own signature to change the *would* to *will.*

Some writers overuse the subjunctive, as in this:

> If AFSCME *were* elected, it *would* establish three or four locals to
> represent the various types of workers, Myers said.

The sense of the statement is better phrased this way:

> If AFSCME is elected, it will establish three or four locals to represent
> the various types of workers, Myers said.

The situation is similar to that found in the sequence of tenses, and the same rule prevails: Let logic guide you.

Verb Voices

Verbs have two voices, active and passive. The active is preferred in all writing and broadcasting because it puts the doer of the action out in front. Here is an active verb:

> The Senate *defeated,* 61-30, an amendment that would have required
> coal-mine operators to meet the final safety standards a year sooner than
> the bill required.

The doer of the action, *The Senate,* precedes the action, *defeated.* Here is that sentence again, only in the passive voice. Notice how the sentence limps along and hides the doer of the action and the action.

> An amendment that would have required coal-mine operators to meet
> the final safety standards a year sooner than the bill required *was*
> *defeated by the Senate,* 61-30.

The journalist's penchant to get the news out front in any one sentence sometimes forces the use of the passive voice. The results can be absurd.

Teaching assistant Penny Chaucer, 28, was discovered pinned beneath a
desk by firemen.

The firemen really ought to be fighting a fire or inspecting the damage, not pinning
female teaching assistants beneath desks—which is what the sentence says. The
passive voice forces the doer of the action into a prepositional phrase that is difficult
to fit harmoniously into the sentence. The sentence is short enough that the active
voice will not bury the news.

Firemen discovered teaching assistant Penny Chaucer, 28, pinned
beneath a desk.

Sheridan Baker's criticism of the passive voice tells what's confusing about the
preceding examples.

The passive voice puts the cart before the horse: the object of the action first, then
the harnessing verb, running backwards, then the driver forgotten, and the whole
contraption at a standstill.

If Baker's sentence makes you ill at ease, fine; it's supposed to. You're not supposed to feel comfortable with the passive voice. The advice to any writer is to write
in the active voice. It is forceful and direct. Besides, active voice verbs are shorter,
which makes for tighter sentences. Here are three paragraphs from a student's
paper; they are followed by a rewrite—in the active voice.

Two teachers were hired at the Corl Street Elementary School.
One will teach fifth and sixth grades, making the class size 26
students per class, 10 less than the previous size of 72 students between
two teachers. A teacher was also hired for the first and second grades.
Before, there were three teachers for 92 children, a class size of 30.67
students a class. The new teacher will bring the size of each class to 23
students, the average elementary class size in Cadbury.
At Park Forest Elementary School a teacher was added to teach the
third and fourth grades, where previously four teachers were divided
among 165 students. The new teacher will bring the class size to 27.

The rewrite shifts to the active voice and cuts out 11 words. In addition, another fact
was added, which took 12 words.

The board hired two teachers at the Corl Street Elementary School—one
for the first and second grades and one for fifth and sixth grades. The
additional fifth-sixth grade teacher will reduce class size from 36 to 26
students, which is one under the ideal set by the board last month.
The additional first-second grade teacher will reduce class size from
30.67 to 23, which, according to board member Barbara Dillon, is the
average for those grades throughout the district.
The third teacher, who will work at Park Forest Elementary School,
will reduce the class size of the third and fourth grades from 41 to 33.

Then there is this additional advice: Don't switch voices, especially in the middle of a sentence. Doing so is similar to violating parallel construction.

The president approved the bills, but the resolutions were ignored.

In that sentence our focus has been shifted from *president* to *resolutions,* yet we are concerned with the actions of the president, not the inaction and passivity of the resolutions.

The president approved the bills but ignored the resolutions.

That maintains the focus the sentence started with. Here is one that doesn't:

Alaska scored the national high of $10,178 and the national low of $4,575 was registered by Mississippi.

See how disconcerting it is to begin a sentence with one focus only to be jarred when the focus changes. Correctly written:

Alaska scored the national high of $10,178 and Mississippi registered the national low of $4,575.

Passive voice is acceptable only when you want to focus on the object of the action, not the doer. It appears most often in leads when the doer is not as important as what has been done.

A veteran who did not serve in any war *was nominated* yesterday by President Reagan to head the Veterans Administration.

Here is an active voice lead to consider:

Barrington City Council last night approved an ordinance that bans dogs from all sidewalks during daylight hours.

There is nothing wrong with that lead. It is short enough that the reader will not be lost. But what if we are more concerned with the ordinance than the approval?

An ordinance banning dogs from all Barrington sidewalks during daylight hours was approved by City Council last night.

The passive voice gets the ordinance up front. Focus is the central concern. Which of the following provides the correct focus?

An automobile struck and killed a 10-year-old Swayzee boy last night.

A 10-year-old Swayzee boy was struck and killed by an automobile last night.

Journalists don't care about automobiles; they care about people. The focus of the story is the boy, not the automobile, so the passive voice is justified. To continue the focus, however, does not mean to continue using the passive voice. The second paragraph:

> Johnny Johnson, the son of William and Mary Johnson, ran in front of
> a car driven by Harry Collins, Schuylkill, in the 500 block of Sunset
> Road, police said.

Usually a writer will shift to the active voice in the second paragraph. Take note, also, that the first name given in the second paragraph is the name of the victim. Some reporters writing accident stories put the name of the driver first while the focus of the story (as established in the lead) is the victim.

Here is a paragraph in which the passive voice puts the focus or stress where the writer wants it:

> In 1976 nearly 36,400 seats were used on a seasonal basis by non-
> students. An additional 18,260 seats were sold to students for each
> game.

The stress is on the number, then the buyer.

Sometimes the passive voice is used when there is no practical subject to head up an active verb.

> Thomas F. Williams of Madera was admitted to Hope Hospital
> Tuesday.

You don't want to say

> Hope Hospital admitted Thomas F. Williams of Madera Tuesday.

or

> Hope Hospital officials admitted Thomas F. Williams of Madera
> Tuesday.

Not all passive verbs have to remain passive. They can be changed without any recasting of the sentence. The solution: Find an active verb to substitute for the passive.

> The Shamokin Area School Board last night *was given* a budget.

Retaining the same subject, you can still write that sentence in the active voice:

> The Shamokin Area School Board last night *received* a budget.

Be cautious of the false passive. If you remember that a passive verb acts on the subject, you will not write:

> John Rucker was awarded the Golden Gloves Trophy last night.

Rucker received the trophy; it is the trophy that *was awarded.*

Passive voice, incidentally, is formed by adding the correct tense form of *be* to the past participle of the verb, giving you: *is grown, was killed, were injured, will be approved, has been postponed.*

Exercise 4.2

Convert the following story into the active voice (where appropriate) and turn in the edited version to your instructor for evaluation.

Name _____

Americans were told last night by President Carter that the United States is confronted with a crisis as serious as war and can be met only by inconvenient and painful sacrifice.

A doubtful audience was told by Carter that the unbridled consumption of past years cannot continue, that the crisis is real and that Americans are to support a program he will detail to Congress tomorrow night.

A week-long blitz intended to sell Congress and the people on a series of stringent steps to reduce gasoline consumption 10 percent by 1985, slash total energy growth by more than half to less than 2 percent a year and cut in half the use of imported oil was launched by the president's talk.

His speech was laced with strong language—terms like "national catastrophe," "a problem unprecedented in our history," "the moral equivalent of war."

Less than half the nation was shown in a recent Gallup poll considering the energy shortages "very serious." The skepticism Carter faces was acknowledged by him.

The people have no stomach for higher gas taxes was stated by members of Congress, just back from their Easter recess.

Strong Verbs

Journalists should use strong verbs. Any form of *be* is considered taboo, except where it links a subject and its modifier (a *complement*). So while *be* has its place, it is not in this clumsy sentence:

> Morocco *is to add* six missile boats to its navy, doubling the size of its combat fleet.

To fix the above, you have at least two choices: You can change the italicized part to *will add,* or if that's too definite for what might be a proposition rather than a fact, try *plans* in place of *is.* Here is another example:

> Reasons given for moving *were,* for the home owners, health, and for the renters, security.

It is a terrible sentence all around. The fact that the writer inverted normal order got him into the mess. Rewritten:

> Home owners said they would move for health reasons and renters said they would move for security reasons.

Do not be deluded into using some form of *be* just to tighten a sentence. A student converted this strong verb

> Boyer *posted* a 6-3 record last season.

into this limp one

> Boyer *was* 6-3 last season.

> Economical writing has virtue, but so do strong verbs.

Verb Classes

Be is a linking verb. When one of its forms is used alone, it connects the subject and whatever follows.

> The sky is blue, the fields are green.

That sentence contains no action, just the description of a condition.

The other verb classes are transitive and intransitive. *Transitive* verbs are followed by an object.

> The senator sought *assurances* the bill would not be voted on unless he was present.

Assurances is the object of the verb *sought.*

Intransitive verbs do not have objects; there is no noun to receive the action started by the subject because one isn't needed.

> The horse neighs.

That sentence is complete; it needs nothing more to fill it out, unlike the sentence with the transitive verb. You could not write:

> The senator sought.

Anyone reading that would ask: What did the senator seek?

Dictionaries tell which verbs are transitive and intransitive and which can go either way. If a sentence sounds wrong, it could be because the writer misused an intransitive or transitive verb.

Irregular Verbs

All principal parts of regular verbs are formed the way you were shown earlier in this chapter. But we also have irregular verbs, irregular because they do not follow the normal pattern. Children just learning the language are the most common culprits in not recognizing irregular verbs. ("I falled down" is a phrase parents hear often from young children.) The children are imitating what appears to be a logical language pattern that really shifts helter-skelter. There is nothing intuitive to guide them through the irregularities. Eventually, though, they learn them—or change them. The approximately 200 irregular verbs in our language may disappear someday. But because they haven't yet, you have to know them or be able to recognize them. Here are some of the more common ones; any good dictionary gives them all.

Present	Past	Past Participle
arise	arose	arisen
awake	awoke	awakened
be (am, is, are)	was, were	been
bite	bit	bitten
catch	caught	caught
do	did	done
drink	drank	drunk
drove	drove	driven
eat	ate	eaten
find	found	found
get	got	got (gotten)
go	went	gone
hit	hit	hit
know	knew	known
lead	led	led
leave	left	left
lie	lay	lain
mean	meant	meant
put	put	put
ring	rang	rung
say	said	said
tear	tore	torn
write	wrote	written

False Verbs

The technique of combining a noun and a participle into a compound modifier has generated a new verb form that despite its known parentage is still a bastard both in form and in function. Given recent history, it's not surprising that the phrase "court-ordered busing" has become common. Someone converted it to a new verb form—the noun-verb or adjective-verb (usually with a hyphen) in which the verb is modified, not by an adverb, but by a noun. The result:

The limitations were court-ordered in 1979.

A journalist once wrote about people at a party who had "gate-crashed," a clunker more socially affronting than the uninvited party-goers. A second journalist told of a political leader who had performed many favors and "index-carded" each one so he had a file when the time for collecting those favors came up. A sportswriter wrote about a sprinter who "false-started" and was disqualified.

The abuse is not limited to journalists. (The abuse is not journalist-limited!) A theater critic wrote about an actor who "cold-shouldered" another actor on the set; a biographer wrote that Walt Whitman journeyed to New York and "job-hunted"; a sign on a bus assured passengers, "This bus is restroom equipped for your convenience" (The company doesn't know any better; it didn't use a hyphen); a mother complained that part of the travails her daughter suffered as a newspaper carrier came about because she had to "roll the papers, rubber-band them, and door-knob them each week" (if that doesn't sound unnatural . . .); a professor advised his readers that he had "tape-interviewed" about 200 sources.

The origin of such abominations is hard to trace. No doubt contemporary critics would lay the blame on Madison Avenue. ("This car is sticker-priced at $10,000 and is factory-equipped for the most discriminating driver." And of course, all of that was done only after the product was "test-marketed.") Dating the form is difficult. My earliest example comes from *Desolation Angels* (copyright 1960), in which Jack Kerouac wrote: "We come walking out of the racetrack and past the parkinglot [sic] to where the little coupe is free-parked by a railroad spur-track." In *The Careful Writer* (copyright 1973) Theodore M. Bernstein calls the form the "home-made compound," although his examples derive from condensing a verb and a prepositional phrase into a false verb. Despite that, his condemnation of the result remains valid.

Presumably, what the form accomplishes is economy of expression; it is briefer to write that the limitations were court-ordered" than "the limitations were ordered by the court." But that doesn't excuse the graceless result, which says more about the writer who would use such a combination than it does about the action it purports to describe. The noun-verb or adjective-verb form is one of those writing tics that should be avoided by all caring writers.

Chapter 5

Modification

Positioning Modifiers Correctly

Modification problems arise when modifiers are misplaced. By now you should have a clear idea of what modification is. You have already seen in Chapter 2 how ideas can be expanded through modification from a basic pattern (subject-verb) into the most complex structure. The positioning of modification (which can be a word, phrase or clause) is crucial. Consider this:

> They maintain that the highway would create a barrier separating
> Crystal City from the adjoining residential area.

That sentence tells us little. Why would the highway create a barrier? And what is so significant about Crystal City that it can't be separated from adjoining residences?

What is lacking is modification at the right place, an explanation of the significance of the highway and Crystal City. The significance cannot be explained two paragraphs later, for you have no guarantee the reader will continue reading past the unexplained information. Nor can you explain the significance two paragraphs earlier in the story because the explanation will lack a context. What must be done is not only modifying but modifying at the right place and time. Here is the sentence as it appeared in *The Washington Post:*

> They maintain that the highway, *sections of which are to be elevated on walls 30 feet high,* would create a barrier separating Crystal City, *with its shops and offices,* from the adjoining residential area [italics added].

Even before we read that the highway would become a barrier, we get a description of the highway, a description telling why the highway would become a barrier. And even before we read what Crystal City would be separated from, we read what Crystal City contains. When we finish the sentence, we know that the people who live in the adjoining residential area will be separated from Crystal City, where they shop and work.

It cannot be stressed enough that modifiers, be they single words, phrases or clauses, must be placed as close as possible to—if not next to—the word or phrase they modify. If they can't be closely placed, rewrite the sentence. Here is a headline error involving misplaced modification:

3 REBELS SEIZED
WITH A CAR BOMB

That certainly suggests that whoever did the seizing used a car bomb (in place of revolvers?). The fact is, the rebels had the car bomb. Correctly modified:

3 REBELS WITH
A CAR BOMB SEIZED

Some editors, however, would forbid that headline because the prepositional phrase (*with . . . bomb*) is split over two lines—a taboo at certain newspapers.

Similarly, the following sign on an interstate highway approaching Baltimore contains misplaced modification:

NO TRUCKS ON EDMONDSON AVE.
IN BALTIMORE CITY OVER ¾ TON

It should say:

NO TRUCKS OVER ¾ TON ON
EDMONDSON AVE. IN BALTIMORE CITY

An editor once argued that the important proximity in any sentence is between the subject and its verb, not the noun or verb and its modifiers. That results in sentences like this:

Opposition was expressed *to this plan* when it was learned the water
level of the dam might go up.

Actually, a phrase and a clause are out of place. The italicized phrase modifies *opposition;* the adverb clause (*when . . . up*) modifies the verb *expressed*. Putting all modification in its place results in:

Opposition to this plan was expressed when it was learned the water
level of the dam might go up.

Following the "rule" of keeping the subject and its verb as close as possible results in sentences that are more awkward than the preceding.

A *bill* was introduced in February in the House of Representatives *that
stated the methane should belong to the federal government.*

The italicized clause modified *bill*—yet we must read 9 words before we find out what the bill is about. Here is a rewrite:

A bill stating that the methane should belong to the federal government
was introduced in the House of Representatives in February.

Now everything is in its place.

Sometimes correcting a modification problem is not a simple matter of moving a clause next to the word it modifies. Sometimes only a full rewrite can save a sentence.

> Generally, the *requirement* in cases in which the family chooses not to have the body embalmed is *that the final disposition of the corpse must occur within 12 to 72 hours of the time of death.*

That sentence contains too much modification and is made worse by the weak verb *is*. The solution is subordination—a complex sentence.

> Generally, when the family chooses not to have the body embalmed, the law requires that the corpse be disposed of within 12 to 72 hours of the time of death.

Now everything is where it belongs; the sentence has a strong verb (*requires*) and is six words shorter than the original. Usually, though, modification misplacement is not as far off base as the preceding.

In improving the placement of modification, you will find that some sentence structures sound better than others. Here is a misplacement:

> I couldn't let the *opportunity* pass *to work for any newspaper*.

One ragged rewrite would be:

> I couldn't let pass the opportunity to work for any newspaper.

But even though the modifying infinitive phrase is next to the word it modifies, the cluster of verbs (*let pass*) is awkward, primarily because the object of *let* is not close to that verb.

> I couldn't let the opportunity to work for any newspaper pass.

Sometimes all the moving around in the world won't save a sentence. In that case, try more precise words.

> I couldn't pass up the opportunity to work for any newsapaper.

It is important, then, to view the whole sentence and not just parts of it. The proximity of objects to their verbs is as important as the proximity of modifiers to the words they modify.

Sometimes a misplaced adverb creates illiterate sentences.

> Turn *on* it.

> Put *down* it.

> Daddy's always knocking *down* me.

> I'm going to close *up* that.

Those examples come from the mouth of a 3½-year-old child. But a college student produced the following:

> Let me look the book through.

The student's error was converting a preposition into an adverb. Her request should have been:

> Let me look through the book.

The 3½-year-old will someday correctly say:

> Turn it on.

> Put it down.

> Daddy's always knocking me down.

> I'm going to close that up. (I'm going to close that.)

Another misplacement put a high school teacher out of work when all he did was quit coaching. A student referred to him as a:

> *former* coach and biology teacher

To get the teacher back in the classroom but keep him out of coaching, the structure should be:

> biology teacher and former coach

Dangling and Misplaced Modifiers

All modifiers have that mischievous habit of appearing in the wrong place. When they do, they are dangling or misplaced—just hanging there not clearly attached to what they modify. For the most part, their misplacement is more humorous than damaging. If they damage anything, it is the writer's credibility. Readers may pause, chuckle, and then continue. But they will also question the writer's attention to detail. If readers decide the writing is sloppy, they may stop reading.

The problem of dangling and misplaced modifiers often arises because writers want to say too much too quickly and forget how they've started a sentence. They get into a jam because they don't like to write simple and direct sentences, because they are too lazy to rewrite poor sentences, or because they are trying to avoid writing a series of similarly structured sentences. While it is true that sentence variety is desirable, it should not be achieved at the expense of clarity. Here are some examples of dangling modifiers.

> *Running through the woods,* the low branches were not seen by the boy. (That says the low branches were running when it was really the boy.)

> *As a Unitarian,* I want to ask you about your church. (The speaker is not a Unitarian; he is asking a question of a Unitarian. This is a common speech error.)

> *To win a football game,* the ball must cross the goal line. (Actually, it's the team that must get the ball across the goal line.)

> *Soon to join the journal's editorial board as an associate editor,* Sharon Sheehe Stark's fiction and poetry have appeared in . . . (The phrase modifies *fiction and poetry,* not *Sharon Sheehe Stark.*)

More grievous are modifiers with nothing to modify.

> As a devoted word processor user, my dusty typewriter hasn't seen light for five years.

Missing is the personal pronoun *I.*

> As a devoted word processor user, I haven't used my typewriter for five years.

Not all misplaced modifiers appear at the beginning of sentences.

> Pope Paul also forbade cardinals to bring in assistants, *except for those gravely ill.*

The modifying phrase goes with *cardinals* and should follow it immediately.

> Pope Paul also forbade cardinals, except for those gravely ill, to bring in assistants.

If that is clumsy:

> Pope Paul also forbade cardinals to bring in assistants. He excepted cardinals who are gravely ill.

> A misplaced attribution tag can create a dangling modifier.

> Referring to the board's fundamental problem, it became evident that a structural defect exists, Williams said.

The best fix for that sentence is moving the attribution tag because the modifying phrase refers to *he.*

> Referring to the board's fundamental problem, he said it became evident that a structural defect exists.

As that example shows, although the error is labeled a *dangling modifier,* the word being modified can be the element of the sentence that is actually out of place. Fixing the error requires moving it.

The second—and more typical—way of correcting a dangling modifer is moving the modifier. The Unitarian sentence suffices as an example.

> As a Unitarian, I want to ask you about your church.

To fix that, move the modifier.

I want to ask you, a Unitarian, about your church.

Now the modifier is properly placed. Think as you modify and danglers won't hang your credibility.

Other Faults

Some writers pile a long list of modifiers in front of a noun. The result is a monster.

Majority-supported university residence hall rules that prohibit door-to-door canvassing do not abridge freedoms guaranteed by the First Amendment.

The student who wrote that could have dropped some of the modifiers and brought in the information in later paragraphs. Thus:

University rules that prohibit door-to-door canvassing in residence halls do not abridge First Amendment freedoms.

Piling a long title in front of a name is also a modification fault.

Managing Director of the Central States' Festival of the Arts Lurene Hunt said that the First Lady will visit the festival on Friday.

Better to make the title the subject of the verb and place the name in apposition.

The managing director of the Central States' Festival of the Arts, Lurene Hunt, said that the First Lady will visit the festival on Friday.

Another problem is created by using a modifier without first introducing information to provide a context. In a first reference to a custody agreement that was being disputed, a student wrote:

A 1973 custody agreement . . .

Besides suggesting that 1973 was a vintage year for custody agreements, the phrase also suggests there were other agreements, say, in 1970, 1975, and so on. The proper phrasing:

A custody agreement reached in 1973 . . .

There is a difference in meaning and it was the latter meaning the student was after. A few extra words are better if they create a more precise meaning.

A similar fault is using a possessive form in first references, resulting in phrases such as ''last night's meeting'' before informing the reader or listener there was a meeting last night.

Sometimes the close-as-possible guideline is not followed for idiomatic reasons. We begin our mornings with a *hot cup of coffee* instead of a *cup of hot coffee*.

Some people would rather wear an *old pair of glasses* than a *pair of old glasses.* And few speakers say they are going shopping for a *pair of new shoes;* they say a *new pair of shoes.* Acceptable or not, idioms should usually be ignored in writing. To my ear an idiom sounds all right when spoken, but to my eye an idiom looks strange when written.

Self-Diagnostic Test 5.1

To determine how well you understand misplaced modification, correct the following sentences so that the modifiers are in the right place. The answers appear in the back of the book.

1. Such a case caused a typical example of strained police-press relations earlier in the day, he said, involving two suspects wanted for robbery and murder.

2. Entranced, the fire was watched by the arsonist.

3. It's relatively easy for this reviewer to complain, who divorced Heathcliff some decades ago.

4. Freed Russian dissident Alexander Ginzburg strolled down the country road near the home of Alexander Solzhenitsyn Wednesday puffing cigarette after cigarette.

5. The preferential treatment afforded the president's peanut business was revealed in a special report Wednesday by two directors of the bank.

6. USE OF TORTURE CALLED WIDESPREAD AGAINST DETAINEES IN SOUTH KOREA

7. VOTING RECORDS DETAILED OF CONGRESSMEN FROM REGION

Words and Phrases

Articles

The difference between *a(an)* and *the* is the difference between a general reference and a definitie one. *A(an)* is an indefinite article usually used in the first reference to something.

> A violent storm caused millions of dollars in damage as it plowed through Watkins Island late yesterday afternoon.

The, on the other hand, is a definite article and whatever *the* refers to should have been previously mentioned or be generally familiar to most readers. Thus, the next paragraph in the violent storm story:

> *The* storm started with soft winds that quickly built up to hurricane
> force, ripping up trees and blowing roofs off houses.

Here is an example of *the* incorrectly used (the report referred to has already been explained in a preceding paragraph):

> The board recommended that local government not develop a housing
> project for the elderly because *the* survey indicated no need for such an
> undertaking.

The writer was on firm footing when he used *a* before *housing project for the elderly;* there was no specific project. But he slipped on *the survey* because it was the first reference. Seeing such a construction, the reader is likely to return to the preceding sentence or paragraph to find out what survey the writer is talking about. Imagine what can happen if the error is made in the lead. Here are two examples:

> *The* decline in the number of daily newspapers in Pennsylvania is due to
> family problems, a changing economy and too many dailies to begin
> with, a journalism professor said yesterday.

> *The* breakdown of small-town identity has caused *the* decline in the
> number of daily newspapers across Pennsylvania, a journalism professor
> said yesterday.

All italicized *the's* should be replaced with *a.* The writers of those leads assumed the reader was familiar with declining newspaper sales and small-town identity breakdown. The reader was not; he or she had to be introduced to the subjects.

Introduce an issue or topic with *a(an).* Once that is done you can refer to the subject with *the* in all other references. *A(an)* is usually correct in leads. It is the lead that introduces a subject to a reader, as in the first example of this section—the storm story. Here is a lead with two unnecessary *the's* that could be dropped (dropping one also gets rid of a preposition):

> The Cadbury School Board last night approved *the* hiring *of* three
> teachers to relieve *the* overcrowded conditions at two elementary
> schools.

The *the* that begins the lead is correct because *the* is often used in first references to subjects or issues very familiar to readers. Cadbury taxpayers don't have to be told about the Cadbury School Board. Only one exists. With all omissions:

> The Cadbury School Board last night approved hiring three teachers to
> relieve overcrowded conditions at two elementary schools.

Similarly, *the* can be used in first references to long-standing organizations:

The Federal Bureau of Investigation

The Congress

The AFL-CIO

The University of Maryland

The president of the United States

To use *a(an)* would suggest there is more than one of each of the preceding, which isn't so.

Issues that have been in the public domain or are continuing news stories don't usually need *a(an)* because of the assumption the public is reading right along.

The on-going controversy between the Grays Knob City Council and the Grays Knob Planning Commission took a new turn last night.

Likewise:

The war in Vietnam . . .

The Watergate scandal . . .

People who are well known and in the public view are usually also *the* references.

"I don't think a vice president will ever be given a serious job by a president," said Arthur Schlesinger Jr., *the* historian [italics added].

What you must remember is what you are referring to.

The death of a Kansas man

A death in the family

The is used in first references when the noun it modifies is specifically identified immediately.

Rightist artillery bombarded leftist positions in *the* mountains *east of Fez* today.

The *Fittleton* was sailing to Hamburg, West Germany, on a goodwill visit after participating with other allied nations in *the* NATO exercise "Teamwork '76" off *the* coast *of Norway*.

The two scientists will report their findings in the journal *Science* next week.

The spokesperson gave no indication how quickly indictments could be presented to *the* grand jury *that has taken evidence in the case.*

Here are four paragraphs modeled after a newspaper story. Only one *the* is misused. Identify it.

Jason Proctor, describing himself as a participant in a "family affair" to win the governorship, had some harsh words for his father's opponent Friday.

Proctor, in a news conference preceding the rally on his father's behalf, said Gov. Rackowski is running "an absolutely filthy campaign."

Proctor, at the rally, said he expected personal attacks on his father because he is the candidate.

"But I take offense when Governor Rackowski cuts down my mother and my brother," he said.

The misused *the* is in the second paragraph. Because the writer was making the first reference to *rally,* the correct article is *a.* Some writers drop *the,* much to the consternation of some editors. I am a *the*-dropper, meaning I *usually* write:

Council agreed . . .

Congress approved . . .

However, I wouldn't drop *the* before *House of Representatives* or *General Assembly.* It rubs my ear the wrong way. Here is a sentence in which the writer dropped *a* and created confusion.

As secretary of education, he won a court decree granting the right of handicapped and retarded children to free education.

Without the article *a, to free* reads like an infinitive. Correctly written:

As secretary of education, he won a court decree granting the right of handicapped and retarded children to a free education.

Whether to use *a* or *an* gives some writers trouble. Generally, *a* precedes words that begin with a consonant sound while *an* is used before words beginning with a vowel sound. Note that sound is the key. The most confusion results with words that begin with *h.* If *h* is pronounced, use *a;* unpronounced, use *an.*

A *h*ouse is not a *h*ome but it is an *h*onor to own one.

The italicized letters are the first sounds pronounced and determine whether you use *a* or *an.*

Adjectives

Adjectives are words that modify nouns, phrases and other adjectives. They are not common to news stories because they can interfere with a reporter's "objective" account of an event or an issue. Describing a school board meeting, a reporter once wrote:

In a stormy session last night . . .

The entire phrase (*in a stormy*) was removed because it is opinionated. Later, someone who was at the meeting said that for that particular school board, the meeting was relatively calm. The reporter who covered the meeting had never attended any of the board's previous meetings.

If not opinionated, adjectives are often unnecessary or vague. They add words to a sentence without enhancing its meaning. Some of the adjectives (italicized) in the following sentences are examples of opinion, waste or vagueness.

The previous day had been one of those *cool, crystal* times.

These are *critical* times.

Political investigations are always interesting.

Stars gleamed like *spikey* chips of ice.

The *frail* man walked across the street.

Notwithstanding *widespread* reliance on the tractor, systems involving *extensive* cultivation of the land do have *certain* disadvantages.

A buffalo hide covered the *wiry* corpse.

A *heavy* snowfall was recorded last night.

It is difficult to latch on to those adjectives with a firm sense of what they mean. A heavy snowfall in Miami, Fla., may not measure the same as a heavy snowfall in Laramie, Wyo. Miami natives, no doubt, would consider two inches heavy; Laramie residents probably wouldn't notice a snowfall until it measured a foot.

Adjectives of color (*red* barn, *green* grass) and number (*11* council members, *three* senators) provide concrete descriptions and are more acceptable. Also acceptable are those adjectives whose descriptive powers are neutral enough not to interfere with a story, such as *presidential* race, *North American* diplomats, *Midwestern* politicians, *downtown* businessmen, *congressional* sources, *governmental* (or *government*) agencies, *martial* law, *automatic* lights.

Any adjective is probably acceptable if it's backed up with an explanation.

The president may resign and the vice president is gravely ill. These are *critical* times such as the nation has not seen since the Civil War.

Such a sentence probably would appear in an editorial rather than a news story. But whether you're writing a news story, an editorial or a feature story, use few—if any—adjectives.

Adjectives (and adverbs) come in three degrees—*positive, comparative* and *superlative.*

Positive	Comparative	Superlative
wise	wiser	wisest
smart	smarter	smartest
weak	weaker	weakest

As you can see, the ending of each is different, depending on the degree. Adjectives in the comparative degree add *er* to the positive form; in the superlative, *est*. There are irregularities, such as:

Positive	Comparative	Superlative
good	better	best

Adjectives of more than one syllable do not usually show their degree by their ending. Instead, we put *more* and *most* before the positive form to indicate, respectively, comparative and superlative.

Positive	Comparative	Superlative
astonishing	more astonishing	most astonishing

Treated that way, multisyllabic adjectives don't become tongue-twisters.

Your teacher is *astonishinger* than mine.

That doesn't mean *more* and *most* don't work with one-syllable adjectives. However, their use is primarily for emphasis.

Who is wiser? She is *more wise* than I.

Likewise, short two-syllable adjectives don't require *more* and *most*.

Positive	Comparative	Superlative
pretty	prettier	prettiest
funny	funnier	funniest

Comparative degree is used when comparing two persons or things; superlative is used with three or more.

She is *wiser* than I.

Of the five, she is the *wisest*.

Remember that the superlative puts someone or something in a category all alone. The person or thing has no equal.

Adverbs

Adverbs share some of the characteristics of adjectives: They can be stated in degrees (*wisely, more wisely, most wisely*); their use steals strength from verbs (the way adjectives obscure nouns); they are not common to news stories; and they are easily identified by function. While adjectives modify nouns and other adjectives, adverbs modify verbs, verb forms and adjectives.

With a Verb

He *ran quickly* down the field for a touchdown.

With a Verb Form (Verbal)

The *easily constructed* building can be used as a second home.

The secretary of state's quest for peace in the *racially troubled* country has been upstaged by a surprise summit of rebel leaders.

With an Adjective

My dog is *adequately faithful.*

The *ly* adverb form is not often used in news stories. The sentence about the secretary of state is a good example of when to use it. However, like some adjectives, the *ly* form can be more vague than concrete, more interpretive than descriptive, which could raise the issue of unobjective, unbalanced or unfair reporting.

The candidate's forces scrambled *grimly* today along the slopes of the Allegheny Mountains.

The president *exuberantly* predicted victory.

In both instances the adverbs are open to debate. In the first example the candidate's forces could argue that what appeared to be grim to the reporter was seriousness on their part. In the second some observers could argue that the exuberance was conduct typical of a candidate in a tight race.

Journalists, who are supposed to be as fair as is humanly possible, are also constrained to keep value judgments out of their stories. A television newscaster once said:

Unfortunately, there were more deaths today . . .

Let readers or listeners make that decision; give them the information on which to base their own decisions. This journalist did not need to use the adverb.

Fire extinguishers were of no use, but *luckily* everyone managed to flee the building.

Adverbs are sometimes used for emphasis, although no real need exists in the following, especially since the direct quotation shows what the adverb is saying.

To critics who suggested Linder's version may not have been Adley's, the AP newsman replied *briefly:* "Sour grapes!"

Perhaps the writer didn't trust readers to make their own judgments. In some instances, though, reporters make a judgment because they cannot reveal their sources.

The candidate's strategists were *reliably* reported to be considering two other approaches.

At other times, reporters interpret information for readers, as in these sentences:

The economic news was certain to cheer the administration, which has been *deeply* worried over price reports in previous months that showed inflation increasing at a worrisome 10 percent annual rate since Jan. 1.

Prices were reported *sharply* lower for grains, eggs, green coffee, cocoa, tea, soybeans and live poultry. But the decreases were *partially* offset by higher prices for livestock.

The problem is, you have to take the reporter's word for all three adverbs; the reporter never provided concrete information to support them. The reader does not know precisely what *deeply, sharply* and *partially* mean. All three adverbs are vague.

Most adverbs are formed by adding *ly* to a root form, which is usually an adjective.

Adjective	Adverb
quick	quickly
smart	smartly
virtual	virtually
grim	grimly
exuberant	exuberantly
medical	medically
political	politically

Note that the *ly* ending does not affect the spelling of the root form.

When forming the comparative and superlative degrees, use *more* and *most*. To use *er/est* endings would create tongue-twisters beyond comparison.

quicklier	quickliest

If when using adverbs, you follow the more-than-one-syllable rule that applies to adjectives, you won't have any problems. Many adverbs, by virtue of the *ly* ending, contain two or more syllables.

Adverbs are classified according to the meaning they express—place, manner (how something is done) and time. Adverbs of place (such as *where, in, off, by, down, under*) are often redundant.

How did he get *down?* He jumped *off.*

In the first sentence *down* is necessary to complete the sentence. But *off* in the second sentence adds nothing; in fact, it weakens *jump.*

Adverbs of manner usually have the *ly* endings. Adverbs of time, on the other hand, include *later, often, sometimes, then, earlier.* Paul Roberts, author of *Understanding English,* says that when all three occur after the same verb, the order is place, manner, time.

One sticky division among editors and teachers concerns where to place the adverb in a two-verb form (an auxiliary verb and a main verb)—in the middle or at the beginning or at the end.

> The lawyer for the former prime minister said his client will *probably* be hanged Tuesday or Wednesday.

> The lawyer for the former prime minister said his client *probably* will be hanged Tuesday or Wednesday.

> The lawyer for the former prime minister said his client will be hanged *probably* Tuesday or Wednesday.

Because there was no question a hanging would take place, the adverb was needed to modify the time—Tuesday or Wednesday—making the third example the correct one. The third example gains clarity with the insertion of a comma after *hanged* (The lawyer for the former prime minister said his client will be *hanged,* probably Tuesday or Wednesday.) Had there been a question about the method of execution, examples one or two would have been better.

The same debate covers the placement of adverbs with infinitives. A split infinitive from the television series "Star Trek" exemplifies the differences:

> The crew of the Enterprise was ordered *to boldly go* where no man had ever gone before.

> The crew of the Enterprise was ordered *to go boldly* where no man had ever gone before.

> The crew of the Enterprise was ordered *boldly to go* where no man had ever gone before.

In the third sentence *boldly* might be read as modifying *ordered.* Were that the case, I would write:

> The crew of the Enterprise *was boldly ordered* to go where no man had ever gone before.

Here is another example in which the meaning changes with the placement of the adverb:

> He suggested hiring a design professional to plan *further parking spaces.* (That suggests more spaces.)

> He suggested hiring a design professional *to further plan* parking spaces. (That suggests more planning.)

Likewise, the title of a magazine article about photography was:

TO SIMPLY SEE

Someone wanted to unsplit the infinitive so it would read:

TO SEE SIMPLY

The split infinitive prevailed, which preserved the author's meaning.

Once again, logic should help the writer determine where to place the adverb. Try to place the adverb as close as possible to the word it modifies. Looked at another way: Place the adverb where it accurately conveys the correct meaning. What is correct, of course, depends on the writer's intention. Here is an exercise from Jack Cappon of the Associated Press showing how *only* moved around in a sentence changes its meaning.

> Only I hit him in the eye yesterday.
> I only hit him in the eye yesterday.
> I hit only him in the eye yesterday.
> I hit him only in the eye yesterday.
> I hit him in only the eye yesterday.
> I hit him in the only eye yesterday.
> I hit him in the eye only yesterday.
> I hit him in the eye yesterday only.

You must also make a distinction between an adverb and an adjective when using certain verbs like *smell, taste, speak, feel, hear,* and *look.* Are you modifying the verb's action or the verb's condition?

> I smell good.

The adjective means my body gives off a good-smelling odor.

> I smell *well*.

The adverb means my nose is superior in sniffing odors.

If the modifier is working on the subject of the sentence or some other noun— that is, describing the condition of the verb rather than modifying it—use an adjective. The following advice concerns the comments you make, not how you make them:

> *Speak good of the dead.*

But to advise on how to make such comments, a person would use an adverb to modify the verb.

> *Speak well of the dead.*

Apposition

Appositives do a lot of work in newspapers. In fact, no journalist could do without them. Their function of giving identity or authority to a noun is crucial to any news story. They are coupled with nouns and are usually noun phrases.

> American Motors Corp., *the nonconformist in an industry where sameness is a virtue,* once again is financially out of step with its larger Big Three auto competitors [italics added].

Without the phrase in apposition (italicized), the importance of the rest of the sentence would be lost on most readers. The readers must first be told what American Motors is before they can be told what the company is doing. Naturally, the phrase in apposition changes to suit the meaning.

> American Motors Corp., *long a manufacturer of low- and medium-priced cars,* announced today it was going to build a luxury car similar to the Cadillac and Lincoln Continental.

Appositives appear in many forms but serve only one purpose—providing identity peculiar to a particular story. Here are two appositives stacked one after the other:

> Prince Stanislaus Radziwill, 61, *Polish-born former husband of Lee Radziwill, sister of Mrs. Jacqueline Onassis,* died Sunday in London after a brief illness.

First there is the phrase in apposition to the subject of the sentence (*Radziwill*). Then you are assaulted with a phrase in apposition to the first phrase in apposition. Such writing crams too much into one sentence, which makes clarity impossible to attain. Two sentences and some careful thought on the clearest way to describe the prince's relationship to Mrs. Onassis are needed.

> Prince Stanislaus Radziwill, 61, former brother-in-law to Mrs. Jacqueline Onassis, died Sunday in London after a brief illness. The Polish-born Radziwill was once married to Mrs. Onassis' sister, Lee Radziwill.

Titles, when following names, are in apposition to names.

> John Monahan, president of the Fix-It Tool Co., said today . . .

Sometimes names are put in apposition to titles. This is common in news stories about people not well known to the general public.

> The superintendent of instruction, Susan Avon, announced plans today for three new courses.

The same thinking can be applied to phrases and clauses.

The person who knows more about this subject than anyone else, Sam Goodman, won't be at tonight's meeting.

Some editors feel uncomfortable (note adjective use) making such a long phrase the subject of a sentence. They routinely exchange the phrase and its appositive so the name becomes the subject. (For an explanation on punctuating appositives, see "Apposition" under the *Comma* section in Chapter 6.)

Prepositional Phrases

Prepositional phrases should appear immediately after the word they modify. When they don't, they make no sense at all or they create humor where none is intended.

The Allen controversy erupted last week when the governor asked her *to respond* to published reports about her absences *in writing*.

The italicized prepositional phrase modifies the italicized infinitive, yet six words separate them. The writer of that sentence, when he wrote the words *to respond,* should have asked: Respond how? Had he done that, he would have written:

The Allen controversy erupted last week when the governor asked her *to respond in writing* to published reports about her absences.

Here is an example of unintended humor:

All board *members* approved a decision to post signs and let the contract *except Dillon.*

To get Dillon back onto the board:

All board *members except Dillon* approved a decision to post signs and let the contract.

The misplacement of a prepositional phrase can sometimes be libelous.

Harry Sneer, head coach of the Kearney Tigers, discusses his personal and professional life *with producer-hostess Mary Rubin* on a PBS interview series.

The prepositional phrase was meant to modify *discusses,* but instead it modifies *life*—Sneer's life with Rubin. Correctly put:

Harry Sneer, head coach of the Kearney Tigers, *discusses with producer-hostess Mary Rubin* on a PBS interview series his personal and professional life.

But that is awkward, so make two sentences, saving the information on the PBS interview series for the second sentence.

Another misplacement caused some laughter among the readers of an advice columnist who had discussed the problem of a nurse who was "ashamed to take her child to a *doctor with recurring pinworms.*" However, the child, not the physician, had recurring pinworms. Placing the prepositional phrase immediately after the noun it modifies would clearly connect the patient with the ailment. To the columnist's credit, she announced the error, which a newspaper editor had pointed out, in a later column.

Here is another example, this one based on the style of a sloppy reporter:

> T. T. Smith was arraigned on charges of committing sodomy *before District Magistrate Harry Jones* yesterday.

The italicized prepositional phrase modifies the prepositional phrase immediately preceding it. How can Smith avoid conviction if the district magistrate witnessed the crime? Better written, the sentence would say:

> T. T. Smith was arraigned yesterday before District Magistrate Harry Jones on a charge of sodomy.

Other examples:

> A woman told police yesterday that a man had assaulted her as she left an elevator at the Sparks Apartments. The victim was grasped from behind *between 12:30 and 12:45 p.m.*

> Brooke Shields, the controversial teen sex symbol, talks with Joe Baltake about her new movie, "Endless Love," and how she wishes her teeth were straightened out *in tomorrow's Daily News.*

A wire service writer unintentionally put secret payments into a book.

> The CIA several years ago went to court to block former intelligence officials Victor Marchetti and John D. Marks from revealing the names of foreign leaders who have *received secret payments in their book* "The CIA and the Cult of Intelligence."

Correctly structured, the sentence would read:

> The CIA several years ago went to court to block former intelligence officials Victor Marchetti and John D. Marks from revealing in their book "The CIA and the Cult of Intelligence" the names of foreign leaders who have received secret payments.

Some prepositional phrases can be moved around in a sentence to change the meaning.

> The children *by the public fountain* pointed to the heap *of stones, boards, tin and broken glass* as if it were a national monument.

The second phrase cannot be moved; it modifies *heap*. Moving it would be confus-

ing, even illiterate. But the first phrase can be moved to the beginning of the
sentence *if a different meaning is wanted*.

> *By the public fountain,* the children pointed to the heap of stones,
> boards, tin and broken glass as if it were a national monument.

The first example indicates the children were standing next to the public fountain.
The second indicates that the children were walking and when they reached the
fountain, they pointed.

Prepositional phrases indicating time rather than place can be moved around
more safely.

> We'll leave here *in the morning*.

> *In the morning* we'll leave here.

As with other modifiers, the stress you want determines where some prepositional
phrases are placed.

> *At the outset of the war,* there were few volunteers. But as the war
> dragged on, more and more people joined the army.

A prepositional phrase can be placed at the beginning of a sentence to signal
transition. For example, a story detailing the major action of a group might shift to a
lesser action.

> *In other business,* the agency board decided to change its next meeting
> from Tuesday to Wednesday.

A fault common with prepositional phrases is trying to make the noun in the
phrase the subject of a verb. In the following the subject and the verb are italicized:

> The *fad* of job-oriented training will not *open* students to the broader
> experiences of life.

Fads don't open anything. The writer of the sentence had *job-oriented training* in
mind for a subject, but that is the object of the preposition. Objects don't function as
subjects. Had the writer forgotten about *fad* altogether and not tried to pile so many
thoughts into the sentence, the blunder wouldn't have occurred.

> Job-oriented training will not open students to the broader experiences
> of life.

If *fad* had been essential to that sentence, the word could have been fitted in like
this:

> Job-oriented training, which is a fad, will not open students to the
> broader experiences of life.

Prepositional phrases are often overused to the detriment of tight writing. There
is no reason to write *in the week just passed* when *last week* will do nicely.

Nouns

Nouns function as modifiers more often than some purists would prefer to admit. We speak of *journalism schools* without one thought that we might really mean *journalistic schools*. *Governmental agencies* is not as comfortable as *government agencies*. And who will call to the defense the dictionary that lists *news* as a noun with the next entry being *news agency?* After that comes *newsboy* and *newscast*. What newspaper doesn't have its *news editor?* And have you ever watched the news on a *television set?*

The problem with nouns as modifiers occurs when an abundance of nouns piles up before the main noun. In this example, a verbal contributes to the clunking result: *non-preregistered degree student time schedule*. Before cluttering your writing with such clunkers, make sure a word does not have an adjectival form or that one can't be created before you go the all-noun route. That advice still stands. But it doesn't mean nouns cannot be used as adjectives in stories and in headlines. Here are some nouns functioning as adjectives:

Grade deflation is slowly replacing *grade* inflation.

"Some of your ideas may find their way into the classroom," the *college* professor told the *alumni* gathering.

A simple *telephone* system is the best.

As far as the *justice* system is concerned, the worst political scandal in American history will be over. (There is an adjective—*judicial*.)

The *police* officer, while looking for the youth, opened the *closet* door and heard the cry: "Shut the door, the cops are chasing me."

The *surprise* decision to release the pair followed six hours of meetings Saturday.

The campus is so large the university needs a *campus police* force.

A *speech* defect can be very traumatic to a child.

Some *price* increases are easier to understand than others.

In headlines a noun modifier can be awkward. But the curse of not enough space to correctly say something forces headline writers to improvise by compacting phrases into single words. Prepositional phrases are almost always converted into grouped nouns in headlines. Because this headline wouldn't fit

UTILITIES DROP COAL PLANT FOR IOWA

the writer chose

UTILITIES DROP IOWA COAL PLANT

Sometimes a prepositional phrase fits.

PRESENCE OF PAROLEE IRKS JONES

But if it hadn't, that headline would have been best modified with a possessive form

PAROLEE'S PRESENCE IRKS JONES

and not a noun

PAROLEE PRESENCE IRKS JONES

Sometimes a noun as a modifier is not offensive

DEMOCRATS TAKE REGISTRATION LEAD

but other times it's overdone as a mouthful of modifiers

SOVIET GRAIN IMPORTS DROP UNLIKELY

UNIVERSITY PROPOSES TUITION BENEFIT CUT DELAY

Stumbling on those should make you more aware of the problem. Journalists who are aware of such abuses don't make such mistakes.

Verbals

Because they are derived from verbs and thus denote action, verbals are ideal modifiers. And, as noted in Chapter 4, entire clauses can be turned into strong verbal modifiers that increase the power of a sentence. A *stalking foe* conjures up a stronger image than *a foe who stalks*.

Reviewing Chapter 4, verbal forms are: the *infinitive* (to stalk), the *present participle* (stalking) and the *past participle* (stalked).

The *stalking* soldier hid in the bushes.

The *wounded* soldier awaited help.

The soldier went on patrol *to stalk* the enemy.

Infinitives modify verbs while present and past participles modify nouns.

The error most frequently made with verbals as modifiers is in the past participle. Some writers forget the *ed*, which results in incorrect constructions like this one from a restaurant's menu:

mash potatoes

You get alcohol from mash, but if you mash potatoes, they are mash*ed*. Likewise, a *toss salad* sounds like something made from *toss*, the way a tuna fish salad is made from tuna fish. The correct word is *tossed*, to describe something that was done (like *mashed* in *mashed potatoes*) to the salad.

Clauses and Phrases

Generally speaking, a *clause* contains a subject and predicate. Sometimes, through elliptical writing, for example, a subject or predicate may not be repeated; then the clause is labeled "reduced." A *phrase* is a combination of words that does not contain a subject and predicate. For this book's purposes, if you spend a lot of time debating whether something is a clause or a phrase, you will surely go mad. If you want to know the many permutations that clauses and phrases can take, please consult the current edition of *Writer's Guide and Index to English,* by Wilma R. Ebbitt and David R. Ebbitt. They explain in detail.

Verb Phrases

Verb phrases are phrases whose initial word is a verbal. Verb phrases can appear after the word they modify

> The congressmen made available letters *received* from the Moroccan ambassador in Paris.

> The press release *announcing the councilman's candidacy* was filled with attacks on the mayor.

or before

> *Weakened by the long hike,* the soldier staggered into camp.

> *Taking his cue from his brother,* Bill helped pick up the debris.

Along with other forms of modification, verb phrases cause the most problems when they dangle. Another problem occurs when an unthinking advertising writer loses control. Try this soggy sandwich:

> Italian steak grinder
> smothered in cheese
>   and
> cup of homemade soup

Relative Clauses

Relative clauses are clauses introduced by relative pronouns: *who, which, that, what.* Because they show a relationship, they should be as close as possible to the word they modify in order to avoid confusion.

> Monahan is a president *who likes to wear sweaters.*

> The hospital, *which was built outside the town,* can be reached by taking Mountain Avenue.

> The plan *that pleases Sen. Williams the most* is the one on comprehensive tax reform.

> Do you know *what he wants?* (In this sentence the clause functions as the object of the verb *know.*)

Misplacing any of the clauses in the preceding sentences would be illiterate or confusing. In the following sentence it would be fatal:

Dillon said, however, that to soften water, *salt* must be added to it,
which is a health hazard.

Once again, common practice is to get the clause as close as possible to the word or phrase it modifies. Otherwise you may get results like these:

None will be accepted who are handicapped either mentally or
physically.

The bride was escorted to the altar by her father which was decorated
with bouquets of red and white mums.

Quipped the contributor of the second example: "Dad must have been gorgeous!"
Sometimes the problem isn't the placement of the clause, but of something else. A student wrote:

The United States, *according to Walsh,* which represents 5 percent of
the world's population, must curtail its consumption.

The attribution tag (italicized), because it comes between the clause and the word it modifies, fouls that sentence. Put the attribution tag at the beginning or end of the sentence so the clause immediately follows *United States*.

According to Walsh, the United States, which represents 5 percent of
the world's population, must curtail its consumption.

The United States, which represents 5 percent of the world's population,
must curtail its consumption, according to Walsh.

Adverb Clauses

Adverb clauses function the same way adverbs do—they modify verbs, verbals and adjectives. No absolute rule governs where they should appear in a sentence. Usually, though, an adverb clause makes the important modifications or qualifications in a sentence, so it should be placed in such a way as to tip the reader.

When the president enters a room, the press corps always *rises.*

The italicized clause modifies *rises.*
In elliptic writing the adverb clause is often written without the similar words of the main clause. Hence, the adverb clause, to be clear, must appear after the main clause.

The president left Washington *earlier than the press* [left Washington].

Essential and Non-essential Clauses

All clauses are either *essential* or *non-essential,* which some usage books call *restrictive* and *non-restrictive.* They are recognized not by the word that introduces them but by the way they function. An essential clause is one that is needed to complete the meaning of a sentence.

> The plan *that pleases Sen. Williams the most* is the one on comprehensive tax reform.

Dropping the clause (in italics) changes the meaning of the sentence, if it will have any meaning at all. ("The plan is the one on comprehensive tax reform.") Additionally, the essential clause tells readers that more than one plan exists but this sentence is about "the one that pleases Sen. Williams the most." Thus, the clause restricts the rest of the sentence and cannot be discarded without doing violence to the sentence's meaning.

A non-essential clause, on the other hand, can modify a noun or the main clause, but it is not needed to complete the meaning of the main clause.

> The bookshelves, which are gray, take up five feet of valuable space in my office.

Dropping the non-essential clause would not make the main clause incomplete.

> The bookshelves take up five feet of valuable space in my office.

The writer's intended meaning determines whether an essential or non-essential clause is used. Compare:

> Legislators *who were briefed on the governor's preliminary budget* said it is a mixture of bad and good news. (essential)

> Legislators, who were briefed on the governor's preliminary budget, said it is a mixture of bad and good news. (non-essential)

In the first sentence, the essential clause restricts the action to only those legislators who were briefed. In the second sentence, the non-essential clause suggests that all legislators were briefed.

When most people think of the pronouns that lead off essential and non-essential clauses, they usually think of *that* and *which*. Other pronouns can begin such clauses too. For example:

> The man *who served as our first president* will also be remembered for his military ability. (essential)

> The columnists agree he would win the most votes in the Northeast, *where he is strongest.* (non-essential)

> When I retire, I want to live *where nobody has lived before.* (essential)

Single words can also function as essential or non-essential modifiers.

> The two scientists will report their findings in the journal *Science* next week. (essential)

Coach Smith's husband, *John*, has packed and moved the family three times during her career. (non-essential)

The distinction between the modifiers in the preceding sentences centers on whether the italicized word is needed to complete the meaning of the sentence. In the first, dropping *Science* would leave the reader wondering which journal was going to carry the findings. In the second, because Coach Smith may legally have only one husband, dropping his name will not affect the sentence. Adding his name provides more information, of course, but his name is not essential to the meaning of the sentence.

Following are two statements made by a person who works most weekends and who is planning to move on a weekend when she doesn't have to work.

I am moving the first weekend in February,
which I have off. (non-essential)

I am moving the first weekend in February
that I have off. (essential)

In the first, the woman has said she is not working on the first weekend of February and that is when she will move. But in the second, she does not say which weekend she has off, only that when she gets a weekend off, she will move. It could be the last weekend of February, which would make a big difference to the person hearing the statement, especially if that person is going to help the woman move.

Punctuation   Non-essential words, phrases and clauses are set off by commas (or by one comma when the modifier comes at the beginning or the end of a sentence), whereas no punctuation separates an essential clause or phrase from the word it modifies. Punctuation, however, is secondary to function and intent. Adding commas does not always make a clause or phrase non-essential.

That, Which   Many of the pronouns that begin essential and non-essential clauses are not interchangeable. No writer would use *who* for *where* and so on. But *that* and *which* can interchange, although the interchange is discouraged—with certain exceptions. The rule is: Use *that* to begin an essential clause and *which* a non-essential clause. The exceptions: Substitute *which* for *that* when otherwise the sentence would contain two *thats*.

Some rules exist despite inconsistencies *that* seem to indicate *that* similar-looking words shouldn't be spelled similarly.

Rewritten:

Some rules exist despite inconsistencies *which* seem to indicate *that* similar-looking words shouldn't be spelled similarly.

From *The Associated Press Stylebook:*

He said Monday *that* the part of the army *which* suffered severe casualties needs reinforcement.

Some editors, relying on rhythm more than rules, would allow a sentence with two *that*s. Generally, follow the substitution guideline stated earlier.

That is never used to introduce a non-essential clause. The next chapter, under the discussion on the comma, contains a debate that centers on punctuation but would have been avoided had someone distinguished between *that* for essential clauses and *which* for non-essential clauses.

Self-Diagnostic Test 5.2

To determine how well you understand the various types of modifiers, name the type of modifier that is italicized in the following sentences. The answers appear in the back of the book. Review what you miss.

1. Members of the House of Representatives, *elected every two years,* find themselves campaigning more often than senators, *who face election every six years.*

2. The *injured* football player hobbled to the sidelines, *where the team's trainer looked after him.*

3. Filled *with the excitement of competition,* our track star ran *swiftly* to *the* finish line.

4. The typewriter, *long a fixture in newsrooms,* will soon become a *museum* piece.

5. Professional *football* teams must announce the *medical* status of all players several days *before a game.*

Exercise 5.1

Identify the modifiers by circling single words and short phrases and by underlining clauses and prepositional phrases. Turn your work in to your instructor for evaluation.

Name _____

1. Government officials said they had been unable to decide whether Israel's reprocessing move was in contravention of a triangular agreement between the United States, Israel and the World Atomic Energy Administration.

2. Morocco's heavily guarded borders are more relaxed and open now than at any time since the end of the two-month war with Algeria.

3. Her street clothes ragged and rumpled, her unshined shoes bursting at the seams, a social worker masqueraded as a welfare recipient and helped document what her superiors say is massive waste and mismanagement in San Francisco's huge welfare program.

4. Returning to the famous redwoods in the national park where he worked as a park attendant 20 years ago, the governor outlined a park acquisition and development plan that he called an environmental gift to future park lovers.

5. The number of demonstrators engaged in protests has not been large anywhere.

6. The Security Council resolution on the Middle East gave small victories to each side.

7. Iowa State's star runner, who earlier in the game had appeared hobbled by a slight leg injury, burst off tackle, eluded two safety men, then moved swiftly into the end zone for the winning touchdown.

8. Using a radial arm saw and a variable speed drill, she fashioned a bookcase that all agreed was superb in craftsmanship, excellent in design and functional in use.

9. The angry fans stormed the referees' dressing room intent on finding out why the touchdown that would have won the game for their team was nullified by a penalty nobody saw.

10. Defensively, the young professor explained why he had given the student's paper a D grade.

11. The pink, red, green and yellow bookcases that line the walls of her den contain many of the books she acquired as a college student.

12. The mayor heatedly responded, then quickly sat down amid a firm round of applause from the small audience in the council chambers.

Exercise 5.2

Some of the modifiers in the following sentences are misplaced or misused. Correct them. Turn your work in to your instructor for evaluation.

Name _____

1. The fact that there were children in the audience born since "Star Trek" stopped filming illustrated Nimoy's idea that the show's reruns appeal to all generations.

2. Tied to a tree, the police found the kidnapped woman two days after she had been forced from her home by two men.

3. The senator said he, turned off by politics, would not seek reelection.

4. Five persons with a rifle were shot by a policeman.

5. Bugliosi has a signed statement from one of two Los Angeles policemen who were shown pointing to a bullet lodged in a hotel door jamb in a photo taken the day after the murder.

6. A president of the United States said today relations with China and Russia are improving.

7. The emotional charged statement was a further indication of how wide the gap has grown between the mayor and the council.

8. Sen. Williams is the exuberantist senator I know.

9. The inmate surrendered when the guards fired tear gas quickly.

10. Harry T. Williams, the new superintendent of Cadbury Schools, was introduced to the public for the first time today.

Chapter 6

Punctuation

Establishing Relationships

The writer is ready to go All lessons have been learned He sits before his typewriter paper in place and begins to type at first slowly as he thinks about his words but then faster faster as he picks up the pace and his great writing flows Someday these words will be discovered on this dog eared paper in a multiuse library the writer says outloud in a somewhat gleeful somewhat arrogant voice What could be better to be discovered later or discovered now A thought Perhaps though it would help if I knew how to punctuate That way people would understand what I am writing

Punctuation establishes the relationship between words in sentences and paragraphs. The preceding unpunctuated paragraph vividly demonstrates the incommunicative horror that results when standard punctuation marks are not used. The writer who misuses punctuation does so at the risk of comprehension, of diluting a sentence's meaning or changing a word's nuance. A comma in the hands of a klutz is just another punctuation mark; in the hands of someone who appreciates how words can collide, a comma cushions the blow.

Unhappy with some out-of-focus prints he had received, an amateur photographer returned the negatives to a camera store and asked that new prints be made. The clerk agreed. He placed the negatives into a new envelope and wrote on the outside:

redo

out of focus

Fortunately, the clerk realized that he had asked the film-developing company to make new prints *out of focus* rather than make new prints because the old ones were out of focus. A comma after *redo* cushioned the words and defined their relationship.

These headlines, punctuated differently, mean different things.

NICARAGUAN	NICARAGUAN	NICARAGUAN TROOPS
TROOPS FIRE	TROOPS FIRE	FIRE AT
AT CROWD,	AT CROWD	CROWD-WOUNDING 10
WOUNDING 10	WOUNDING 10	

The first says the troops wounded 10 people; the second says the crowd was wounding 10 people when the troops fired; the third says the crowd has wounded 10 people but not necessarily when the troops fired. The correct punctuation mark helps the reader understand. (The correct headline is the first.)

The difference between a hyphen and no hyphen can be the difference between gang war and a change of heart, between a gang of delinquents that had broken up deciding to re-form or reform. No small difference, yet it hangs on the thread of a hyphen—and the knowledge of someone who knows how to punctuate.

Even the much abused semicolon, misplaced, alters meaning. Compare the following:

The drinks are free; unfortunately, the pizza isn't.

The drinks are free, unfortunately; the pizza isn't.

There's a third possibility, albeit incorrect, one common with novice writers—no semicolon at all.

The drinks are free, unfortunately, the pizza isn't.

How will readers know which meaning the writer intended?

Finally, the much overused dash can be used to make meaning clear. Consider the following photo caption, where the dash is needed:

HOME STRETCH: These runners, students and townspeople,
near the finish of a 10-mile race held to raise money
for Sun Day.

On first reading, the initial comma suggests a series of people—runners, students and townspeople. The second comma helps show the apposition, but not strongly enough to avoid a second reading. What is really meant is that the runners comprise students and townspeople, and dashes in place of commas would make that immediately clear.

HOME STRETCH: These runners—students and townspeople—
near the finish of a 10-mile race held to raise money
for Sun Day.

If you've ever examined something written two or three centuries ago, you will notice that writers then punctuated more than we do today. The style at that time was to write longer sentences, which in turn required more punctuation. Modern style demands briefer sentences that need less punctuation. However, less punctuation does not mean no punctuation at all. Rather, it means a precise use of punctuation.

End Punctuation

The Period .

End of Sentence   The period indicates the end of a declarative sentence.

Officials are baffled about the cause and nature of the disease.

It also indicates the end of an imperative sentence.

Give me your notes.

The period also appears at the end of a polite request that sounds like a question.

Would you give me your notes.

Abbreviation   Sometimes called a *point* by printers, the period is used in abbreviations.

The Middlemen Inc.
J. C. Penney Co.
U.S. government
Harrisburg, Pa.
Los Angeles, Calif.

It also serves as a decimal point.

1.3 percent
$2.5 million

With Quotation Marks   The period ending a sentence usually appears in front of an ending quotation mark.

He called the mayor a "redneck."

With Parentheses   The sentence-ending period appears outside a closing parenthesis when parentheses enclose only a word or fragment.

It is a rare newspaper usage (although *Editor & Publisher* follows that style).

A period appears inside when parentheses enclose a complete sentence.

He called the mayor a "redneck." (*Redneck* is a derogatory term.)

Ellipsis   When the period is used in a series of three (. . .), it indicates the omission of some words in a direct quotation. The series of three periods is called an *ellipsis*.

To be, or not to be . . .

Whether 'tis nobler in the mind to suffer

The slings and arrows of outrageous fortune,

Or to take arms against a sea of troubles . . .

Journalists, of course, don't usually quote Hamlet. Often they quote people whose statements were spoken only to them or to a small group, and the public has no idea if something is omitted from a direct quotation. In those circumstances journalists don't usually indicate omissions because the reader won't know what the ellipsis signifies. Here is a direct quotation from a news story:

We expect the IRA to hit back at any moment. . . . The terrorists have already publicly stated they plan a bombing campaign far worse than anything they have done before.

There is no reason for the ellipsis. What reader would know what was missing? Furthermore, the reader probably wouldn't care. If you do use an ellipsis, remember that it is three periods and is in addition to the final punctuation of the sentence. See the IRA quotation, above, for an example.

Headline writers sometimes use the ellipsis in two headlines to indicate that two stories, one below the other, are related.

YOUNGSTOWN STEEL UNION ASKS

FOR PRESIDENT'S ASSISTANCE . . .

. . . WHILE STEELHAULERS BROOD

Note that the ellipses are used at the end of the first headline and at the beginning of the second.

Some broadcasters use the ellipsis to indicate where the news reader should pause or change pace.

The president signed into law today a bill that will lower everyone's income tax next year. . . . In Madison, Wisconsin, 10 people died when an early morning fire leveled an apartment building. . . . And in London the prime minister devalued the pound. . . . Details after these messages.

The Question Mark   ?

This mark appears at the end of a question. Not using it when it is needed can alter the meaning of a sentence.

Know what's happening.

That is a command telling you to know what is happening. The question mark makes it a question.

Know what's happening?

That means, do you know what is happening?

Whether or not the question mark appears inside or outside the quotation mark depends on whether the question mark belongs to the quoted matter or the entire statement.

"Is the mayor going to run for re-election?" council member Pearson asked.

Did you see the movie "All the President's Men"? When Bill asked me that, I replied: "No, did you?"

Putting the question mark inside the quotation mark in the first sentence of the above example would change the title of the movie to

"All the President's Men?"

Exclamation Mark *!*

The exclamation mark is an indication of intensity or excitation.

Watch out!

Had that been a calmly made statement, such as a piece of advice, a period would have been used.

Watch out.

The exclamation mark is used cautiously in good writing. Used too much it is weakened, its intensity made meaningless through numerous appearances. In stories the exclamation mark does not appear outside direct quotations because it could be taken as a reporter's opinion.

Jones was charged with murder!

And even within quotation marks it is seldom used. People do not go through life exclaiming many things (unless they have children). My comments do not preclude the exclamation mark's use in a direct quotation, an editorial or a column of opinion.

Self-Diagnostic Test 6.1

To determine how well you understand the use of the period and the question mark, do the following exercise. Insert the appropriate punctuation mark or place the punctuation mark already in the sentence in the correct place. The answers appear in the back of the book. Review what you miss.

1. Average attendance was 76 percent, down from 938 percent for last

   season

2. She said, "The US government is bursting at the seams".

3. "What did she say" the reporter asked.

4. They shipped the faulty product to Hillsboro, Ore, where it was

   made

Punctuation Within a Sentence

The Comma   ,

The comma is the most widely used punctuation mark, yet some of its uses are hardly absolute. The comma avoids confusion, although misused it can create confusion, as when a writer puts one between a subject and its verb. Here are several sentences whose meanings depend on the comma.

Robert Williams, junior chairman of the English Department, spoke
about Chaucer.
Robert Williams, junior, chairman of the English Department, spoke
about Chaucer.

On the platform were Victor L. Marchetti, a former CIA officer and six
students.
On the platform were Victor L. Marchetti, a former CIA officer, and
six students.

My wife, Karen, makes many of the children's clothes.
My wife Karen makes many of the children's clothes.

The highway project list for discretionary funds, approved by the
Transportation Commission yesterday, gave link-to-link resuscitation to
the Cadbury bypass.
The highway project list for discretionary funds approved by the
Transportation Commission yesterday gave link-to-link resuscitation to
the Cadbury bypass.

The Democrats who run Congress gave him a standing ovation.
The Democrats, who run Congress, gave him a standing ovation.

The day was, well, up in the air.
The day was well up in the air.

He was first governor of Ohio.
He was, first, governor of Ohio.

Most of her story is clear and honest, but before she's done it gets a bit
fuzzy.
Most of her story is clear and honest, but before she's done, it gets a bit
fuzzy.

The differences between the sentences in each set or the problems with them are discussed throughout this section.

Items in a Series   The comma separates items in a series.

> The students studying football games asked *fans, coaches, players, league officials* and *any other persons who were at the games* to answer 15 questions.

> He can, when necessary, be serious or funny, believing or cynical, even believing and cynical.

More formal punctuation conventions call for the comma to be used before the word *and* in a series. When the comma there would eliminate confusion, by all means use it. Here is such a sentence.

> Some of the students are majoring in journalism, *history and health* and physical education.

A comma after *history* would make it clear that the italicized portion of that sentence does not belong together.

> Some of the students are majoring in journalism, history, and health and physical education.

Titles After Names   The comma sets off titles or suffixes after names.

> **Title**
>
> Miriam DeHaas, *the mayor,* celebrated her third year in office by holding an open house.

> **Suffix After Name**
>
> Robert Williams, *junior,* chairman of the English Department, spoke about Chaucer.

The comma in the last sentence changes both Robert Williams' name and his authority in the English Department. Without the second comma, Williams becomes *junior chairman*. Newspapers do not use junior and senior in those forms, but instead abbreviate to Jr. and Sr. (or jr. and sr.). Furthermore, most newspapers do not set off suffixes with commas. A reporter following the stylebook of the wire services would write:

> Robert Williams Jr., chairman of the English Department, spoke about Chaucer.

Titles as Subjects   The comma also sets off titles preceding names when the title, not the name, is the subject of the sentence.

> The mayor, Miriam DeHaas, celebrated her third year in office by holding an open house.

Short titles are placed before names without any punctuation.

Mayor Miriam DeHaas celebrated her third year in office by holding an open house.

Secretary of State Joseph Shaw appeared before a congressional committee today.

Apposition   The comma sets off modifying words or phrases in apposition to a noun.

The ceremony, *a contrast to the policies of the past,* had special meaning for Josephine M. Williams, *the college's 32-year-old sociology professor.*

The second photograph, *a sweeping panorama shot of Viking 2's new neighborhood,* showed an uneven horizon.

China's leader, *Deng Xiaoping,* told Japanese Prime Minister Zenko Suzuki today there will be no fundamental warming of chilly Sino-Soviet relations.

Ed Dunham, a longtime copy editor, spoke to the local chapter of the Society of Professional Journalists last night.

Clarity   The Marchetti sentence in the list at the beginning of this section easily produces confusion. The comma can decide how many people are on the platform.

On the platform were Victor L. Marchetti, a former CIA officer and six students. (There are eight people—Marchetti, a former CIA officer and six students.)

On the platform were Victor L. Marchetti, a former CIA officer, and six students. (There could be seven people, which is what I would count, or eight, which is another possible count. By my count there is Marchetti, who is a former CIA officer, and six students.)

The following could lead the reader to believe there are three speakers.

In a speech at Kansas State, Fran Lee, a former consumer editor and a broadcaster said she warned the president against a nationwide vaccination program.

A comma after *broadcaster* makes it clear that *editor* and *broadcaster* modify *Lee.* Likewise, from a non-fiction book the numbers problem appears:

He, in turn, communicated it to two more people, the Governor General, Lord Mountbatten and Field Marshall Auchinleck.

That reads like three people unless you know that Lord Mountbatten was also the governor general.

Restatement   A modifying phrase is often a restatement or further explanation, only from a different perspective. It is still set off with commas.

> The meeting will be held Wednesday, *Nov. 10,* in City Hall.

The italicized portion of that sentence defines Wednesday further.
Don't be fooled into believing that just because a sentence has a connective it doesn't need a comma. Again, the restatement guideline applies.

> The Cadbury Tigers, who have not scored a touchdown in 33 straight quarters, *or since the first period at Clive nine weeks ago,* could not make a 3-0 lead stand up, despite holding Bakersfield without a touchdown.

Without the comma after *quarters,* the sentence would lose its clarity because it would read as though there are two different times.

> The Cadbury Tigers, who have not scored a touchdown in 33 straight quarters or since the first period at Clive nine weeks ago, could not make a 3-0 lead stand up, despite holding Bakersfield without a touchdown.

The reader might wonder which is correct—33 straight quarters or since the first period nine weeks ago. They are the same thing: the second being a restatement of the first from a different perspective. Only commas make that perfectly clear.

Non-essential Words, Phrases and Clauses   The comma sets off non-essential material (material that can be dropped without damaging the meaning of the main clause).

> The house, *built in 1857,* was sold twice to family members before an outsider bought it.

> My wife, *Karen,* makes many of the children's clothes.

All the word between the commas does is further identify the subject of the sentence. Karen can be discarded in the sentence but she will still be my wife.

> My wife makes many of the children's clothes.

In that sentence, my wife remains Karen. But in the following, with no commas, the word *Karen* restricts the word *wife*.

> My wife Karen makes many of the children's clothes.

Without commas, that sentence suggests the existence of my wife Mary, my wife Sue, my wife Anne, and so on.
Here are two sentences that are identical except for two commas. The commas change the meaning.

> The highway project list for discretionary funds, approved by the
> Transportation Commission yesterday, gave link-to-link resuscitation to
> the Cadbury bypass.

> The highway project list for discretionary funds approved by the
> Transportation Commission yesterday gave link-to-link resuscitation to
> the Cadbury bypass.

The first sentence says a list for discretionary funds exists and that it was approved yesterday. The second suggests more than one list exists and one of them was approved yesterday.

Similarly, the Democrats are the majority party in the House; they control the House.

> The Democrats, who control the House, gave him a standing ovation.

But if only some of the Democrats in the majority control the House, then the clause is essential and goes unpunctuated.

> The Democrats who control the House gave him a standing ovation.

That suggests that not every Democrat stood and applauded—just the ones in power.

The misuse of a comma has caused debate in the U.S. Senate. In 1977, when Paul C. Warnke was before the Senate as President Carter's nominee to be the country's chief arms control negotiator, a comma became headline news. From the floor of the Senate, Sen. Henry M. Jackson of Washington pointed to a statement Warnke had made in 1972.

> Under those circumstances, it seems to me, Mr. Chairman and Senator
> Cooper, that the continuation of the missile numbers game is in fact a
> mindless exercise, that there is no purpose in either side's achieving a
> numerical *superiority, which is not translatable into either any sort of
> military capability or any sort of political potential* [italics added].

As punctuated, what follows *superiority* is a non-essential clause and it can be dropped without doing damage to the meaning of the sentence. Jackson told his colleagues there was a contradiction in the 1972 statement and he asked Warnke for a clarification. Warnke replied, in writing,

> I specifically stated that "numerical superiority *which is not translatable
> into either any sort of military capability or any sort of political
> potential* has no purpose [Warnke's emphasis]."

As punctuated, the italicized portion of the preceding is an essential clause and cannot be dropped without changing the meaning of the sentence. Warnke blamed the comma problem on a sloppy typist; Jackson said it was an intentional distortion, magnified by the alteration of the original sentence. The comma aside, the statement could have been clear from the start had Warnke used *that* to lead off an essential clause (if that's what he intended) or *which* to lead off a non-essential clause (if that's what he intended). But because *which* is sometimes used for *that,* the solution for this case lies in correct punctuation.

Parenthetical Expressions   The comma distinguishes parenthetical expressions.

> The day was, *well,* up in the air.

Without the commas, the condition of the day changes.

> The day was well up in the air.

Commas also make the difference in these sentences.

> "This is a good budget for our investigation," the congresswoman said; "any cut, *in my opinion,* will weaken what we are trying to do."

> "This is a good budget for our investigation," the congresswoman said; "any cut *in my opinion* will weaken what we are trying to do."

Another way of not cutting the congresswoman's opinion is to use parentheses, although it is a second-rate approach.

> "This is a good budget for our investigation," the congresswoman said; "any cut (in my opinion) will weaken what we are trying to do."

Dates   The comma sets off the year in a complete date.

> July 4, 1776, is the birthday of the United States.

However, a comma is not needed in month-year combinations, such as *July 1776.*

Addresses and Ages   Addresses, names of towns, and ages, when placed immediately after a person's name, are set off with commas.

> William Marconi, 39, of 310 March St., Cairo, Ill., died today of congestive heart failure.

Transition Markers   The comma sets off standard transition words at the beginning of sentences and in the middle of sentences.

> *Nevertheless,* the president's change of heart on foreign aid will do little to endear him to his party.

> The president's change of heart on foreign aid, *nevertheless,* will do little to endear him to his party.

However is also set off by a comma when its meaning indicates that a contradiction or contrary information is to follow.

This car is just the right size for our family. *However,* I don't like the color.

But when *however* means *no matter how,* it is not set off by a comma.

However great he may have been, historians will never rank him with the greatest.

No matter how great he may have been, historians will never rank him with the greatest.

Here is one final example of transitional markers with commas. In this case—as in many other examples—the absence of commas changes the meaning.

He was, first, governor of Ohio.

The story goes on to explain that *he* was later a senator and then a newspaper publisher—all within recent history. But the absence of commas sends the time back approximately two centuries.

He was first governor of Ohio.

Introductory Phrases   A comma sets off long introductory phrases at the beginning of a sentence.

In an attempt to learn more about the crowds at football games, the students conducting the study asked fans, coaches, players, league officials and any other persons who were at the games to answer 15 questions.

Introductory Modifiers   The same principle applies to introductory modifiers, such as a verbal, verb clause or prepositional phrase (which begins the preceding example).

Running through the woods, Jack tripped over a rock in the middle of the path. (verb clause)

With much less fear than we had expected, Tracey bravely entered the hospital for an ear operation. (prepositional phrase)

Blindfolded, the kidnap victim could not tell where his abductors drove him. (verbal)

By using three steps, we can get to the room before they do. (prepositional phrase)

Here are four more sentences whose italicized portions are misleading or unclear because of a missing comma. Correct versions follow in parentheses.

To eat the survivors of the plane crash had to dig up roots. (To eat, the survivors of the plane crash had to dig up roots.)

After the large coal mines *closed the economies* of the towns died.
(After the large coal mines closed, the economies of the towns died.)

If *I published my mask* would disappear. (If I published, my mask
would disappear.)

Most of her story is clear and honest, but before *she's done it* gets a bit
fuzzy. (Most of her story is clear and honest, but before she's done, it
gets a bit fuzzy.)

In all four examples a verb or verbal is involved. Because the reader might read the
word after the verb or verbal as the object of the verb or verbal, the comma is
necessary.

Sometimes clauses not appearing in their normal place in a complex sentence
are set off by a comma, although the decision to use them should depend on clarity,
not convention.

If I were you, I'd take the job.
If I were you I'd take the job.

When we were young, we played stickball.
When we were young we played stickball.

Modifiers in a Series   Modifiers in a series take a comma if you can substitute *and*
without changing the meaning. In such cases, the modifiers have equal rank.

The long, drawn-out meeting ended when the chairman collapsed.

That sentence could also be written:

The long *and* drawn-out meeting ended when the chairman collapsed.

In the following a comma is not needed between modifiers because they are not
equal.

The boys wanted to spend a *five-week summer* vacation with their
father.

When you have doubt, insert *and* and see if the sentence still makes sense.

The boys wanted to spend a *five-week and summer* vacation with their
father.

That sentence makes no sense so the modifiers of *vacation* need no punctuation.
Commas also substitute for *and* in other places.

Go *and* see it.
Go, see it.

Try more *and* shorter stories.
Try more, shorter stories.

The last sentence would be non-standard usage without the comma. The comma-for-and convention also applies to headlines.

TROJANS, RAMS FACE TOUGH TEAMS

Contrasting Ideas   Contrasting ideas are set off with a comma or commas.

Sometimes, clauses not appearing in their normal place in a complex sentence are set off by a comma, although the decision to use them should depend on *clarity, not convention*.

The *mayor, not the vice president of the council,* will preside at tonight's meeting.

The student wants to study *literature, not grammar*.

Natural gas, not oil, may provide the richest payoff in the Atlantic Ocean.

Connectives   Newspaper style usually omits the comma before a connective in a short compound sentence.

The president eats breakfast alone and his wife eats with the children.

The congressman would like to visit our town but his schedule for that day is full.

Long Compound Sentences   However, as in the case of items in a series, the comma should always be used for clarity, especially when you are connecting sentences with *and,* or for reader convenience when you are connecting long sentences.

At all evening meals, the mayor *serves the wine and his wife* serves the meat.

The reader may have to read that sentence twice to understand that the mayor does not serve *the wine and his wife*. The description of a movie on television provides another example.

Chicago underworld boss Al Capone plots *to kill Bugs Moran and the famous St. Valentine's Day Massacre* in which seven of Moran's men are gunned down in a warehouse is recreated [italics added].

The problem develops because of a verb followed by its object, then a connective, and then a noun that could be read as another object of the verb. It reads as a compound object. These don't.

At all evening meals, the mayor serves the wine, and his wife serves the meat.

Chicago underworld boss Al Capone plots to kill Bugs Moran, and the famous St. Valentine's Day Massacre in which seven of Moran's men are gunned down in a warehouse is recreated.

Usually a comma is not used in a simple sentence with a compound predicate, as it is in the following misuse.

The judge found that the husband has assumed parental responsibility, and has shown an interest in his children.

There is no need for a comma in compound modifiers joined by *and*.

The home of the husband and his girlfriend is normal, and morally satisfactory in every respect except for the absence of a marriage certificate.

Elliptic Use   The comma is used in place of a verb to show the verb is being repeated.

Williams had 35 marbles; Smith *had* 10, Jones *had* 5, and Wentzel *had* 2.

Williams had 35 marbles; Smith, 10; Jones, 5, and Wentzel, 2.

Direct Address   Direct address is set off from the rest of the sentence by a comma. Try the first example without.

It's time to eat, Amy.

Amy, it's time to eat.

Placement With Quotation Marks   Commas always appear inside quotation marks.

"This is a very austere budget," the city manager said.

Attribution Tag   A comma gets a lot of use in direct and indirect quotations by setting them off from the speech or attribution tag.

Kusion said, "We need a vote on this proposal tonight or it will be too late."

"We need a vote on this proposal tonight," Kusion said, "or it will be too late."

"We need a vote on this proposal tonight or it will be too late," Kusion said.

"City Council must vote on this proposal tonight," Kusion said.

According to Kusion, City Council must vote on this proposal tonight.

City Council must vote on this proposal tonight, according to Kusion.

City Council, according to Kusion, must vote on this proposal tonight. (Attribution tags are not normally placed between a subject and its verb.)

A comma is not needed, though, in an indirect quotation when the attribution tag is the beginning and (really) the main clause in a complex sentence.

Kusion said City Council must vote on this proposal tonight.

If you remember that the preceding is a complex sentence—a main clause and a subordinate clause—you won't put in a comma. Reporters often discard the pronoun that would begin the clause in more formal writing.

In a similar vein, a comma is not used to separate a partial quotation from the rest of a sentence.

According to Lee, dogs give humans, "a present they'll never be able to get rid of."

That sentence does not need the comma after humans.

According to Lee, dogs give humans "a present they'll never be able to get rid of."

The partial quotation is the object of the verb. A comma is not placed between a verb and its subject or object. The quotation marks don't change anything.

If the direct quotation is a question or (perish the thought) an exclamatory sentence, the appropriate mark is used *without a comma.*

"Do you honestly believe we need this bypass?" council member Williams asked the mayor.
   "Yes!" the mayor screamed.

The unnecessary comma would appear as such:

"Do you honestly believe we need this bypass?", council member Williams asked the mayor.
   "Yes!", the mayor screamed.

If the order of the sentence quoting council member Williams is reversed, a comma or a colon could be used.

Council member Williams asked the mayor: "Do you honestly believe we need this bypass?"

Council member Williams asked the mayor, "Do you honestly believe we need this bypass?"

Masquerade   Sometimes the comma masquerades as a punctuation mark in a series when it is really setting off a phrase in apposition. How many people were arrested in the following?

Scotland Yard today announced the arrest of 10 alleged slayers, seven Irish terrorists and three Palestinians.

If you said 20, you are wrong. Try 10. Also try a dash or a colon.

Scotland Yard today announced the arrest of 10 alleged slayers—seven Irish terrorists and three Palestinians.

A similar example:

Bulgaria has already concluded friendship treaties with at least two other Western countries, the United States and Canada. (That's four countries.)

Bulgaria has already concluded friendship treaties with at least two other Western countries: the United States and Canada. (That's two.)

Clarity There are countless examples of how a dropped comma can change or fuzz the meaning of a sentence. I misread the following sign in my oral surgeon's office.

Because of the nature of *oral surgery appointments* are for the approximate time only.

Because of the nature of oral surgery, appointments are for the approximate time only.

The place of a person's death can hinge on a comma.

The American Legion Auxiliary of Mapleville Post 261 will hold a memorial service for Mrs. Mary C. Linn, *who died Sunday at the T.F. Williams Funeral Home* in Mapleville today at 7:30 p.m.

The American Legion Auxiliary of Mapleville Post 261 will hold a memorial service for Mrs. Mary C. Linn, who died Sunday, at the T.F. Williams Funeral Home in Mapleville today at 7:30 p.m.

A comma can make a difference to a vote-counter.

The tally shows Carter with *1,526 delegates more than the 1,505 needed to win the nomination.* (That gives Carter 3,031 delegates, but he really had 1,526—or 21 more than needed to win the nomination.)

The tally shows Carter with 1,526 delegates, more than the 1,505 needed to win the nomination.

Erroneous Omission Sometimes reporters write such involved sentences they forget to punctuate non-essential clauses at both ends.

TMSA's decision apparently ends more than three years of on-again off-again negotiations among several parties, including TMSA, the county commissioners and the hospital authority (which owns Sunbank) aimed at finding an answer to the problem of how best to use Sunbank.

A comma is needed after the parenthetical phrase. But because that is such a long sentence, it should be made into two.

TMSA's decision apparently ends more than three years of on-again off-again negotiations among several parties, including TMSA, the county commissioners and the hospital authority (which owns Sunbank). The negotiations were aimed at finding an answer to the problem of how best to use Sunbank.

Instead of a Semicolon   Usually a semicolon is used in a compound sentence when a connective is not used. But when both sentences are very short and their forms are similar, a comma suffices.

The people lost, the bureaucracy won.

If the door is closed, don't knock, don't bother me.

Self-Diagnostic Test 6.2

To determine how well you understand the comma, insert commas where appropriate or move commas to their appropriate places in the following sentences. The answers appear in the back of the book. Review what you miss.

1. In its April order the court directed the district to further desegregate the city's school system and the district responded with the plan to merge 11 predominantly white and 11 predominantly black schools at the beginning of the next school year.

2. "While we must look to ourselves to avert a crisis we do need help from the federal government", said New Orleans Mayor Ernest N. Morial.

3. President Reagan's wife Nancy dresses nicely.

4. Some people however wish she would be more outspoken on some issues.

5. Students majoring in journalism study in a variety of areas, reporting editing international communication ethics and law.

6. The meeting one of the longer ones in council's history lasted 4½ hours.

7. According to policy, Francine Jamison 22 378 Broadway Ave.

Apartment 7 stopped the purse-snatcher by tripping him as he ran by her an act police said showed quick thinking and courage.

8. Bombarded Americans like their messages to the point.

9. Some journalists feel according to a recent survey that they don't get enough time to write their stories.

10. The leading candidate for the post Mary T. Harrison has such high visibility among voters that she doesn't need to conduct much of a campaign.

The Semicolon ;

The semicolon's primary function is to separate complete but coordinating sentences (called *compound* sentences) that are not joined by a connective.

The house is big enough; I think there's room for everyone.

It wasn't the subfreezing playing conditions or a matter of being outplayed; the game was decided by puck luck.

Among unanswered questions, Foege said, are: "How did it get to the people; why didn't it spread among individuals; were other factors needed for it to spread?"

Some writers—newspaper and otherwise—will put in a period where a semicolon could be used and go on to a new sentence. That doesn't make the preceding examples wrong or uncommon. In fact, they are very good examples of situations in which the period might jar the reader because it would disjoint tightly related ideas.

One place in newspapers where the semicolon is called for is after an attribution tag that separates two coordinating sentences. Often a reporter will make an attribution tag do double work, letting it refer to a statement just made and a statement to follow. Misuse occurs when a comma appears in the place of a semicolon.

"It was an even game," Jones said, "I felt both defenses were strong."

Correctly punctuated, that sentence would read

"It was an even game," Jones said; "I felt both defenses were strong."

"It was an even game," Jones said. "I felt both defenses were strong."

Conditioned as they are to attributing, some journalists are afraid to allow a direct quotation stand by itself because they fear the reader will not tag it correctly.

In stories with only one speaker, the fear is unfounded. The quotation marks make the attribution clear.

With a Series   A second necessary use of the semicolon is with items in a series in which some items have apposition. Count the number of people in this sentence.

> Present at the party were John Jones, the butler; Mary Smith, a private secretary; two attorneys; Bill Jackson, a former judge; Karen Harpster, a maid and a horse trader.

Now in this one.

> Present at the party were John Jones; the butler; Mary Smith; a private secretary; two attorneys; Bill Jackson; a former judge; Karen Harpster; a maid; and a horse trader.

By using semicolons to clarify the ambiguities of possible apposition, the writer shows 11 people at the party, not six.

In the following examples note how the semicolons neatly keep sets of related items separate from other sets of related items.

> In addition to the congressional pay increases, other pay raises include: vice president, chief justice, House speaker, from $65,000 to $75,000; associate Supreme Court justices, $63,000 to $72,000; cabinet members, $63,000 to $66,000; majority and minority leaders in Congress, $52,000 to $65,000; district judges, $42,000 to $54,000.

> The provost said that recommendations will be made in 11 areas: the purpose and place of the college; enrollment, admissions and probable distribution of students; mix and quality of students; scope of academic offerings; quality of teaching; research effort and emphasis; direction and scope of public service; faculty personnel policies; college governance and administrative organization; student housing; and funding efforts, including tuition policies.

> Their roles on the paper were typical of their relationship: Apte the fast-dealing businessman, Godse the outraged editorialist; Apte the chairman of the meeting, controlling its flow, Godse the fiery orator; Apte the formulator of their political schemes, Godse their vocal proponent.

Note that in the second example semicolons appear where commas are normally slotted. That happens because very quickly a comma is needed in a series (*enrollment, admissions and probable distribution of students*). Thus, the writer started with semicolons in place of commas.

Placement With Quotation Marks   Semicolons always appear outside quotation marks. For newspapers that don't italicize or bold face book titles, this is correct for titles:

Some of the better modern authors and their books are Tracy Kidder, "The Soul of a New Machine"; Jonathan Schell, "The Fate of the Earth"; John McPhee, "Coming into the Country"; Tom Wolfe, "The Right Stuff."

The Colon   :

The colon is used to show a relationship. Think of it as an equals sign—whatever follows it is equivalent or similar to what precedes it or is an explanation of what precedes it.

With the outbreak of war, another style of dress is common on campus: green army fatigues.

Students' grades in writing courses reflect a dramatic change: The basics are being taught again in high schools, which shows up in better written term papers.

Note the difference in capitalization. The initial letter that follows the colon in the first example is not capitalized while it is in the second example. When what follows a colon is a complete sentence (subject-verb construction), the initial letter is capitalized. When what follows a colon is a series or list, do not capitalize the initial letter.

You have three choices: the Army, college or work.

The colon is also used to separate a long introduction from a direct quotation that follows.

The president did not speak during the applause. After the crowd had quieted, he resumed: "I stand here today to explain my energy plan in full."

He said he was confronted by Mrs. Jones, who told him: "I did it. I hope he doesn't die."

The Hyphen   -

The difference between the hyphen and the dash is a difference in function: a hyphen connects, a dash separates. The two create problems because some people use them interchangeably. However, they not only function differently but they are also not the same length. The hyphen, which every typewriter has, is -, while on a typewriter the dash (—) is two hyphens --. To add to the problem, the dash on a video display terminal is a function separate from the hyphen, yet typewriter-trained journalists still strike two hyphens to make a dash, and the error appears in print. Printers routinely convert double hyphens to dashes so that they appear correctly in print. But printers aren't mind readers, so journalists must learn to make the distinction on their copy.

In a Compound Modifier   The hyphen is used in a compound modifier that precedes the word or phrases it modifies.

> The new department store was particularly crowded yesterday because of a one-of-a-kind sale on free-standing mirrors.

If the hyphen were dropped in the second modifier, a reader might misread the modification and believe the sale involved free *standing mirrors.*

The hyphen is extremely crucial when a noun and a verb function as a compound modifier. Without the hyphen a person might read the noun as the subject of the verb.

> U.S. RUN TRUCE
> QUIETS LEBANESE
> AND ISRAELI GUNS

Granted the verb *run* does not agree with *U.S.* in number, but the addition of the hyphen would clear all doubt.

> U.S.-RUN TRUCE
> QUIETS LEBANESE
> AND ISRAELI GUNS

Do not hyphenate when the compound modifier is an adverb and a participle. For example:

> the heavily guarded road
>
> the well built fort
>
> the happily married couple
>
> the well known composer

Readers understand the function of adverbs; it is unlikely they will get confused without the hyphen. That is why the hyphen should be used only when necessary for clarity. In football, some players are *running backs* and play in the *running-back position.* That is not the same as the *running back position,* which sounds like somebody running backward. Likewise, there is a difference between a *child-teaching expert,* which suggests a child teaching an expert, and a *child-teaching expert,* an expert who teaches children.

With a Prefix   The hyphen is also used to attach a prefix to a proper noun. It is *anti-American,* not *antiamerican* or *antiAmerican.* Similarly, you should use the hyphen when the prefixed word might be misread. A favorite example of one editor is *anticrime,* which he says could be mispronounced as *an-TICK-re-mi.* Another tongue twister: *antimale.* No, it's not the opposite of tamale. The following eye baffler appeared in headline type: *multiemployer.*

With a Repeated Vowel, For Word Distinction   When a vowel is repeated in the prefixing process, use a hyphen, as in *re-election*. That convention, however, isn't absolute, as *cooperation* shows. (But you need the hyphen in *co-op* lest you write *coop.*) Sometimes a writer uses the hyphen when adding an ending to a word to create a new word.

One listener complained that reception was "echo-ey."

The reader might have difficulty with the hyphenless word *echoey*. Similarly, the reader would have difficulty realizing you meant *co-inmates* if you wrote *coinmates*.

The hyphen distinguishes between two words that look the same. Hence, you *recover* from an illness but you *re-cover* a book; you *recount* a story but *re-count* the results of an election. To duplicate a painting is *re-creation,* which you might do for *recreation* if contact sports aren't for you. Likewise, you might *resent* it when your grades are missent, but you'll be happy when they're found and *re-sent*.

Imagine if one of those words was hyphenated at the end of a typewritten line of copy, with *re-* on one line and the rest of the word on the following line. What does the person setting type do if the word fits on one line? Will the person know the difference? Rather than hope so, the person writing on a typewriter should not hyphenate any word at the end of news copy (VDTs don't require end-of-line hyphens). If anyone or anything is going to make a mistake, such as *the-rapist* for *therapist,* let it be the computer.

Other Uses   *Self* is followed by a hyphen when it begins a word. Likewise, the hyphen is used in some compound nouns, such as *chess-player* and *well-being* and a host of others that are in any dictionary. Some compound nouns also function as verbs; then the hyphen is not used. The noun *fade-in,* to mention one of many, is *fade in* as a verb. (Some compound nouns, following the traditional process of many of our words, are written solid—*breakout, shutdown*—but the verbs remain two words—*break out, shut down.*)

Most prefixes (which precede a word) and suffixes (which follow) are not hyphenated when attached to words (except proper nouns). *All* as in *all-star, ex* as in *ex-governor* and *non* as in *non-restrictive* seem to be the only hyphenated ones. As a prefix, *in* is not hyphenated (*insatiable*) when it means *not.* But it is hyphenated in such constructions as *in-service,* where it does not mean *not.* As a suffix, it is *sit-in* and *break-in.* Most other prefixes and suffixes are not hyphenated.

Clarity   The hyphen can make a difference in a headline or sentence that begins with the article *a.*

A-BOMB EXPLODES	A BOMB EXPLODES
IN CITY SUBWAY	IN CITY SUBWAY

And it can make a difference in those words that function as nouns when hyphenated but function as verbs when written as separate words.

BREAK-IN WEATHER   BREAK IN WEATHER
WON'T EASE CRISIS   WON'T EASE CRISIS

GALLUP REPORTS   GALLUP REPORTS
CHURCH-GOING UP   CHURCH GOING UP

In the following example the lack of a hyphen creates confusion, but not until you've read about half of the sentence, at which time you must start again to get the meaning.

After tax earnings last year were reduced by about $2.3 million because of interest not recorded on some loans.

Read the sentence again with a hyphen in the compound modifier *after tax* and you'll get the message.

After-tax earnings last year were reduced by about $2.3 million because of interest not recorded on some loans.

In the following a hyphen would make the sentence clearer by creating a paired noun.

Still pictures were allowed only before the president went on television.

Still-pictures were allowed only before the president went on television.

Without the hyphen the first sentence appears to need a comma.

Still, pictures were allowed only before the president went on television.

But what is meant is *still-pictures,* the kind you see in newspapers or have in the family album.

The hyphen is also usually used in constructions like this:

The people paid the 50-cent fares.

Without the hyphen the sentence could mean the people paid *50 one-cent fares.* Likewise, don't hyphenate *50 dollar bills* if you mean *50 one-dollar bills.* The hyphen would mean *$50 bills.*

The hyphen is also used to show a person with two jobs or identities.

Harry Sneer, head coach of the Cadbury Tigers, discusses with *producer-hostess* Mary Rubin . . .

And:

When the two-hour show began in February 1969, *actress-interviewer* Mary Todd was co-host.

The 1970 stylebook jointly prepared by *The Associated Press* and *United Press International* contains a good example of how a hyphen can change a meaning.

The 6-foot man eating shark was killed. (the man was)

The 6-foot man-eating shark was killed. (the shark was)

Suspensive Hyphenation   Suspensive hyphenation is the tying of two prefixes to one word by using hyphens.

The 20- and 30-degree temperatures common to this area do not suit me.

Theodore M. Bernstein suggests, however, that writers avoid the opposite construction.

University-owned and -operated airplanes are always an issue at budget hearings.

There's nothing wrong with repeating *university*. It makes the sentence clear.

University-owned and university-operated airplanes are always an issue at budget hearings.

Ages   The hyphen is also used in ages functioning as compound modifiers and nouns.

Tracey, an 8-year-old girl, won the prize for 8-year-olds.

The hyphen is used in fractions (four-tenths, eight-tenths) and in numbers when the first word ends in *y* (seventy-five, sixty-eight).

Broadcast Copy   In broadcast copy the hyphen appears between letters of abbreviations when the letters should be read individually. A broadcast newswriter would use the hyphen like this:

Y-W-C-A
C-I-A
F-B-I
U-C-L-A
U-S Information Agency
U-S Supreme Court

Where there are hyphens each letter is pronounced. The newspaper equivalent is the period, although the period is not used as much in abbreviations as it once was.

The Dash   —

The dash is used for emphasis, usually to set off material a writer wants to stress. Journalists tend to overuse the dash, sometimes making it do the work of the colon or parentheses.

With the routine business out of the way, the chairman introduced the two candidates—T.F. Stein of Clive and Leonard E. Tressler of Cadbury—and began the interview by asking the first question.

Lengthy Apposition   The dash is used in lengthy lists in apposition to a noun.

Members of the trustee advisory committee—Michael Baker Jr., chairman; Harry R. Ulrich, Ralph Hetzel, Walter J. Conti, Helen Wise, Samuel F. Hinkle and J. Lewis Williams—will screen persons for the provost position. (Note the use of the semicolon.)

Stress   The dash is also used to stress a word or phrase at the end of a sentence.

A 25-year-old Visalia man was charged yesterday with possession of cocaine and attempting to conceal it—in his stomach.

The dash also completes or sums up an involved sentence.

The senator said the amendment failed on the floor for two reasons—he had failed to make a last-minute check of its pledged voters and he could not counter the feeling that the bill would not work.

As a Colon   Journalists often use the dash where a colon could work as well.

The contributing factors fall in three groups—natural conditions, the type of materials used and the design elements of the day.

or where parentheses might also fit.

Under apartheid the ''coloreds''—people of mixed race considered neither black nor white—live apart from the other races and have more advantages than blacks but fewer than whites.

Misused   Occasionally dashes are used where commas are better.

Proving assault will be difficult—T.L. Holt, the chief of police, said— because the alleged victim had no marks on him when he made the charge.

Lists   Dashes are used by some journalists to indicate a continued subject and verb throughout a list.

The Council also:
    —voted not to meet next week.
    —postponed action on May Day plans.
    —set June 21 as the date for a public hearing on the proposed sidewalk ordinance.
    —told James H. Andrews he could proceed with his plans to clean up Walnut Spring Park as part of a Boy Scout project.

The Council voted to:

—keep meeting the first Monday of the month;

—call special meetings when necessary;

—ban smoking in the meeting room.

Because continuity from line to line is desired, some editors punctuate all but the last line of such a list with semicolons. Others prefer periods. Whichever, it is a matter of newspaper style, not some convention of punctuation.

Self-Diagnostic Test 6.3

To determine how well you understand hyphens and dashes, do the following exercise. Insert a hyphen or dash where appropriate or change a hyphen to a dash where appropriate. The answers appear in the back of the book. Review what you miss.

1. The city's aviation division has awarded a multiyear contract for the first construction in a two year project designed to ease traffic congestion at the airport.

2. The division proposes to build a three lane roadway near the baggage claims area-the second such road in the area.

3. The well being of airport users prompted the division to propose the project originally.

4. With traffic congestion reduced, division officials feel the airport will become smoothest running one in the country a boast no other airport operator is willing to make.

Parentheses ( )

Information enclosed within parentheses is usually an explanation, a qualification or an example. Such information is not usually crucial to the main thought of the sentence. Journalists use parentheses to enclose explanatory information where it is immediately useful.

Scientists believe that if the icebreak drift begins soon, it will contribute to the first worldwide experiment of GARP (the Global Atmospheric Research Program).

Most ethologists (students of animal behavior) contend that genetic patterning determines how all creatures except humans behave.

Other Uses A journalist will use a parenthetical insert to call attention to something the journalist wants stressed, as John Sherwood of the late *Washington Star* did in an interview with Theodore A. Wertime, a Smithsonian research associate.

The affluent American way of life as we knew it (he uses the past tense) is already over.

And from a front page story:

Ten men were in the mine when the explosion occurred at 4:40 p.m. Pacific Coast Time (7:40 p.m. Eastern daylight time).

Parentheses also set off information that is not part of an official name but is necessary for complete identification.

Warren (Pa.) Times Observer
Tamaqua (Pa.) Historical Society

Sometimes editors will insert two or three paragraphs of local information into a wire story. The information is set off by parentheses in the following manner.

Todd accused Hill of choosing this weekend to call a strike because Hill knew 35 percent of the drivers would have pulled off the highway for the holiday weekend.
(No protesting or striking truckers were reported at the Bald Eagle Truck and Auto Plaza at the Milesburg interchange of the Keystone Shortway this morning.
(Milesburg state police said truck traffic on the Shortway appeared to be normal today.
(They said it generally tapered off a bit over long holiday weekends.)
Early reports on truck traffic were mixed.

The convention is the same one used for direct quotations continued uninterrupted over two or more paragraphs—a parenthesis at the beginning of each new paragraph and a parenthesis also at the end of the last paragraph.

One place a parenthetical insert does not belong is in a lead. If information is worth being in the lead, then it is worth showing off, not hiding within parentheses—a structure that disrupts the lead's flow.

The present New Mexico Power Company line could be improved without any sizable expansion (which would considerably lower the cost), a Taos Planning Commission member said last night.

The parenthetical information rates its own sentence, perhaps leading off the second paragraph.

Holding down on expansion would also lower the cost, William Kitchen said last night.

Broadcast newswriters use parentheses to insert a phonetic spelling behind a word or name.

W. Somerset Maugham (mom)

When a name is uncommon, the phonetic spelling is repeated every time the name appears.

Abuse Despite the valuable function of parentheses, journalists use them sparingly. In addition to disrupting sentence rhythm, parenthetical inserts are considered non-essential and can be discarded. The good writer doesn't want to hide information inside parentheses, as this writer did:

> Other large expenditures in the taxi budget are drivers' labor ($1,330); gasoline and oil ($23,400); dispatching services ($22,000); maintenance ($11,800); insurance ($7,850).

The parenthetical information in that sentence is part of the main information and should not be hidden.

> Other large expenditures in the taxi budget are drivers' labor, $41,330; gasoline and oil, $23,400; dispatching services, $22,000; maintenance, $11,800; insurance, $7,850.

Brackets [ ]

Brackets indicate to the reader that a reporter or editor has inserted something into quoted matter. The reporter or editor may do this to substitute a name for a pronoun where the antecedent is unclear or to give additional information to the reader.

> "I don't think he [Zelenski] has been on top of the situation the way a public official should be," the candidate said.

Some editors would discard the pronoun in the interest of rhythm, but no rule governs the usage.

> "I don't think [Zelenski] has been on top of the situation the way a public . . ."

In the following sentence, the material inside the brackets provides additional information:

> "I think the secret to this team's success [Baltimore is 6-1] is that we don't have any one guy we rely on," the coach said.

Other Uses When reporters quote a grammatical error or misuse of the language, they tell the reader by doing the following.

> "After what I read in that newspaper, I'm going to sue them for slander [sic]," the council member said.

The council member apparently meant *libel*.

Brackets are sometimes used to set off *refers*—phrases at the end of paragraphs indicating where a story giving more detail on the paragraph appears.

Meanwhile, a presidential aide announced that the president would take a vacation next week. [Story on Page 6.]

Abuse   The problem with brackets lies in their intrusive nature and their overuse. At one time journalists were conservative about inserting anything into quoted matter. Instead, they paraphrased any statement that otherwise needed bracketed inserts for clarity. Unfortunately, that is no longer true. It now seems that journalists the country wide are competing to see how many miles of bracketed inserts they can work into a story. Here are two paragraphs from a 14-paragraph story.

> "[Dallas Coach] Tom Landry is a genius. Why do you think he has a shifting offense? Well, it's to confuse the defense."

> "It's a lot like the Cowboys' [offense] except they put [Roger] Staubach back in the shotgun. With Fran, we don't have to because he can get back fast enough [to pass]."

If journalists stopped acting like tape recorders, they wouldn't create such messes. Instead of bracketing, clarify and paraphrase.

> Tarkenton called Dallas coach Tom Landry a genius. "Why do you think he has a shifting offense? Well, it's to confuse the defense."

> Grant compared the Vikings' offensive strategy to the Cowboys' and found the only difference in the Cowboys' use of quarterback Roger Staubach in the shotgun. "With Fran, we don't have to because he can get back fast enough" to pass.

Is there a rule for the use of brackets? No, but it helps to remember that clarity rules the written word. Too many bracketed inserts grind the gears of clarity. Use bracketed inserts sparingly.

The Apostrophe   '

The apostrophe, which is a sign that a letter has been omitted, is used to indicate possession. A few centuries ago, possessive forms were made like this:

> the presidentes spokesman

> the kinges English

> the boyses tent

Today we use the apostrophe.

> the president's spokesman

> the king's English

> the boys' tent

Generally, it is not necessary to add *'s* to show possession when the singular noun ends in *s*. *Charles'* and *Charles's* are both acceptable, although the trend is toward the apostrophe alone.

The apostrophe also shows omitted letters in contractions.

wouldn't for would not

don't for do not

can't for cannot

she's for she is

he's for he is (avoid he's/she's for he has/she has)

it's for it is

won't for will not

The apostrophe also indicates the omission of the current century in a date.

Spirit of '76

a child of the '50s

The plural of singular letters is formed by adding *'s*.

mind your p's and q's

dot all the i's, cross all the t's

Some editors don't use the apostrophe to form plurals of capital letter abbreviations and acronyms or numbers. They favor POWs over POW's, GIs over GI's, and '50s over '50's. Regardless, it is pros and cons, not pro's and con's.

Quotation Marks   " and '

When journalists quote someone, that is, report the person's words exactly (or as exactly as it is humanly possible to transcribe), the person's words are enclosed in quotation marks.

> "A woman can never become a great mathematician," a math professor said recently.

The misuse of quotation marks makes editors scream. One misuse is called *orphan* or *fragmentary quotations*. To understand the misuse, you must first appreciate the convention of using quotation marks around single words to signal an ironic or sarcastic use, a misuse, a shading of meaning or a slang use of a word.

Here is a sarcastic use:

> "When you remove all the fancy words from my opponent's campaign 'promises,' you'll see he really hasn't committed himself to do anything," Sen. Smith said.

Promises is not what Sen. Smith meant. He was denigrating his opponent's campaign statements by suggesting they weren't what his opponent said they were.

In the following sentence, quotation marks surround a misuse of a word:

The editor told the cub reporter to get a lot of ''quotes'' for his story.

What the editor meant was *quotations; quote* is a verb used as a noun only in newsrooms.

Here quotation marks surround a shading of meaning:

Back in 1970 there were four men on the Supreme Court who took the ''absolute'' view of the First Amendment.

Relative to the other justices, the four were absolutists. But there has never been a pure absolutist on the Supreme Court, at least in First Amendment decisions.

Quotation marks are also used around slang:

As a consumer advocate, Lee is constantly on guard against being ''taken'' and is now in court with 14 cases.

And around coined words:

The budget problem has been ''overmediated,'' the economist said.

The economist believed that the problem had received too much coverage in the news media. Labor problems can be overmediated, perhaps, but the word has nothing to do with intensive news coverage.

Usually, the quotation marks around slang and coined words are dropped in subsequent references.

Sometimes writers use quotation marks around a single word or short phrase to make it clear that they are using some else's words, not their own.

An ''astoundingly'' large number of children are mistreated by their parents, and a new study of child abuse says mothers are more likely to do the mistreating.

Considering all of the uses that have been cited above, the journalist who places quotation marks around single words risks confusing the reader. For example:

The mayor said he is ''angry'' with council member Blair.

If the mayor is indeed angry, drop the quotation marks so the reader doesn't believe the word is misused. If the mayor is being facetious, make the context clear and use the quotation marks. It is puzzling to read news stories of someone's retirement or resignation that include this phrase:

The resignation was accepted with ''regret.''

The reader might read between the lines, although the writer wasn't aiming for that.

Single quotation marks are used in place of double quotation marks in newspaper headlines. In a story, they are also used to indicate a quotation within a quotation.

> The speaker said: "It was Hamlet, I believe, who said, 'To be or not to be.' Well, that is the question facing us tonight."

Quotations continued from one paragraph to the next are used in the following way:

> "We're not necessarily looking for a direct tie," Hillard said.
> "Those cases may be another disease that we have to thoroughly investigate. [No closing quotation marks.]
> "They wanted to call it a sort of virus or flu."

The joint stylebook of the wire services calls for quotation marks around titles of books, operas, plays, television programs, works of art, songs, movies, lectures and speeches. Newspapers, however, seem to be very selective in applying that guideline, enclosing the titles of books but not the titles of movies, or the names of newspapers but not the names of magazines. The trend seems to be moving away from using quotation marks when the meaning is clear. More and more newspapers also seem inclined to use italics in place of quotation marks, which is book style.

> The story first appeared in the November edition of *More* magazine.

Finally, there is this warning on something quotation marks don't do—they don't get a newspaper off the hook in a libel case.

> "She's a no-good whore," Petyak said of his daughter-in-law, the former Mary T. Meade.

While it is true that the speaker can be sued for libel, so can the newspaper. Quotation marks don't change that fact.

Self-Diagnostic Test 6.4

To determine how well you understand the major points made in this chapter, do the following exercise. Repeated here is the unpunctuated paragraph that began the chapter. Insert the appropriate punctuation marks. The answers appear in the back of the book. Review what you miss.

The writer is ready to go All lessons have been learned He sits before

his typewriter paper in place and begins to type at first slowly as he thinks

about his words but then faster faster as he picks up the pace and his great

writing flows Someday these words will be discovered on this dog eared

paper in a multiuse library the writer says outloud in a somewhat gleeful

somewhat arrogant voice What could be better to be discovered later or

discovered now A thought Perhaps though it would help if I knew how to
punctuate That way people would understand what I am writing

Exercise 6.1

Punctuate these sentences according to standard newspaper usage and turn them
in to your instructor for evaluation.

Name _____

1. Public property losses in New Mexico included initial estimates of
   up to $7 million

2. "Maybe we could dance to Frosty the Snowman."

3. For breakfast I had toast bacon and eggs fried potatoes grapefruit
   and a glass of milk

4. Mary Sue Nelson the movie star will appear here next week

5. "It was assumed that I got the piece of mail a statement of fitness
   to serve and there was no way for me to prove I did not get it I
   find the conviction in your own words inherently incredible."

6. The superintendent of education Lawrence Johnson said the new
   program will begin in the middle of the school year

7. The spokesman said the workers had won a cost of living increase a
   new issue in bargaining talks this year.

8. Requiring everyone to pay taxes which was not part of the measure
   will increase the Treasurys revenues by $10 billion a year.

9. The touchdown that won the game came on a quarterback option a
   new play in Clive's playbook.

10. People, who live in glass houses, shouldn't throw stones.

11. The highway department expects to complete the bypass by April 1,
    1994 a spokesman said

12. The proposal however does not consider what the department will
    be doing 15 years from now

13. In answer to a question today Dr. Eugene Kellner director of the
    bureaus research division said the serum will be available in four
    weeks.

14. When the bank shut down the town died too.

15. Since the vaccination program began there have been no flu outbreaks.

16. They said they intend to live together arguing that a marriage certificate does not make a marriage

17. The big fast football player also likes dancing

18. In a long editorial the new leaders of Excelsior said they ''would continue the newspapers policy of informing the people.

19. Both facilities officials said are crowded.

20. The conservative dissidents, who last night ousted the editor of the newspaper cooperative Julio Schere Garcia and 200 of his top staff were apparently encouraged and assisted in their move by the government.

21. On stage at Harrisons Williams told joke after joke after joke

22. ''John when are we going to get off dead center and do something'' the mayor asked.

23. The president likes the bill he will sign it into law.

24. Here are my suggestions give the map to Jim, the shovel to Amy and the pick to Tracey.

25. The network's proposed schedule thereby looks like a corporate giant surrounded by business as usual fillers.

26. Recounting the votes from the last election will take about three weeks the county commissioners said.

27. But some middle class area residents have challenged these figures saying that a number of low income welfare receiving families are living in apartments that the city counts in its middle income and moderate income totals.

28. The recently-elected congressmen are not familiar with all of the procedures of Congress.

29. The news editor Thomas L Jones will rewrite the stylebook.

30. There are five mile relay teams entered in the mile relay competition.

31. There is only one man who can lead this country out of the depths of despair Thomas F. Williams

32. City Council will vote tonight on a proposal to ban dogs from public streets the first such proposal on the issue.

33. The president called for removing some of the burdens the public must bear in reporting taxes Story on Page 8

34. I said, Isnt it enough that Jims idea was discussed

Chapter 7
Meaning

Pinning the Meaning Down

"Words are inexact tools to say the least," the late Supreme Court Justice William O. Douglas once said. As the cause of inexactitude, Douglas cited the different experiences each person brings to a word. He could have also blamed the ever-changing meaning of words. Nothing is as old as yesterday's meaning of a word. Nor is anything as uncertain as what its meaning will be tomorrow. To rely on the past to define a word is not as secure a practice as some believe. S. I. Hayakawa says:

> In choosing our words when we speak or write, we can be *guided* by the historical record afforded us by the dictionary, but we cannot be *bound* by it, because new situations, new experiences, new inventions, new feelings are always compelling us to give new uses to old words. Looking under a "hood," we should ordinarily have found, five hundred years ago, a monk; today we find a motor car engine [italics in original].

L.M. Myers, a college English teacher, provides an example of a change that occurred within four generations (approximately 120 years).

> To my grandfather, who was born in Ireland, the "natural" meaning of the word *car* was a small horsedrawn vehicle; to my father, it was a railroad coach; to me, a street-car. Of course all of us had to recognize new meanings as conditions changed. To my son, the natural meaning is an automobile; and it is quite possible that to his son it may seem the obvious word for what we now call airplanes, especially if our roads get so full of automobiles that they can't move any more.

Hayakawa's interest is that of a *semanticist*, a person who studies the meanings of words. A semanticist will never tell you what a word must mean, only what it means to the people who use it. Edwin Newman, on the other hand, is not willing to accept every change that occurs. Known as the house grammarian at NBC-TV, Newman is both eloquent and witty—and upset with the dilution of words in the English language.

Hayakawa could tell us that at one time *disinterested* and *uninterested* meant two different things but that today the distinction is seldom made. Newman would argue persuasively that we shouldn't let the distinction die because we have no substitute for *disinterested* and we need it.

The meaning of a word is not sacred. Any word can change, like *hood,* to fit the times. Written 200 years ago the following sentence would have had nothing to do with tennis:

The shot *killed* Jones, and Sweeney served an ace for the coup de grâce.

Thirty years ago a *camper* was a person who camped in the forests; today a *camper* is also a motorized vehicle people can live in. A *capsule* once did nothing more than hold medicine. Today space technology has added another definition. If the man who invented the diesel engine had been named Rudolf Schultz instead of Rudolf Diesel, we would have cars powered by schultz engines instead of diesel engines. Nothing in the history of any word preordains its meaning for eternity. A word's meaning is not inherent. Linguist Ronald Langacker calls the relationship between a word and its meaning "a matter of convention." S. Leonard Rubinstein and Robert Weaver, authors of *The Plain Rhetoric,* see it as "a social contract whereby persons agree on the meaning occupied by a word."

The social contract is handed down to us in dictionaries, which are put together by people who *record* and *report* the meanings in current use. Dictionary-makers do not determine meanings. The meaning (or definition) given in any dictionary is denotative; it is the objective fact of a word's meaning stated as dryly and impartially as possible. From *The American Heritage Dictionary of the English Language:*

bee: Any of various winged, hairy-bodied, usually stinging insects of the order Hymenoptera, including many solitary species as well as the social members of the family Apidae, and characterized by specialized structures for sucking nectar and gathering pollen from flowers.

Ask anyone who has been stung by a bee or chased by a swarm of bees to tell you what a bee is.

You may have trouble getting someone to define the next word for you, but be assured there's more to it than this:

copulate: To engage in coitus.

And the definition of *coitus* is no less objective.

Still, we know more about bees and copulation than the dictionary tells. We can speak from our own or someone else's experience about these words, and when we think of the words later, those experiences will mean more to us than the dictionary's definition. The experiences or associations people add to a word are a word's connotative meaning, which is far more crucial in communication than any dictionary definition could hope to be. It is the difference between a house and a home—a physical structure and a state of mind.

An article in *Smithsonian* magazine began:

Neighborhood: the very word is pleasant. Its syllables flow with deliberation and warmth, connoting a realm of peace, stability and fellowship.

According to the dictionary, a neighborhood is "a district considered in regard to its inhabitants or distinctive characteristics." That doesn't make the *Smithsonian* article incorrect. The author apparently feels this way about *neighborhood*. He did include *connoting* in his second sentence. But not everyone feels that way about the word *neighborhood,* and we would have to know more about any person using the word and the sentence in which he or she uses it to understand better what is meant. Does this use not mean something different?

The damn neighborhood ruins everyone who lives in it.

You have now seen *neighborhood* in two different contexts. It is in the context that the meaning of a word can go astray, but it is also in the context that a precise meaning can be conveyed. You know what the word *light* means. But before you produce 10 definitions from a dictionary, read this sentence from *Scientific American:*

Light can appear dim or bright but not light or dark.

Do you still need a dictionary? You shouldn't. The context says it all. And if you had to define the second light as it related to dark and dim or bright, you were relying on context. Here are similar examples:

As they *tear* down the old hotel, it brings a *tear* to my eye.

Show me a *bear* who can *bear* to be held in captivity and I'll show you one tough *bear*.

Take the words *since* and *because*. Although few make a distinction today, the two words don't always mean the same thing, as shown in this sentence from the now-defunct *More* magazine:

Since—if not because—Hayes left, ad linage has dropped disastrously, to little more than half the 1,280 pages the magazine had in 1973.

Despite the difference, people still use *since* for *because,* which is acceptable if the usage isn't ambiguous.

Since I'm the oldest member, I'll serve as president.

The context makes the preceding clear, but context isn't enough to help in the following:

Since we're considering this topic for the first time since classes began, we should open with a review.

The first *since* should be *because*.

In the following example, *doctor* (meaning to treat or tamper with) is misused. But the reporter first provided a context to make the intended meaning clear.

> He asked Mr. Bernier to justify the number of specialists recently admitted to the hospital's staff. ''At what point will you become over-doctored?'' he asked.

The first sentence gives the second its context.

The italicized portion of the following example does not mean what it says, yet the context gives it the meaning the writer wanted to convey.

> Most are connected with other dailies, and, with the Times' bureaus around the world, they form a global net through which *little news* passes unnoticed [italics added].

A memorandum telling faculty members that a maintenance crew was going to wash their venetian blinds included this humorous phrase:

> Please care for papers, books, etc., which might be lost in the movement of equipment by the *blind crew* [italics added].

Nobody who read the memorandum believed the maintenance crew was sightless.

Context sometimes deprives us of using words that are otherwise okay. In a court trial, where charges are made, the following use of *charged* for *attacked* is confusing:

> Williams also said that one day Jones *charged* the judge.

When Walter Cronkite of CBS News asked the American public ''to declare a honeymoon'' with President Gerald R. Ford, the late Jean Stafford, a staunch defender of pure usage, asked:

> How is a honeymoon declared? Who has vested in Mr. Cronkite the power to let precision of speech go to hell in a handbasket?

She argued that in the strict sense of the language, you cannot ''declare a honeymoon.'' But I like the phrase—I like it now; I liked it when I heard Cronkite use it. It evokes the history of a troubled presidency, of a constituency turned against the presidency and of a president who resigned from office (Richard M. Nixon). We could have declared a truce, but there was a new man in office. In effect, it was a new marriage. And because of the embattled condition of the office of the president, Cronkite knew the bitterness of the past might continue. By asking us ''to declare a honeymoon,'' Cronkite effectively combined the language of war and the language of domestic joy. It worked because the events of the time provided the context.

The good writer is aware of context and is extremely careful with it. Nothing angers an editor more than to be told someone has been ''quoted out of context'' by a reporter. People who have been quoted out of context may wonder if the press is completely fair.

Still another problem arises when the context changes; then the thought you want to convey may also change. Yesterday's meaning is dead. *Urchin* on the lips of a social worker may be someone to be helped; to a police officer an *urchin* may be a juvenile delinquent.

Different groups give different meanings to the same word. To a photographer, *agitate* means a gentle but steady motion intended to distribute chemicals evenly around film, whereas to a protester *agitate* might mean stirring emotions to their most intense. A journalist might use the word *research* to mean gathering information for a story, whereas a college professor might mean systematically studying a problem in an effort to find an answer. Writers who wish to write clearly for their audiences must first know what their sources' words mean.

When you find yourself in a situation where a person is putting great stress on connotation, try getting the person to be specific. You obviously can't say, "Would you be more denotative than connotative, please." But you can ask the person to be more precise by explaining what he or she means. Journalists aim for denotation; they can't afford to give the reader even a slight chance of interpreting any word differently. To guard against misinterpretation, the journalist has to keep context in mind at all times.

Tampering with Meaning

Many journalists would deny that they unintentionally do harm to the meaning of words. In reality, they are no more or less guilty of tampering than anyone else, but they'd like to believe their purity. Regardless, journalists should be extremely cautious of the way they use their language. Tampering with meaning devalues the language, leaving, for example, *disinterested* and *uninterested* as synonyms when, in fact, we need to preserve the original distinction between the two.

Journalists have been criticized for changing meaning. Consider, first, the complaint of H.L. Mencken:

> The copy-reader accordingly makes heavy use of very short words . . . and these words tend to be borrowed by the reporters who must submit to his whims and long for his authority and glory. Their way into the common speech thus comes easy.

Those copy-readers are also headline writers who need short words, not only because they fit in a limited space, but also because they can be readily understood during a fast-paced scan by the reader. But, as Mencken says, headline writers are not satisfied with existing short words so they extend the meanings of some (just as they change nouns into bastard adjectives) to cover every possible news story. Objects of Mencken's scorn include (all italics are his):

> *Ace.* In the sense of expert or champion it came in during the World War. It has since been extended to mean any person who shows any ponderable proficiency in whatever he undertakes to do. I have encountered *ace* lawyers, *ace* radio-crooners and *ace* gynecologists in headlines.

> *Car.* It is rapidly displacing all the older synonyms for *automobile*, including even *auto*.

Chief. Any headman, whether political, pedagogical, industrial, military or ecclesiastical. I once encountered the headline *Church Chiefs Hold Parley* over a news item dealing with a meeting of the Sacred College.

Drive. Any concerted and public effort to achieve anything.

Fete. Any celebration.

Head. It means whatever *chief* means.

Plea. It means *request, petition, application, prayer, suit, demand or appeal.*

Slate. Any program, agenda, or list.

Talk. Any discussion or conference.

Mencken was equally disturbed by clipped forms of words in headlines. He observed that *ad, confab, duo, exam, gas, isle, mart, photo* and *quake* were common. Four decades later, when there was a shortage of natural gas and gasoline, the clipped word *gas* became confusing. Today we have clipped, for example, *airplane* to *plane, memorandum* to *memo, telephone* to *phone, omnibus* to *bus, bicycle* to *bike, smoke* and *fog* to *smog,* and *coeducational* to *coed*—and changed that word's meaning to boot. Headline writers and imitative reporters are still at it. In addition to using many of the words Mencken mentioned, today's headline writers and reporters have added the following:

Air. Takes up less space than *discuss.*

Back. It means *support, endorse,* even *approve.*

Bogus bills. Synonymous with *counterfeit money,* but a lot shorter.

Decry. Often a substitute for *criticize,* the word really means *belittle.*

Eye. As a verb, it replaces *study.*

Feds. For *federal officials,* as in this headline: "FEDS BATTLE MEDS IN AIR FRAUD CASE." Obviously, *meds* are doctors.

Grill. A substitute for *question,* it means *intense questioning.*

Gyn. From a headline, "ROUTINE GYN EXAMS HARD TO GET," it was clipped from *gynecological.* Fortunately it wasn't used in the story.

Hike. Not a long walk in the woods, but an *increase.* The word has infiltrated news stories to the point that one reporter wrote this lead: "A tax hike is a tax hike." People don't talk like that; writers shouldn't write like that.

Ink. Sports page talk for *sign,* as in "ROOKER INKS CONTRACT." Despite the fact it's a verb usage going back at least a century, one contemporary dictionary ignores it, listing *ink* only as a noun. You will also hear the word in newspaper pressrooms when press workers ink the presses.

Loom. Large storms *loom,* but to headline writers, anything in the future *looms,* including meetings. For reporters, it's inflation, as in: "Inflation has loomed suddenly as an increasingly important administration concern in recent months."

Meet. Short for *meeting;* also more common to headlines than news stories.

Nip. The misfortune of this word is in its misuse, as in this headline: "DODGERS NIP GIANTS, 10-3." The word should be preserved for close scores and short drinks.

OK or *OKs.* It takes in all the meanings of *approve.*

Pen. Perhaps to give a quill-and-ink effect, headline writers use this verb to describe the labor of authors of books and songs. After all, *pen* is shorter than *write.*

Pick. As a noun, it means *choice, selection, nominee.*

Rap. What happens when somebody criticizes your *pick.*

Rip. When you rebut the critic of your *pick.*

Set. A shorter version of *slated,* which is a shorter version of *scheduled.*

Slap. No harm intended; it takes the place of *rip* and *rap.*

Tap. When you select a *pick.* "REAGAN TAPS SHULTZ AS STATE PICK."

Unit. Indicates part of a whole—"HOUSE UNIT OKS PLAN." But it can get confusing, especially with the Justice Department, which is both a whole and part of a whole (the federal government). "JUSTICE UNIT PLANS PROBE" could be anything from the entire department to one subdivision of the department.

Up. Another verb for *hike;* never a noun.

Vie. Usually seen in political and sports stories, it is a shortended form of the Middle English *envien,* to challenge. "CHAUCER VIES FOR FAVOR."

From headlines to text, language abuse continues. A novice journalist once wrote that a business had had "mediocre success," at the least a contradiction in terms. Despite seemingly thousands of jokes, "surrounded on three sides" still appears in war stories. (Maybe they were trapped in a triangle!) And one night an actor told a talk show host that there was a "direct parallel" between an actor's physical condition and the condition of his voice. Could it still be parallel if the connection were "indirect"? What suspicions pass through the mind when a jewelry store advertises class rings made of "real gold"? What were the previous rings made of? Maybe they were "free gifts" to distinguish them from "paid gifts."

The thoughtless affixation of "pre" to any number of words and phrases has created silly or impossible conditions. A news release said that a company official had been admitted to the hospital for a "pre-existing eye condition." Existing previous to what? "On-going" is the desired modifier. A firm once held a reception followed by a dinner with a "preplanned menu." What the author meant was that the diners were not going to get a choice; the selection of the entree was made in advance. "Set menu" sounds like a better term. Given the attention that college football gets, is a coach's future any more secure if on any given Saturday he has a "preconceived game plan"? It's better than conceiving a plan after the game, of course, but before the game, "plan" says it best. And what "pre-expectations" do fans have before the big game? Are they different from their "expectations"? Based on a newspaper column by a school teacher, this sentence makes a point about misused words:

> Kingman Area's programs in reading, writing and mathematics are
> *spearheaded* by teachers [italics added].

The word means to be the leader of a drive or an attack and is more apt in the description of a movie on television that said "a police investigator is assigned to spearhead the search for a mad bomber who has terrorized the city."

Words are misused when writers don't think about what they are writing. Here are more examples:

> *Conclusive* evidence has been found of the *possibility* of a second gun
> in the senator's death.

Perhaps the writer wanted to protect herself against any eventuality. But if the evidence is conclusive, how can there be any doubt?

> "We understand three bodies have definitely been *visualized* in the
> debris," Allegheny County Coroner Cyril Wecht said.

The coroner meant *seen*. The obligation of the journalist in such instances is to paraphrase the speaker rather than quote abominable language.

> A Utah State fraternity has been *sanctioned* for an alleged hazing
> incident.

When something is sanctioned, it is approved. Only in the realm of law does it mean penalized.

> He *alluded* to a secret charter.

An allusion is a vague or oblique reference. Actually, the person referred to a secret charter by naming it and telling who authorized it.

> Covert action ranges from propaganda to *coups de grâce*.

The correct phrase is *coups d'etat,* a foreign word that probably shouldn't appear in newspapers.

The government pressures journalists not to pursue *exposés* of the CIA.

An *expose* is something already revealed, not something that can be revealed.

The CIA *catalyzes* wars.

The word is too technical; it has a very special meaning to scientists. The second sin is that it is an uncommon word; what's wrong with *instigates?*

Dr. Thomas criticized the scientific *instinct* of reductionism.

Because instinct is innate, it's difficult to imagine people born with scientific instinct. Better words are *approach* or *method.*

A negative word mixed poorly might have confused the readers of this caption:

No parking would be allowed at any time . . .

How does the police department "allow no parking"?

How does a person change the place of his or her birth, as in this:

Mehrin is *originally a native* of San Francisco.

Maybe that's what the song "I Left My Heart in San Francisco" means—double nativity. People are natives of the place where they are born and remain a native of that place no matter where they later live.

A thoughtless headline writer committed this foul:

DEATHS *TOLLED* AT 42

Bells toll; deaths are totaled.

Some words seem the same but when misused turn honest people into dishonest people.

Legislators accused the university administration of *duplicity* of services.

Duplicity means *double dealing,* not *duplication.* The writer meant *duplication of services.*

Finally, an editor took the following sentence and changed its meaning by changing one word:

She went to Buenos Aires alone on their 15th wedding anniversary *early* this month.

She went to Buenos Aires alone on their 15th wedding anniversary *earlier* this month.

The first sentence appeared in a story published in the last week of the month. It means that during the first week (approximately) the action took place. But when *early* is changed to *earlier* it could mean any time in the first three weeks of the month.

The same editor changed the meaning of the following

The council voted to urge a review by the pope of a recent declaration *against allowing* admission of women to the priesthood.

by substituting

The council voted to urge a review by the pope of a recent declaration *prohibiting* admission of women to the priesthood.

The distinction is this: The pope's declaration reaffirmed a centuries-old ban on the admission of women to the priesthood; it did not, for the first time, ban women from the priesthood. Unfortunately for good reporting, the editor changed history.

The lazy journalist may ask: What's one more *fete,* one more *hike,* one more *free gift?* But measured against the many times they are used, they are meaningless; they say nothing and do nothing except take up space. As a journalist, you must be alert. Make sure that one writer's well turned phrase does not become your cliche. Find your own phrases and use them precisely. Don't use a word whose meaning you don't know for sure; look it up. Don't rely on sound and sight; *fortuitous* does not mean *fruitful* or *fortunate; fulsome* doesn't mean *bountiful; essay* does not mean *to write an essay* and *mitigate* does not mean *militate.* As Emily Dickinson wrote:

A Word that breathes distinctly
Has not the power to die.

High-Sounding Words and Phrases

The Washington Post reported one day that a designer had difficulty getting anyone at the U.S. Department of Transportation to listen to his proposal on taxis. "But when he said 'para-transit vehicles' they were all ears."

According to The Associated Press, "People in government find that you can get things done by using the right words." When officials of one state feared that a needed swimming pool at a state police academy would not be approved, they scratched the words *swimming pool* in favor of *water training tank.* The academy got its swimming pool.

Madison Avenue produces its share of high-sounding words. After all, when most products are generically the same, what can an advertiser do to get customers to buy one bar of soap instead of another? Don't call it soap; call it a "skin care bar." Who doesn't want to take care of his skin?

The government abounds with examples of language abuse, either in the name of making something sound better than it is or for the sake of hiding something. I'm not sure which applies to this statement by a governor:

You know, when we were talking about budget, perspectively, it's easier to talk retrospectively with specifics than prospectively.

A wrestling coach:

> I would like to build a national power that can compete with
> competition from a national level at a consistent year-in and year-out
> basis.

No matter the speaker, the practice of saying obscurely what could be said plainly is all too common. Politicians and bureaucrats are infamous for toying with the language. They have discovered that the wrong word at the right time often escapes the notice of a public numb to language abuses. During testimony about a massacre in Lebanon in 1982, Israel's defense minister said one of his field commanders had told him that "during the Phalangist operation in the camps, the Christians harmed the civilian population beyond expectations." "Beyond expectations" meant 328 dead and 991 people missing and presumed dead.

The preceding quotation is an example of a euphemism—describing something unpleasant in pleasant or neutral terms or terms that mask the truth. Euphemisms abound. Students who misbehave in school are sent to "motivational resource centers"; if they've been cheating, their parents are told that they "depend on others"; if they are below average, they're "working at their own level"; if they lie, they "show difficulty in distinguishing between imaginary and factual material."

Those cover-ups come from education sources; politics provides other examples of semantic changes. Such was the case in the 1976 presidential campaign when Jimmy Carter was seeking the Democratic Party's nomination. At the time, much was made of Carter's pronouncement to give "full pardon"—but not amnesty—to draft evaders. Carter kept trying to put distance between *amnesty* and *pardon,* contending that *amnesty* meant he would be condoning draft evasion while *pardon* merely meant forgiving—right or wrong—what had been done. But at least one dictionary uses *pardon* to define *amnesty,* so Carter's distinction is offbase. Regardless, Carter granted the pardon-amnesty and within months the issue was forgotten.

Carter's successor, Ronald Reagan, also toyed with words to his own advantage. Reagan, a practicing tax-reducer in a land of rising taxes, supported a plan to raise taxes on gasoline. Had the president reversed his position on taxes? No, he said, the increase wasn't a tax; it was a "user's fee." It was also a "public works revenue enhancement," but most people still say *tax.* Elsewhere in the federal government, an official in the Environmental Protection Agency did not like the name of its public relations office—so she changed it to "Office of Public Awareness." It sounds good, but does it provide information?

On the state level, a letter from the New Hampshire Executive Council said a grant would:

> Develop groups of evaluation modules for several types of programs to
> consist of sophisticated and quantitatively oriented research designs to
> be used in evaluation programs.
> Establish minimal data requirements as required by the evaluation
> modules and set in place a system through which a continual flow of
> empirical data will be directed toward the commission's evaluation staff.

Establish through the use of computer analysis modules a highly empirical and quantitative means for policy makers to make decisions about programs.

The Associated Press said: "Approval was unanimous."

The AP also reported about a parent in Houston, Texas, who received the following from his child's high school principal:

Our schools' cross-graded, multi-ethnic, individualized learning program is designed to enhance the concept of an open-ended learning program with emphasis on a continuum of multi-ethnic, academically enriched learning using the identified intellectually gifted child as the agent or director of his own learning.

Major emphasis is on cross-graded, multi-ethnic learning with the main objective being to learn respect for the uniqueness of a person.

United Press International quoted a communiqué from the Arms Control and Disarmament Agency:

Under the previous arrangement, the Verification and Analysis Bureau had theoretical responsibility for all verification questions of interest to the Arms Control Agency. However, its separation from operational activities creates a bureaucratic gap between the area (in ACDA) that handled SALT and MBFR, for example, and the verification experts.

The journalist's job is to restrain from quoting the miscast pomposity of experts and at the same time find out what it means. So that you will be familiar with such language, here are several other examples. They are a mixture of obscurity, euphemism and ignorance. Ignorance may be an excuse for talking and writing like this, but it is not an excuse for journalists reporting such nonsense.

advance downward adjustments. A reduction in social services.

adjustment centers or mediation rooms. Solitary confinement, which is sometimes also called segregation.

cost effective. Economical.

precipitation protective contrivance. What Archie of the comic strip says is an *umbrella.*

perspiration garment. A *sweatshirt,* Archie says.

mandatory flotation device. Which turns out to be a raft in "B.C.," also a comic strip.

extremely adverse operating environment. Sounds like a serious crisis magnified.

device system benefit. Computer talk to be avoided.

idea sharing and governance input. Not something for computers.

locational preference. Where you choose to live.

interpersonal and academic improvement houses. Coeducational dormitories.

communication feedback loop. A gives his views; B can't give her views until she summarizes A's to A's satisfaction, and vice versa.

circular area possibility. The chance that civilian buildings near military targets might get bombed.

inverted aerial maneuvers. Every skier knows they are *flips.*

semi-independent living environment. No, it doesn't mean the college student living away from home; I don't know what it means.

facilitation of professional development. Advance upward adjustment made easy.

pedestrian-oriented improvements. Sidewalks.

spatial mean-wage-salary disparity. Some people make more money than others.

forward-looking aspects of the programs. Futuristic?

crisp memoranda. An admission, finally, that many aren't.

his desires relative to his future residence. Forward-looking locational preference, in case it isn't clear.

acute grief situation. When final grades are given.

general salary distributional pattern. Has nothing to do with how salaries are disbursed by employers.

methods of activating the cluster. How to teach in kindergarten.

motorized attendance module. A school bus.

attitude centers. Police cruisers.

distance sensitive basis. The greater the distance the person you're telephoning is from you, the more the call will cost. Charges are calculated on a distance sensitive basis.

over-deliverability situation. More supply than demand.

combat emplacement evacuator. A shovel.

vertical transportation corps. Elevator operators.

recycled funds. Not money used over, but money shifted from one part of the budget to another. The phrase hides the fact that a service is about to be discontinued.

urban transportation specialists. Cab drivers.

energetic disassembly. Explosion.

rapid oxidation. Fire. (Try yelling "rapid oxidation" in a crowded theater and see if anyone leaves.)

operational programs or activities. Watch out for inoperational ones.

operational responsibility. A person with this responsibility is really in charge, not a figurehead.

marital experience. Marriage, according to a court decision.

mature woman. Another way of saying *fat.*

queen size pantyhose. For mature women.

power system. Used by one company to describe the batteries it sells.

language contact situation. When two or more languages collide.

injury situation. What football coaches hope to avoid.

fire suppression system. Despite the suggestion that it puts out fires, it can also be a heat or smoke detector that only warns people.

automotive replacement products. Auto parts.

emotional marginality of teenagers. Immaturity.

aesthetic relationism. Any *ism* is abstract.

index of work alienation-indifference-attachment. At least the sociologist who made that up wasn't struck by the noun plague.

internalize a set of moral values. Beware of externalized ones.

periodicity and chronicity in criminal careers. A detective from any television program won't solve it in an hour.

a meteorological prognosis. Weather forecast.

learning process. What college students endure. (To get there they had to pass through a *reading situation.* In elementary school, during recess, they enjoyed a *play situation.* To which Edwin Newman adds: "If children who go through play situations and learning experiences have nothing to look forward to but being in a hostage situation, what will it do to their self-image? What will happen to their potential to develop a potential?")

hostage situation. I found it in a wire service story and called it to Newman's attention, which resulted in the preceding communication situation with the author of this book.

Here are some very high-sounding sentences, but they need an introduction. If anyone caused the type of language derided here to get a new public awareness, it was Alexander M. Haig Jr., a former Army general who became a U.S. secretary of state. Haig's convoluted pattern of speaking could fill a book, but for this book he gets just one entry.

And this could have been at a very low level of competence and motivation in the context of the issue itself. But the facts on this are not clear enough for anyone to draw a definitive conclusion.

Moreover, to go beyond the vital and most conspicuous, to interpret imprecisely the plethora of apparently irrelevant minutiae would be to indulge in unnecessary turgidity, and to becloud the vivid pattern of that fabric. The enumeration of additional influences is therefore restricted to a minimum. (From an urban geography course.)

Kline, who has been endorsed by the association's political action committee for the Democratic gubernatorial nomination, and Dwyer, ranking Republican on the Senate Education Committee as well as its policy chairperson, will interact with the master plan as developed to date from an election point of view. (They're going to debate.)

The candidate lacks a recognition factor. (Nobody knows her.)

In approving purchase requests we must walk a line between a policy of flexibility—to be able to take advantage of advances in technology—and a policy of constraints sufficient to prevent rampant proliferation of vendors' computer hardware and software.

Proof of any resident disposing items in the commodes that create the sewer blocks will be terminated. (After the manager terminates the proof, how will he prove who blocked the commodes?)

The income distribution seems to indicate that on a mean/total basis there was a disproportionate distribution of basic manufacturing wages/salaries. (Sounds like a case for the National Labor Relations Board.)

Health-wise, the region's senior citizens enjoy a high degree of good health. (They're healthy.)

We recommend that the company consider the current and future feasibility of buying or leasing fleet coal trains. (Current and future! Also, *feasibility* is jargon and is overused and vague, like *input*.)

It is very often the case, however, that apparent morphological irregularities turn out to be regular phenomena when examined carefully in relation to the entire phonological system. (Spelling is related to pronunciation.)

It is not apparent to me she is socially inadequate and certainly her educability under the ordinary acoustic environment is not jeopardized. (An ear specialist telling a family doctor one of his young patients can hear.)

Because approximately 50 percent by volume of refinery output is now exempt, increased costs allocated to those products on a pro rata volumetric basis but historically recovered through sales of gasoline may no longer be recovered through such sales because the regulations do not afford a means for refiners to reallocate to gasoline amounts of increased costs allocated to a pro rata volumetric basis to exempt products. (Courtesy of the Federal Register)

Synonym Problems

Synonyms are words that have a similar meaning. Note that *similar* does not mean *identical*. Synonyms cause problems when an editor or writer tries to avoid using the same word twice in any one sentence or paragraph. Synonym faddists might write:

> The five-mile *bypass* is the best *road* in the state. The *highway* can handle 55,000 cars daily, which is twice the capacity of any other *autobahn* in the immediate area. When the latest *expanse of concrete* is filled to capacity, it can be expanded.

Of course, my made-up example borders on the ridiculous. But I was encouraged to include it after seeing a journalist use four different words in seven paragraphs all to mean. . . Well, that's just it; I don't know what the writer meant. He started his story by writing about *missile boats,* then shifted to *vessels.* Later he used *craft* and still later, *ships.* I'm confused because, as a former sailor, I know that a boat and a ship aren't the same, and that craft are landing or pleasure, but not missile carrying. And vessels can hold water or ride on top of water. I'm not discounting the use of synonyms. Using them aids you in varying your writing. But don't toss them into sentences just because you don't want to repeat a word. Have a better reason first.

Value Words

> *A Journal of the Plague Year* by Daniel Defoe is an outstanding book.
> True or false?

Your response to that question should be: "What do you mean by *outstanding?*" The word suffers from more than just vagueness. It is also a *value word*—it means different things to people at different times. And while we normally associate the word with excellence, reporters have been known to describe disasters as outstanding. Value words are easily identified by their vagueness; there's nothing there for us to set our minds on. Some people also think of value words as relative terms. ("The play was outstanding." "Relative to what? A garbage can?")

Only is a value word (an adverb of opinion, you'll recall) that should be used only when it's necessary to explain a situation or context the reader would not normally understand (such as sports stories for sports fans). *Only* can load a sentence with opinion and show reporter partiality where none is intended.

For example, the state House of Representatives approves a pay raise for its members. "Only five legislators voted against the raises," a reporter writes, perhaps signaling that he or she is angry because more didn't oppose the proposal. Let the taxpayers be angry. Remove *only* from that sentence and you remove the onus.

In many cases where *only* is misused it is not necessary anyway. Suppose five out of 200 persons survive an airplane crash. "Only five survived" or "Five survived"—which is more objective and less emotional? The second one. If you've told the reader 200 persons were in the crash, adding that five survived makes the tragedy clear enough.

Value words can provide both a fact and a judgment simultaneously. A person can express disapproval by using any of the following: *ambulance chaser, atheist, profiteer, drunkard, communist, prostitute.* Imagine, then, what happens when the journalist uses them. Who knows how the audience will accept those words? It should also come as no surprise that some of the preceding words plus hundreds more are libelous by themselves, yet another reason to avoid them.

Still other value words:

abhorrent	easy	lovable
able	fantastic	magnificent
abominable	fearless	massive
beautiful	flashy	progressive
big	good	short
brave	great	slender
cold	handsome	small
conservative	innovative	terrible
courageous	lengthy	terrific
cute	liberal	unfortunately
deserving	little	warm
dynamic	long	wonderful

Note that they are adjectives and adverbs, parts of speech not common to good newswriting.

Nouns and verbs, however, can also be value words, depending on the context. The gymnastics coach asking for an addition to the high school gymnasium to be used exclusively by his or her team may call the addition an improvement to the school. But the school board member who has to approve raising taxes to pay for the improvement may see it as a waste and vote against it. Similarly, the negative connotations of *failed* make it a good word to avoid, especially in this usage:

City Council failed last night to approve next year's budget.

Attribution verbs unfortunately suffer from a dismal reputation because some journalists refuse to use the neutral *said* but instead insist on using a word that has negative connotations. For example:

"To me, this tax is very discriminatory," *harped* the lone dissenter, council member Ted Hun.

Some other nouns, verbs and adjectives that send an extra message to readers and listeners: *advantage, loophole, warn, emphasize, admit, threaten, refute, claim, man, straightforward.* Present the facts and let the readers and listeners decide if the council member was harping or not or if the change in the law is a loophole. Because there are enough neutral words to go around, a journalist doesn't have to resort to value words.

Frame of Reference

Often in writing news stories you are forced to write in abstract or general terms. Such terms cannot stand alone. They must be explained clearly, and part of explaining them clearly is using terms and contexts readers are familiar with. How would you describe a tree to someone who has grown up around cornfields and never seen anything higher than corn stalks? The corn stalks are a possible frame of reference for you and the other person. Describe the rigors of farming in Iowa to a coal miner in Pennsylvania. Before beginning, you need a frame of reference, something the reader can identify with, something you hope is not so rigid it can't ease the reader into your frame. A story on changes in car sizes included this line:

> They are noticeably shorter than their 1976 predecessors—9 to 15
> inches to be exact.

The 9 to 15 inches phrase serves as a frame of reference, something specific for the reader. But numbers don't always work. The following sentence, from a story about India, is without a frame of reference:

> Mr. Narayanan's vasectomy, which took five minutes and earned him a
> government bonus of $11, was one more statistic in what officials say is
> by far their most intensive and successful sterilization campaign yet.

To an American $11 is not a lot of money. Knowing that, *The New York Times* reporter who wrote the preceding gave his American audience a frame of reference:

> Mr. Narayanan's vasectomy, which took five minutes and earned him a
> government bonus of $11—*as much money as he makes in a month*—
> was one more statistic in what officials say is by far their most intensive
> and successful sterilization campaign yet [italics added].

Now you know what $11 means to Mr. Narayanan.

From the General to the Specific

When you use general terms, back them up with specific examples, as this student did with parenthetical information:

> Bugliosi said the interest in the trial, one of the longest (9½ months)
> and most expensive ($962,000) in history, continues because the
> strange, bizarre murders actually happened.

It's not always possible to be specific in one parenthetical swoop, as these paragraphs from an AP story show:

> Under certain conditions, a public body, by a majority vote of its total
> membership, may close the doors to the general public.
> If disclosure would imperil the public safety, disclose the indentity
> of a law enforcement agent or informer or imperil the investigation or
> prosecution of a criminal offense, the governmental body could call an
> executive session.

The public could also be excluded during discussions of personnel matters, collective bargaining or the acquisition of real property.

Now you know what certain conditions are. The next time they may be different. Even if they aren't, you can't take the liberty of never redefining them. Be specific at all times.

Double Meaning

As the headline suggests, a word, phrase or sentence that can be interpreted two ways has a double meaning. The result is called a double-entendre. Usually the second meaning is risqué or salacious.

The National Football League paid approximately $250,000 *to satisfy the needs of the press* in the 1978 Super Bowl.

A complaint that calls mining "the most blatantly discriminatory industry in the country" asks the government to order companies to send *one woman into the mines for every three men.*

[poster] Free V.D. Screening
Thorough, Confidential
Open to the Public

Sex aside, any sentence that might be taken two ways should be rewritten so that it cannot be misunderstood.

Frank and honest state leaders, especially in the Department of Transportation, are *encouraging signs.*

It's not clear if the leaders are encouraging the use of signs or if the presence of "frank and honest leaders" is an encouraging sign. Also, since the sentence involves the Department of Transportation, will the reader see "signs" as a pun?

A photo caption described a defendant as "boxed in" by his attorney. Any attorney who would box in a client isn't a very good attorney.

A columnist once wrote that Martin Van Buren was the "first natural born president," not to suggest that his predecessors had been born unnaturally but that they had not been born in the United States after independence was gained from England. Some presidents had been born here, but prior to the colonies' independence from England.

A headline writer created two meanings in the following:

MINOR INJURIES TAKE THEIR TOLL ON SUPER BOWL FOES

Are the *foes* opponents of the Super Bowl or rivals in the Super Bowl?

Some writers don't think long enough about what they write. A news magazine said presidential aides were checking the president's speeches with "Republican members of Congress with ethnic backgrounds.'' Don't we all have ethnic back-grounds? Another writer, paraphrasing a speaker about Africa, said: "Most Af-ricans, who are 95 percent farmers and 85 percent illiterate, derive little. . ." Finally, the Humane Fire Company erected this sign in its parking lot:

PARKING FOR HUMANE MEMBERS ONLY

It's a wonder anyone could find a vacant space.

The job of the news writer is to make any sentence mean only one thing. Readers and listeners spend little time with the news media, and sentences with two meanings arc liable to make the visit even briefer. Direct sentences that convey one meaning only are the best for any news medium. This section, this chapter, this book all point to a single goal for any news writer: clarity. Without it, the writer will accomplish nothing.

Appendixes

Spelling

A. Here is a list of frequently misspelled words. The trouble spot in each word is, where practical, italicized.

a

accident*all*y
acco*mm*odate
achi*eve*
advis*er*
all*ege*
al*lott*ed
a*n*oint
ant*i*quated
ar*c*tic
arg*um*ent
a*ss*a*ss*ination

b

baby-sit
baloney
ba*rr*oom
ba*tta*lion
bel*ieve*
benefi*t*ed
bologna
bu*s*es

c

can*d*idate
cemet*er*y
chang*e*able
coa*tt*ails
commi*t*ment
commi*tt*ee
con*sc*ience
con*s*ensus

d

defend*a*nt
defin*i*te
depend*e*nt
desirable
develop
dieti*t*ian
discrep*a*ncy
di*ss*ension
dou*b*t
drunke*nn*ess

e

ecsta*s*y

emba*rr*a*ss*

employ*ee*

enviro*n*ment

e*rr*atic

exhi*l*arate

exist*e*nce

f

fun*d*amental

g

gover*n*ment

gramm*a*r

gue*rr*illa

h

hara*ss*

ha*z*ard

hemo*rr*hage

hit*ch*hike

hum*o*rous

i

inadvert*e*nt

indi*ct*

indispens*a*ble

i*nn*oculate

insist*e*nt

inte*rr*upt

irresist*i*ble

j

judgment

k

*k*etchup

kidna*pp*ed

kidna*pp*er

l

le*i*sure

lia*i*son

ligh*t*ning

liqu*e*fy

m

marsha*l*

m*e*mento

mil*e*age

mi*s*spell

mor*t*gage

municip*al*

n

notic*e*able

o

o*cc*asional

occu*rr*ence

p

para*ll*el

passer*s*-by

permiss*i*ble

perseve*ra*nce

perso*nn*el

p*ie*ce

pre*ce*de

p*r*erogative

privi*l*ege

pro*cee*d

proteste*r*

q

qua*ff*

quan*t*ify

quan*t*ity

questio*nn*aire

quorum

r
rec*ei*ve
rep*e*tition
roo*mm*ate

s
s*ei*ze
sep*ara*te
s*ie*ge
siz*a*ble
ster*nn*ess
superintend*e*nt
super*s*ede

t
tota*l*ed
trave*l*ed

u
under way
u*nn*atural

v
vac*uu*m
vene*real*
v*i*cinity
vi*l*ify
vill*ai*n

w
well-being

x
X-ray

y
y*i*eld

B. The following list for the spelling of natives of states is taken from the *Government Printing Office Style Manual*. These forms are not universally accepted by editors and teachers because of their awkwardness.

Alabamian	Kentuckian
Alaskan	Louisianian
Arizonan	Mainer
Arkansan	Marylander
Californian	Massachusettsan
Coloradan	Michiganite
Connecticuter	Minnesotan
Delawarean	Mississippian
Floridian	Missourian
Georgian	Montanan
Hawaiian	Nebraskan
Idahoan	Nevadan
Illinoisan	New Hampshirite
Indianian	New Jerseyite
Iowan	New Mexican
Kansan	New Yorker

North Carolinian

North Dakotan

Ohioan

Oklahoman

Oregonian

Pennsylvanian

Rhode Islander

South Carolinian

South Dakotan

Tennessean

Texan

Utahan

Vermonter

Virginian

Washingtonian

West Virginian

Wisconsinite

Wyomingite

A Glossary of Major Terms

adjective An adjective is a word that modifies nouns, phrases and other adjectives. (Look for *cool* weather this spring.)

adverb An adverb is a word that modifies verbs, verbals and adjectives. (Despite his reputation for being slow, the fullback ran *swiftly* after catching the screen pass.)

antecedent A word or phrase to which a pronoun refers is its antecedent. Although the word means *preceding,* an antecedent can appear after the pronoun that refers to it. (Smith warned advisory commission *members* that the coach would take advantage of them.)

appositive A phrase placed next to a noun to provide identification or explanation of that noun. (The professor, *a member of the advisory commission on athletics,* never participated in sports in high school or college.)

article A modifier that establishes a general reference (*a*) or a specific one (*the*).

complex sentence A sentence that contains a main and a subordinate clause. (The school teachers' strike lasted for 15 days, which is 14 days longer than most people thought it would last.)

compound-complex sentence A sentence that contains two main clauses and at least one subordinate clause. (The school teachers' strike lasted for 15 days, which is 14 days longer than most people thought it would last, but the length indicates how resolved both sides were to get their own way.)

compound modifier Unlike modifiers in a series, in which each modifier refers to a single word that is modified, compound modifiers are usually two-word phrases in which the first word modifies the second modifier rather than the main word. The phrase *two-word* in the preceding sentence is a compound modifier in which *two* modifies *word* and then *two-word* modifies phrases. (See the ''Hyphen'' section in the text for guidelines on punctuation.)

compound sentence A sentence that contains two related main clauses. (The school teachers' strike lasted for 15 days; the length indicates how resolved both sides were to get their own way.)

connective A word used to join two related groups—nouns, verbs, subjects, predicates, sentences—is a connective. (The two hunters awoke early, saw that it was raining, *and* decided to stay in the cabin for the day.)

elliptic writing The omission of repeated elements in a sentence, such as verbs, verb intensifiers, subjects of verbs and pronouns. Words that could be omitted are italicized in this example: Johnstown was cut off from the world, its railroads *were* washed away and *its* bridges *were* destroyed.

essential clause Any clause attached to a noun, verb, verbal or phrase to give it a specific meaning is an essential clause. Also called a *restrictive clause.* (Alexander the Great conquered lands *that had never been conquered before.*)

modifier   Any word, phrase or clause that describes a noun, verb or other clause is a modifier. Modifiers include adjectives, adverbs, articles, verbals, nouns, prepositional phrases, and various types of clauses. See those entries for examples.

non-essential clause   Any clause attached to another sentence element to give it additional but incidental meaning is a non-essential clause. Also called a *non-restrictive* clause. (Alexander the Great, *who died young,* conquered lands that had never been conquered before.)

noun   A word is a noun when it functions as the subject or object of a verb or the object of a preposition. Nouns can also function as modifiers. (The *football player* kicked the *ball* away from the speedy *runner.*)

paragraph   A collection of logically related sentences.

parallel construction   Related items in a series maintain consistent form or function and are said to have parallel construction. (The two hunters *awoke* early, *saw* that it was raining, and *decided* to stay in the cabin for the day.)

person   The distinction among pronouns used as subjects of verbs, with first person being the person speaking (*I, we*), second person the person spoken to (*you*) and third the person spoken about (*he, she, it, they*).

point of view   The perspective from which something is viewed and subsequently written about.

predicate   The predicate is one of two major elements of a sentence (the other is the subject) and contains a verb(s) and related modifiers and objects. (The professor, a member of the advisory commission on athletics, *never participated in sports in high school or college.*)

prefix   An element placed at the beginning of a word to create a related word. (*mis*spell)

preposition   The connecting word that begins a prepositional phrase and links the phrase to what it modifies. (The hunters decided to stay inside *for* the day.)

prepositional phrase   A sequence of words beginning with a preposition and ending with a noun. Prepositional phrases function as modifiers. (The hunters decided to stay inside *for the day.*)

pronoun   A word that substitutes for a noun or phrase in subsequent references. (Smith warned advisory commission members that the coach would take advantage of *them.*)

redundancy   Any extraneous or repetitive word or phrase in a sentence. (The *general* consensus *of opinion* is that the advisory commission is weak.)

sentence   A group of words containing at the least a subject and verb. (The two hunters decided to stay in the cabin.)

sentence fragment   A collection of words that lacks a subject or main verb or independent standing. (Washed out in the seventh. Some storm. Because it rained so hard.)

simple sentence   A sentence that limits itself to one idea or action; i.e., a sentence having no subordinate clauses. (The two hunters decided to stay in the cabin.)

subject   Generally, the noun phrase to which the action of the verb refers is the subject of a sentence. The subject is one of two major elements in a sentence (the other is the predicate). (*The two hunters* decided to stay in the cabin.)

subordinate clause   See *non-essential clause*.

suffix   A phrase added to a word to change its function or create a related word. (foolish*ness*)

tense   The time of an action as shown by the verb. The six tenses are: present, past, future, present perfect, past perfect, future perfect.

transition   A word, phrase or paragraph that makes a smooth bridge from another word, phrase or paragraph.

verb   The word that tells what action the subject or main noun of a sentence is taking. (The school teachers' strike *lasted* for 15 days.)

verbal   A word derived from a verb that functions as a noun or a modifier. The three verbal forms are present participle (*walking*), past participle (*walked*) and infinitive (*to walk*).

Language Usage Test

Advisory

This test has not been validated as a tool for screening students out of a journalism program. The intention of the test is to aid students in identifying their particular language skills problems so they may overcome them. The author discourages anyone from using the test as a predictor of a student's success in a journalism program.

Directions

The following sentences may have errors in grammar, modification, redundancy and punctuation. None contain capitalization errors or errors in proper nouns. No sentence contains more than one error.

Every sentence could be rewritten to make it better. That, however, is not the purpose of this test. The purpose is to find out what you don't know so you can learn from your mistakes.

If a sentence is correct as written, circle the letter E at the end of the sentence. If it is incorrect, circle the letter designating the area of the sentence that is in error. The designated error may not be in error by itself but would be if considered in the context of the entire sentence. Turn in the completed test to your instructor for evaluation.

Name _____

1. (a) U.S. and Mexican industries (b) are integrated with autos and

   parts (c) flowing unhindered (d) across the border.   a   b   c   d   e

2. (a) Even as a native of Raton who lives in a university residence

   hall, it is (b) easy to forget that (c) there is more to life than (d)

   classes, dining halls, concerts, parties and the library. a   b   c   d   e

3. (a) George Washington University, (b) which was named in honor

   of this country's first president, (c) is situated (d) in the nations

   capital.   a   b   c   d   e

4. (a) The article says journalism education (b) inspires idealism in

   students (c) that gradually fade away after (d) the students work in

   the real world.   a   b   c   d   e

5. (a) William Boone has traced the history of the system (b) in detail

   from 900 B.C. through the 14th century, his book is (c)

recommended for anyone (d) who is interested in the history of art.

    a   b   c   d   e

6. (a) When Wentzel stepped to the plate, (b) he hit the first pitch, (c)

    lofting it in a high arc (d) that ended in the centerfield bleachers.

    a   b   c   d   e

7. (a) Nobody in a democracy, (b) regardless of race, creed or

    religion, (c) can be taxed (d) without their consent.   a   b   c   d   e

8. (a) Neither John nor Bill have (b) the good sense (c) to come in (d)

    out of the rain.   a   b   c   d   e

9. (a) When Judy and Sally worked (b) for the Youngs a decade ago,

    (c) they were well-paid (d) by today's standards.   a   b   c   d   e

10. (a) What makes the English so (b) interesting, aside from the

    rhythm of their writing is the (c) serious intensity with which (d)

    they absorb concepts.   a   b   c   d   e

11. (a) A combination of the aging Walt Jones, (b) a rash of injuries

    and a new generation of uncooperative talent (c) are primarily (d)

    responsible for the poor season.   a   b   c   d   e

12. (a) The 15 bears he has shot (b) represent an unusual hunting

    record, "that's pretty (c) good for Montana," the (d) game warden

    said.   a   b   c   d   e

13. (a) Last seen in the vicinity of Bowe Street, police (b) say the

    suspect is dangerous (c) and could assault anyone (d) without

    provocation.   a   b   c   d   e

14. (a) Five persons—Wildavsky, Jones, Phalan, Emerson and me—

    were (b) chosen to research and write (c) the Herald-Republic's first

    series of articles (d) on nursing-home care.   a   b   c   d   e

15. (a) If you want to observe (b) Congress, you must (c) go to

    Washington, D.C. the capital (d) of the United States. a   b   c   d   e

16. (a) The facts of the Watergate (b) scandal will (c) not be learned

    until each major (d) and minor figure write his own book.

    a   b   c   d   e

17. (a) Traditional espionage, such as penetrating (b) the intelligence agencies of other countries and covering up (c) clandestine information is the (d) CIA's function, according to Tressler.

        a   b   c   d   e

18. (a) The following afternoon, (b) which was a Wednesday an Air (c) Force transport landed in an (d) abandoned dirt strip that once was the Clive airport.   a   b   c   d   e

19. (a) When he saw the fire damage, (b) he exclaimed: (c) "That must have been (d) some fire!   a   b   c   d   e

20. (a) Packard suggested closing (b) the loopholes for the rich (c) and rejection of salary increases (d) for government officials.

        a   b   c   d   e

21. (a) When your nerves are frazzled, (b) there's nothing like a (c) soothing tranquilizer (d) to make everything seem right.   a   b   c   d   e

22. (a) The news media is (b) the major source of information (c) in this country (d) and in most other democracies.   a   b   c   d   e

23. (a) One of every five (b) of the state's residents (c) live in the sort of poverty (d) that forced Bert Collins to leave the area.

        a   b   c   d   e

24. (a) The fourth annual conference which (b) was held after the disaster, (c) left the participants as confused and discouraged (d) as before the disaster.   a   b   c   d   e

25. (a) The budget limitations (b) of a newspaper this size (c) prevents the hiring (d) of a staff for investigative reporting.   a   b   c   d   e

26. (a) The project requires cleaning (b) and reconstruction of a water channel, repairing (c) dikes and complying with (d) anti-pollution measures.   a   b   c   d   e

27. (a) During that time, (b) a passing motorist saw the (c) fire in the Garber Mansion (d) and called the fire department.   a   b   c   d   e

28. (a) The survey conducted by two nationally known testing (b)

authorities show that (c) only one of 50 students (d) finds college

less demanding (d) than high school.   a   b   c   d   e

29. (a) If you think she's (b) intelligent, you (c) should meet her (d)

five year old sister.   a   b   c   d   e

30. (a) Pressures that result from arguments and mistrust (b) between

local conservative and liberal groups—as well as (c) the influence

of various local (d) political leaders—brings about this scrutiny.

                                                        a   b   c   d   e

31. (a) To criticize him however is (b) to hold him accountable to a

high standard—indeed, (c) one beyond most journalists, most

researchers (d) and most college professors.   a   b   c   d   e

32. (a) While in Lexington, (b) the Parnells only saw one house (c)

they really liked (d) enough to consider buying.   a   b   c   d   e

33. (a) A proposal to rezone part of Schuylkill Avenue (b) may be

voted on by council (c) tonight, or the proposal may be (d)

remanded back to the planning commission.   a   b   c   d   e

34. (a) Forty hours of work (b) a week tires anyone (c) who has never

worked (d) that much before.   a   b   c   d   e

35. (a) The writing of both authors (b) continue to reflect (c) their

contrasting (d) philosophies on history.   a   b   c   d   e

36. (a) Twain's stories are (b) very interesting, (c) they represent

several (d) styles of writing.   a   b   c   d   e

37. (a) The judge ruled that (b) University of Florida students have the

(c) legal right to vote in the (d) district where they attend college.

                                                        a   b   c   d   e

38. (a) The value of all of Mexico's exports (b) to the United States (c)

are given as (d) 183 million pesos.   a   b   c   d   e

39. (a) The new faculty member (b) proposed the following changes,

(c) discontinue two writing courses, add three theory courses (d)

and increase the length of class sessions.   a   b   c   d   e

40. (a) At twelve noon (b) many university employees (c) go downtown
    (d) to eat lunch and to shop.   a   b   c   d   e

41. (a) The tax collector said that (b) the new tax law, with its many
    exceptions and qualifications, (c) make the tax forms (d) difficult to
    understand.   a   b   c   d   e

42. (a) Collective nouns take a singular verb (b) when considered as
    one unit (c) and a plural verb when (d) considered by its individual
    parts.   a   b   c   d   e

43. (a) The new School Board member (b) asked whether a teacher
    who is not rehired (c) after their first year (d) would be eligible for
    compensation.   a   b   c   d   e

44. (a) Staunton policy allege (b) that the man, who was not identified
    broke (c) into the Smiths' house (d) shortly after midnight.

                                                             a   b   c   d   e

45. (a) Numerous researchers have (b) complained about the time and
    effort (c) that has been wasted trying (d) to replicate shoddy
    experiments.   a   b   c   d   e

46. (a) On the platform were (b) two people—a former FBI agent, who
    is a (c) 1941 graduate of Oregon (d) State and the moderator.

                                                             a   b   c   d   e

47. (a) He found the book a 954-page volume, (c) very difficult to read
    (d) to himself or to his children.   a   b   c   d   e

48. (a) One of his sisters, Lyn, (b) is a old hand (c) at reporting on
    intermediate (d) school units.   a   b   c   d   e

49. (a) Studying is (b) one of those chores (c) that makes college life
    (d) more than just one big social event.   a   b   c   d   e

50. (a) Nebraska Attorney General, Joseph Dalton, (b) argued that it
    doesn't cost (c) the Postal Service 20 cents to deliver (d) a first-
    class letter.   a   b   c   d   e

Review Exercises

The following exercises test a variety of points made throughout the book rather than a specific section at a time. To enable you to get the most use out of them, the points being tested are cross-referenced to the page(s) where you can find the solution. The numbers appear under the problem areas. Fix only the areas that are designated by page numbers, although some rewriting may be necessary to make the desired corrections. After completing each set of exercises, turn it in to your instructor for evaluation.

I.

Name _____

1. The two scientists, who are both experts in physics, will report
   16–17   8

   their findings on their research in the journal, *Science,* next week.
   10   153–155

2. The lone Democrat on the City Council is against the tax increase.
   111–112

3. If the union were elected, it will establish three local units to
   106–107   70

   represent the various types of workers the spokesperson said.
   17–19   159–160

4. Neither Teamsters Local 9 nor the Allied Truck Company of the

   Americas are making any attempt to resume contract negotiations.
   91   10–11

5. Looking out the window today, it may seem hard for you to believe
   118–119

   that trout fishing season gets underway in two months.
   16–17   11–12   203

6. A newspaper story is an example of the end product of such a
   111–112

   process of selection, summarizing and paraphrasing.
   54–56

7. There is a possibility that the US Customs Service may charge
   9   147

   Smith who served a prison term as a young juvenile with
   153–155   11–12   153–155

   smuggling.

8. Readers who browse newspapers, miss mistakes more careful
   112   /   153–155

   readers do not miss.
   14–16

9. Grant who now lives in Belleville, said his memory is cloudy but
   153–155   158–159

   he suspects permission to establish the memorial was never
   16–17

   obtained from the appropriate officials and he recalls "a couple of
   41–42

   different ideas" being discussed, including placing an American

   flag above an engrave marker.
   136

10. The writer, who uses the techniques of literary allusion, may
       153–155   8–9

    discover that the intended meaning eludes the reader.

II.

Name _____

1. What effect the break out at the prison had on the future of the
   167   10

   warden remains to be seen, it will probably be detrimental,
   163

   however.
   43

2. Among the most commonly mispelled words are accomodate
                                      202   201   151

   dependant villin recieve preceed questionaire and unatural.
   201   203   203   202   202   203

3. Members of the Extension Center acting as advisers to the group,
                     153–155

   was at the recently-plowed field to see the new tractor.
   91–92   166

4. "Nobody knows the best way to go, Superintendent of Schools,
                            175   151–152

   Thomas F. Williams said.

5. The news media is calling for a treaty of peace that only is fair to
               94   10   130

   three of the five countries involved in the war.
                  17–19

6. In a two month period, 14 contributions were made by residents.
      166   107–111

7. Two contributions-$589 from a widow woman and $400 from a
               170   11–12

   merchant-accounted for all but $330 of the total.
        170

8. In all the presidents programs are designed to give aid to 5.3
      101   174–175   17–19

   million students, and their parents.
        159

9. Joseph Smathers, head of the Engineering Department says that it
                                                        151

   helps to have a wife in his position.
        132–134

10. Smith supports the program while his opponent Klein is opposed
                                        153–155   111–112

    to it.

III.

Name _____

1. Polsby was arrested by the police and the cocaine was confiscated
   107–111   14–16

   immediately.

2. Marys professor persuaded her to take the job when he told her she
   174–175

   would not only be well-paid but would also recieve a opportunity to
                    166   203   124

   do some editing.

3. Vandals were the cause of the damage in the cemetary.
   111–112   201

4. The board includes seven volunteers, each of whom have a full
                                              90   166

   time job.

5. "Total body burden" is a representation of the total of various
   111–112

   risks, such as smoking eating bacon and the use of hair dye.
                    151   54–56

6. Opponents argue indexing builds inflation in the tax system, hiding
   16–17

   it and undercuts efforts to curb it, because of this, a serious fight
   54–56   163   86–87

   against it is certain.

7. Josephine Doaks, who is a 1958 graduate of Drake Law School,
   16–17

   was immediately admitted to the Iowa bar and then practiced law in
   8–9

   Des Moines until 1979, when she moved to California.

8. Some people prefer a car which does not burn a lot of gasoline.
   140–141

9. Unaware that the gangplank had been raised and that the ship was

   underway, the sailors only saw the mast and believed they had time
   203   130

   still to get on board.

10. The universally-accepted term for this action is "missing
                166   86–87
    movement". Because the sailors were not on board their ship as
                26   8–9
    their ship was leaving port.

IV.

Name _____

1. Neither Bill nor his sons has the sense to walk any farther than the
                                  91
   nearest tree during a thunderstorm.

2. The Traffic Comittee for the two communities makes the contention
                201   10–11
   that converting the 100 block of Clive Street to two way traffic
                                                      166
   would create, ''a parking problem beyond anyone's wildest
                160
   imagination''.
       147

3. The children created a game which according to their teacher
                      140–141 159–160
   ''deserves a permanent place in the schools outdoor program.''
                                        174–175

4. To avoid mellowing a judge must strive to be a combination of
                          161
   sterness and fairness.
      203

5. The horse neighed loud.
               126–127

6. The club's president John T. Snedden selected a delegate to meet
                              151–152
   Dr. K S Jones, who is the executive secretary of the State
       147   16–17
   Historical and Museum Commission and to meet Clifford H. Odett,
                                    153–155 14–16
   chief engineer for the Department of Forests and Waters.

7. Fifteen distinct congressional districts have seperately petitioned for
              11–12   203
   the grant from the federal government.
                10

8. The star high-school basketball player was serious considering the
                                          126–127
   University of Iowa until Minnesota showed him their facilities.
                                                    80

9. A banker, aware of the ''inactive'' state of the fund and fearing
       139–140   175–177   54–56
   that its administration could fall into state hands (due to inactivity,
                                                          171–173
   notified the Jaycees.

10. The attorneys said that they could recall, ''no specific instructions
              16–17   160
to petition the court,'' however.
                43

V.

Name _____

1. In the worst airplane crash in the history of Pike County there were

                                             10   156 9

   no survivors.

2. A visitor to the communitys Mountain Spring Park will find no

                                   174–175

   landscape area, no marker, no momento in honor of the victims.

   136   202

3. The networks gave a report that Begin on Wednesday gave

                              10–11

   instructions to the Israeli team that could lead to a breakthrough.

                    132–134   137–138

4. According to most students, the furthest thing from a student's

   mind during summer vacation is coming back to school.

                                 65–67

5. Referring to the boards funamental problem, it became evident a

                     174–175   202   17

   structural defect existed in the organization, Williams said.

   98–99

6. A 30 to 35 year old smoker can expect to die eight or nine years

     169

   sooner than a nonsmoker.

                   166

7. She is on six comittees.

     111–112   201

8. The girl in the red bikini defected Russia three weeks ago.

                               112

9. The Association for Intercollegiate Athletics for Women have stiffer

                                          91

   rules and regulations than the NCAA has.

      11–12   14–16

10. Food prices which tapered off three months ago, rose last month as

        153–155   11–12

    the cost of beef veal poultry fruits and vegetables moved upward.

        151 151   151   17–19

VI.

Name _____

1. Bill, who once worked in a dairy store likes ice cream, Mary, his
                               153–155   163

   sister, likes cotton candy however.
                   43

2. The canidates expressed different views on the issue.
       201   10–11

3. I have two sisters, my youngest sister likes novels, non-fiction
                     163

   books and works for a watch manufacturer.
       56–57

4. There are 15 reasons she has for not going.
     9

5. Taxpayers will have to dig more deep if they have the expectation
                 125–126   10–11

   that the city will maintain present services the council member said
                         159–160 121–122

   last night.

6. Council member Mary Anne Delphi, speaking to a gathering of the
                         11–14

   Clive Taxpayers League said that the public expects too much from
           161–162

   local goverment-much more than it's willing to pay.
       202 169–170

7. Delphi who is chairperson of the city council's finance committee,
   153–155 16–17

   said new services would have to be paid for out of public tax

   money.
   11–12

8. The homeowners on the West Side, who sees less of the garbage
            10   89–90

   truck than homeowners elsewhere may complain loud at next
              153–155   126

   month's budget hearings, Delphi predicted.

9. Delphi added waste in government has put a strain on the councils
           17   10–11   174–175

   credibility.

10. The talk was sponsored by the Clive Taxpayers League.
        107–111

VII.

Name _____

1. Neither members of the league nor council member Delphi are
                                                              91
   optimistic that the council will be able to "hold the line" on taxes
                                              175–177
   in the next budget.

2. Some beleive laying off 25 percent of the city's work force would
            201
   help to reduce the budget.
        19

3. Others say however that this solution would wreak havoc in the
              155–156   80
   nonpublic sector.
   166

4. "We've got to keep this city together" Delphi said "or we can
                                        159–160   159–160
   forget about winning the next election.
                                        175

5. The $50 the 5 year old found in a tree trunk are safe with her
              169   92–93
   parents.

6. A majority party in Congress controls each and every committee.
   121–122   7–8

7. The armed pair stole $327 worth of cash.
                        11–12

8. The mayor made a promise to examine the sheet of names, which
            10–11
   include the owners of two apartmental buildings.
   94–95   135

9. The tax bill which was drafted by the House Ways and Means
          138–141
   Committee, proposes lowering taxes for middle income families
                                                    166
   only.

10. Cardiovascular diseases were responsible for 61 percent of all
                        111–112
    deaths last year.

VIII.

Name _____

1. The two boys snuck into the football game crawling under a wire
   113   118–119

   fence.

2. Council member Dean James who made the motion to uphold the
                       153–155

   mayor also made the statement that the council must enforce the
     153–155   10–11

   rules if they are to have any control over city employees.
        80 94   10–11

3. He belonged to a well to do Providence industrial family, held a
                166

   management job in the familys iron foundry, and his legal
              174–175   56–57

   experience consisted of three years with a firm specializing in trusts

   and estates.

4. When the senator gave a speech on Labor Day, she said Americans
              10–11

   still beleive, ''in a person's right to receive a full day's pay for a
       201 160

   full day's work''.
        147

5. There were a few people in the audience who booed the senators
   9   174–175

   speech.

6. When the children stopped playing, the jellybeans they had taken

   from the kitchen were eaten by them.
                109

7. Reacting strong to many days of criticism over his silence on the
       126

   nuclear plant accident the president today announced a full fledged
          156   166

   investigation saying ''the people have a right to know.''
    153–155

8. Smokers and nonsmokers clash every day such as John and Sam.
         166   118–120

9. There are 31 gallons in a barrel.
   9

10. The sink in the kitchen is about all that is left at the new house of
    10   111–112
    Mr. and Mrs. T. James Williams.

IX.

Name _____

1. Taxpayers wanting to blow the whistle on fraud in government can
                                                    10

   tip investigators secretly.
            129

2. He said that the ordinance overlooks the need for more parking in
           16–17

   multiresidence zones, the need for greater lighting in parking areas
     166   14–16

   and does not provide for commercial parking.
   56–57

3. The sunlight which dances graceful among the many trees create a
            138–140   126   91

   variety of colors unatural to this area.
                     203

4. "Isn't that pretty?", Jones asked when she saw the sun set over the
                        160

   harbor at San Diego.

5. 'I'd like to see more sunsets," DiMaria said, "I hope we see one
   175   163

   every day were here."
          175–176

6. Because the professor was 10 minutes late for class the students
                                         8–9   156–157

   made a decision to leave and then left.
   10–11

7. The five member board comprises Harry T. James, president,
           166   164

   Charlene C. Williams, vice president, Charles Stewart, treasurer,
                                                 164

   Mary C. Meade and Alfred Thomas.
             164

8. The City Council will make a study of the proposal to eliminate all
                       10–11

   smoking in public buildings, to keep all dogs out of areas, where
                                 14–16   138–140

   children play, and to limit the hours bars may be open.
       14–16

9. Most political observers however don't see much hope for the
                              155

   smoking ban, they also doubt council has the authority to regulate
              163   16–17

   bars.

10. The last time the council wanted to hold a discussion on the ban on
                                    10–11   10

smoking, more than 60 people said they were averse to it.
                                111–112

X.

Name _____

1. In an earlier council meeting James T. McHaven a former US
   156   152   147
   senator appeared before the council and told them that trying to
   7–8   80
   regulate bars would give each member of council a "headache."
                                  10   175–176

2. These words by McHaven were ignored by the council.
   86–87   107–111

3. Did you ever hear the old adage, "Once burned, twice shy?"
                   11–12   165   149–150

4. A number of students majoring in journalism believes that they will
                                  92   16–17
   change the world when they become reporters.

5. When the rate of deficiency went from 66 percent to 33 percent-a
                       10   170
   drop of 50 percent-the Faculty Senate knew that their tutoring
        170   80
   program was working.

6. The obligation of any speaker is to speak clear and not muttering
                                  126   54–56
   through a presentation.

7. We hope the dean will look no further than his diminish staff to see
                                                    136
   what effect the budget cut back has had.
                        167

8. With fewer contestants in this years dance marathon, the comittee
                              174–175   201
   only will raise enough money to cover their expenses.
   120   80

9. The rate of inflation began last year at 5 percent and rose to 10
               10
   percent an increase of 100 percent.
   14–16 153

10. College graduates although technically-ready for employment in
                153–155   166
    their chosen field, may be unprepared for a job change a decade
    from now.

XI.

Name _____

1. The self taught artist did not begin selling her work until she met
   166
   her second husband.

2. Cadbury City Council passed a motion to seek a tax exemption for
   10–11
   their housing project on Clive Avenue in a closed session last night.
   80   118–120

3. After the committee meeting, Parker said that the date, time and
   16–17
   place of the convention has yet to be set.
   90

4. The villins inferred from the victims silence that they had
   203   174–175
   accidently smothered her.
   201

5. The president urged Congress, "to act speedily and quickly before
   160
   taxpayers begin to think relief is nonexistent."
   166

6. City Council last night approved a budget higher than last year's

   budget, then dclays action on the ordinance that will raise taxes to
   14–16   101
   cover the increase.

7. A report showing the school has more female than male journalism
   16 17
   majors indicate how open the field is to women.
   91

8. Here is a suggestion that is sure to please everyone.
   9   16–17

9. To sleep as much as possible and studying as little as possible is
   54–56   89
   important to her.

10. As corporations, the main goal of all newspapers are to increase
    118–120   89
    profits.

XII.

Name _____

1. The council of bishops overwhelming urge a papal review of a
                    126   91

   recent declaration, reaffirming the church's ban on women in the
                    138–140

   priesthood.

2. James R. Kelley, mayor of Clive urged Monday his constituents to
                              151   53

   do more to protect the environment of Clive.
                                        8–9

3. The mayor divided his appeal into three areas preserving what the
                                      169–171

   people have for their descendants, maintenance of their present
                                54–56

   resources for themselves, and keeping alive the heritage of their

   ancestors.

4. Two graduate students and three university employees spoke,

   including Christine Williams a faculty member.
   118–120   152

5. The Society of Professional Journalists are host to many
                                        14

   conventions.

6. School superintendants walk a tightrope between teachers' unions
              203

   and school boards.

7. Iowa Attorney General, David L. Dillon, said he will seek an
                    151   151

   indictment against the two suspects.

8. When he is confident that he has enough evidence and a courtroom
              16–17

   large enough to accomodate the number of spectators which the
                    201   140

   trial is likely to attract, he will act.

9. When faced with a difficult question on a test, ill prepare students
166   136

   write answers that allude to something they read hoping their
153–155

   teachers will give them credit for trying.

10. The variety of situations and events that makes a feature story have
94–95   91

   been suggested in several books.

Answers to Self-Diagnostic Tests

Here are the author's suggested answers for the self-diagnostic tests.

Chapter 1

Self-Diagnostic Test 1.1

1. T.R. Thompson of Cadbury Gardens found the hunter's body by a clump of trees about 200 yards from a tool shed on the Smith farm. (prepositional pile-up)
2. About a dozen people were in the church when the fire started. (weak phrasing)
3. Another weakness Mrs. Williams discussed is a state-required program for gifted students. (to the point)
4. This is a professional course aimed at improving the skills and knowledge needed for effective news work. (omission of pronouns and verbs)
5. A brief controversy flashed last week when Knepper condemned the mayor. (weak phrasing)
6. Tom Drew told the council that he owns five pool tables in his business. (stating the obvious)
7. Sen. Jones said last night that Russia's army is getting stronger. (redundancy)
8. Required conservation measures must be followed. (redundancy)
9. Strokes caused 67 deaths. (weak phrasing)
10. City Council voted to tax pool tables. (verb-noun construction)
11. Another school bus was immediately dispatched. (conventional information)
12. The new store will be more than five times the size of the present store. (stating the obvious)
13. During the trial the jury was sequestered. (needless detail)
14. To help eliminate classroom crowding, the district will also hire teachers' aides at $2,800 each, Superintendent of Schools Thomas F. Williams said. The total cost will be approximately $60,000. (to the point)

Chapter 2

Self-Diagnostic Test 2.1

The traditional sentences are underscored.

> Lights.
> Red blinkers. White spotlights. Neon. <u>On-off, on-off. on-off twin yellow caution lights look down on an ant heap of sweating men clambering across the shattered carcass of a truck—wedged fast in the corner of the house.</u>
> One dead. <u>Five injured.</u>
> <u>The living are gone.</u> Bandaged. Rushed to hospital asepsis.

One remains. In a tangle of broken metal, class, plaster, brick and wood. Wedged fast in the truck in the corner of the house.

Children's bare feet pad across the ridged asphalt of the highway where wheel rims gouged a path.

The crowd.

A boy and girl embrace in the roadway, in the glare of spotlights examining the shafts and tubes of the exposed underside of the truck—the skeleton of some unfamiliar sea beast.

A quiet crowd.

Policemen. "Put out your cigarettes."

Black-booted firemen stand in a slick of diesel fuel and light cigarettes.

Fuel trickles from a ruptured tank, vanishes, reappears in a shimmer on the curb, running in silent counterpoint to the nearby stream, splashing into the light, beneath the bridge, and gone.

Thick odor of diesel fuel.

Knots of men—dark slickers of firemen, white rescue squad coveralls, gray police tunics—form and dissolve.

Firemen in shorts, sneakers and hard hats.

Ropes. Cables. Wires.

Men with pikes gingerly pick away the sagging block facing of the house. Masonry tumbles onto the truck cab, billowing dust, exposing wide-plank inner siding.

Dials. Gauges. A fireman stands for hours beside the truck, hose ready, while a second monitors water pressure.

Lights.

Flashlights. Headlights. Flash bulbs.

A wheel turns slowly, spilling shattered blocks onto the sidewalk.

"Stand back."

An uncut pizza rests on a table in the corner room.

The wreckers arrive. Two, three, the fourth seems half as high as the house. Conference. Debate.

Newcomers edge around the fire trucks, staring. How? Who?

A father carries his sleepy daughter—long blonde hair and sweatshirt—piggyback through the crowd.

The crowd thins. Going home. To rest. For a final day of work before a long weekend.

Labor Day.

Lights.

Self-Diagnostic Test 2.2

The main clauses are italicized; the subordinate clauses are not.

1. *Monahan,* who says he would have had more trouble in the West if Williams had chosen O'Hara instead of Sen. Shaw as his running mate, *scheduled a speech today in San Francisco.*
2. Despite crowds that established records for high attendance with each passing year, *the county event is quieter and more serious.*
3. *Several universities,* because they annually have good football or basketball teams, *lead the nation in the number of people applying for admission.*

4. *Harrison had stated earlier* that he wished to serve only one term if elected.
5. *And now the middle-aged high-school dropout, a maintenance employee at a small college, was reminiscing about the golden moment two months earlier* when he surprised everyone by passing the entrance examinations at the school where he worked.
6. If for any reason the customers wish to discontinue direct deposit or wish to redirect their check to a different financial institution, *it is a simple procedure to make that change.*
7. *Dr. Stanton urged the graduates to be alert in defending their liberties,* which he said "are as precious as life itself."
8. *The United States announced today* [that] it will exchange diplomats with Cuba for the first time in 16 years.
9. Although formal relations may be a long way off, *the diplomats will be in charge of a full range of activities between the two countries.*
10. When demand for electricity is high during the 24-hour period, *the water will be discharged from the reservoir into Cato Dam and will turn turbines to generate power.*

Self-Diagnostic Test 2.3

1. After being injured in a plane crash at the Flagstaff airport last night, Congressmen Evan Evans said: "I am fine. Just a few scratches. Nothing serious."
2. Fifty million people would starve to death if America goes back to organic farming, the president of the Federation of Farmers said yesterday.
3. The president praised American farmers for being so productive that even though the number of farmers is decreasing they create a surplus the government is able to ship to less fortunate nations.
4. The old saying goes, "If you want to dance, you have to pay the piper." When it comes to financing education, that is the belief of many, including the state's legislators.
5. Labeling it "regulatory overkill," the mayor also objected to a section of the ordinance that would ban the parking of recreation vehicles in front-yard driveways.

Self-Diagnostic Test 2.4

1. Under the student regulations in effect in a student government election for the first time, the cost of all on-campus campaigning for all student candidates is paid entirely from the student activities fund. No personal contributions are permitted, except for a limited amount channeled through committees recognized by the Undergraduate Student Government.
2. Last April the commissioners met with hospital officials to discuss a list of possible Elmbank uses. With few exceptions, the hospital officials approved the list before agreeing to further negotiations.

3. A Soviet spokesman initially reported the jet had been seized by five gunmen. But the spokesman later said three were involved—one carrying a Somalian passport, the second, an Ethiopian passport, and the third, a Moroccan travel permit.

4. Clifford has come under mounting pressure from students, lawyers, and more recently, alumni of the school, to appoint an impartial group to investigate allegations of a cover-up at the school. Faculty members there have testified that more than half of last year's engineering class of 250 students could have been involved in collaborating on a take-home test last April.

5. Notices will be sent to about 150 school superintendents—the first to leave their positions since the state's financial crisis forced reductions in the public school system. In some instances the superintendents will be pushed to lower-paying positions than they had. In others, they will be let go altogether.

6. The society said the highest number of species reported by a group in this country was 221 turned in at Des Moines, Iowa. Sixty-two other groups in communities from Virginia to Washington listed 125 or more species.

Self-Diagnostic Test 2.5

1. Parallel construction
2. Non sequitur
3. False series
4. Parallel construction
5. Structure
6. Parallel construction

Chapter 3

Self-Diagnostic Test 3.1

The parts of speech are identified by the following code: N = noun, V = verb, M = modifier, C = connective.

          M   N   V   M

1. The *key* vote on the *proposal came* after only an hour *of debate* in

          M   V

  which *Democratic* senators from the city *contended* that the proposal

          M

  would cut *city* revenues by as much as $65 million a year.

         M   N   V

2. At a *news* conference, Morial said the *mayors* would also *ask* the

         N   C   M

  lame-duck *session* of Congress *and* the administration for a *job-*

     M   M

  creating program *keyed to repairing the nation's roads and bridges.*

         N   V   M

3. Two years ago *Congress ordered* the VA to conduct *scientific*

                                          N   C
    research into Agent Orange's *effects, but* the study has not gotten
                              N
    started because of *difficulties* in designing it.
                                                                M   M
    4. The results showed that Thompson had won an *unprecedented third*
        M
    consecutive term with 1,816,101 votes to Stevenson's 1,811,027—
            M
    a margin of 0.14 percent.
                        N   V   M
    5. An old *man stabbed* his *critically ill* wife twice in the back
            M   M
    with a kitchen knife in an unsuccessful *mercy-killing* attempt at a
                N   N
    nursing *home,* police said *Sunday.*
            M   N   V   M   M
    6. A *federal judge* yesterday *declared unconstitutional* the *only* law in
                                          M
    the nation *that requires teaching the biblical account of creation in*

    public schools.

Chapter 4

Self-Diagnostic Test 4.1

1. his or her
2. it
3. its
4. it
5. its
6. its
7. It
8. it

Self-Diagnostic Test 4.2

1. Sears sells many products, from bedclothes to toggle switches. (singular disguised as plural)
2. None of the players is able to explain the loss. (any, none)
3. The land in addition to the houses was sold. (false plural)
4. Neither the dogs nor their masters hunts very well. (neither . . . nor)
5. Each of the members of our microcomputer club runs four miles daily. (each)
6. The car on the right or the car on the left—I forget which—runs raggedly. (singular connective)

7. The number of students who took the test for the first time and did poorly was large. (collective noun)
8. Three is the maximum number of times a student may take the language test. (numbers)
9. There are too many people driving today. (complement)
10. The region's proximity to the Atlantic Ocean and the Great Lakes explains the moisture and the clouds. (agreement)

Chapter 5

Self-Diagnostic Test 5.1

1. Such a case, involving two suspects wanted for robbery and murder, caused a typical example of strained policy-press relations earlier in the day, he said.
2. Entranced, the arsonist watched the fire.
3. It's relatively easy for this reviewer, who divorced Heathcliff some decades ago, to complain.
4. Freed Russian dissident Alexander Ginzburg, puffing cigarette after cigarette, strolled down the country road near the home of Alexander Solzhenitsyn Wednesday.
5. The preferential treatment afforded the president's peanut business was revealed Wednesday in a special report by two directors of the bank.
6. USE OF TORTURE AGAINST DETAINEES IN SOUTH KOREA CALLED WIDESPREAD
7. VOTING RECORDS OF CONGRESSMEN FROM REGION DETAILED

Self-Diagnostic Test 5.2

1. Members of the House of Representatives, <u>elected every two years,</u> [verb phrase]
   find themselves campaigning more often than senators, <u>who face</u> [relative clause]
   <u>election every six years.</u>

2. The <u>injured</u> [verbal] football player hobbled to the sidelines, <u>where the</u> [adverb clause]
   <u>team's trainer looked after him.</u>

3. Filled <u>with the excitement of competition,</u> [prepositional phrase] our track star ran <u>swiftly</u> [adverb]
   to <u>the</u> [article] finish line.

4. The typewriter, <u>long a fixture in newsrooms,</u> [apposition] will soon become a
   <u>museum</u> [noun as modifier] piece.

noun as modifier   adjective
5. Professional <u>football</u> teams must announce the <u>medical</u> status of all

prepositional phrase
players several days <u>before a game</u>.

Chapter 6

Self-Diagnostic Test 6.1

1. Average attendance was 76 percent, down from 938 percent for last

season.

2. She said, "The US government is bursting at the seams".

3. "What did she say," the reporter asked.

4. They shipped the faulty product to Hillsboro, Ore, where it was

made.

Self-Diagnostic Test 6.2

1. In its April order, the court directed the district to further

desegregate the city's school system, and the district responded with

the plan to merge 11 predominantly white and 11 predominantly

black schools at the beginning of the next school year.

2. "While we must look to ourselves to avert a crisis, we do need help

from the federal government," said New Orleans Mayor Ernest N.

Morial.

3. President Reagan's wife, Nancy, dresses nicely.

4. Some people, however, wish she would be more outspoken on some

issues.

5. Students majoring in journalism study in a variety of areas, reporting,

editing, international communication, ethics and law.

6. The meeting, one of the longer ones in council's history, lasted 4½

hours.

7. According to police, Francine Jamison, 22, 378 Broadway Ave.,

Apartment 7, stopped the purse-snatcher by tripping him as he ran

by her, an act policy said showed quick thinking and courage.

8. Bombarded, Americans like their messages to the point.

9. Some journalists feel, according to a recent survey, that they don't get enough time to write their stories.

10. The leading candidate for the post, Mary T. Harrison, has such high visibility among voters that she doesn't need to conduct much of a campaign.

Self-Diagnostic Test 6.3

1. The city's aviation division has awarded a multiyear contract for the first construction in a two-year project designed to ease traffic congestion at the airport.

2. The division proposes to build a three-lane roadway near the baggage claims area, the second such road in the area.

3. The well-being of airport users prompted the division to propose the project originally.

4. With traffic congestion reduced, division officials feel the airport will become the smoothest-running one in the country, a boast no other airport operator is willing to make.

Self-Diagnostic Test 6.4

The writer is ready to go. All lessons have been learned. He sits before his typewriter, paper in place, and begins to type, at first slowly as he thinks about his words, but then faster, faster as he picks up the pace and his great writing flows. Someday these words will be discovered on this dog-eared paper in a multiuse library, the writer says outloud in a somewhat gleeful, somewhat arrogant voice. What could be better, to be discovered later or discovered now? A thought. Perhaps, though, it would help if I knew how to punctuate. That way people would understand what I am writing.

Bibliography

The Associated Press Stylebook, Rev. ed. The Associated Press, New York, 1980.

Baker, Sheridan. *The Practical Stylist,* 3rd ed. Thomas Y. Crowell Company, New York, 1973.

Berner, R. Thomas. *Editing.* Holt, Rinehart and Winston, New York, 1982.

Bernstein, Theodore M. *The Careful Writer, A Modern Guide to English Usage.* Atheneum, New York, 1973.

Bremner, John B. *Words on Words.* Columbia University Press, New York, 1980.

The Compact Edition of the Oxford English Dictionary. Oxford University Press, New York, 1971.

Copperud, Roy H. *Words on Paper.* Hawthorn Books, New York, 1960.

Flesch, Rudolf. *The Art of Readable Writing.* Collier Books, New York, 1949.

Flexner, Stuart Berg. *I Hear America Talking.* Van Nostrand Reinhold: A Hudson Group Book, New York, 1976.

Fowler, H.W. *Fowler's Modern English Usage,* 2nd ed. Revised by Sir Ernest Gowers. Oxford University Press, New York, 1965.

Hayakawa, S.I., ed. *The Use and Misuse of Language.* Fawcett Publications, Greenwich, Conn., 1962.

Hayakawa, S.I. *Language in Thought and Action,* 3rd ed. Harcourt Brace Jovanovich, New York, 1972.

House, Homer C., and Susan Emolyn Harman. *Descriptive English Grammar,* 2nd ed. Revised by Susan Emolyn Harman. Prentice-Hall, Englewood Cliffs, N.J., 1950.

Langacker, Ronald W. *Language and Its Structure, Some Fundamental Linguistic Concepts.* Harcourt, Brace & World, New York, 1967.

McCrimmon, James M. *Writing with a Purpose,* 4th ed. Houghton Mifflin Company, Boston, 1967.

Mencken, H.L. *The American Language,* 4th ed. Alfred A. Knopf, New York, 1936.

Mencken, H.L. *The American Language, Supplement I.* Alfred A. Knopf, New York, 1945.

Morris, William, ed. *The American Heritage Dictionary of the English Language*. American Heritage Publishing Company, New York; Houghton Mifflin Company, Boston, 1969.

Myers, L.M. *The Roots of Modern English*. Little, Brown and Company, Boston, 1966.

Rank, Hugh, ed. *Language and Public Policy*. National Council of Teachers of English, Urbana, Ill., 1974.

Roberts, Paul. *Understanding English*. Harper and Brothers, New York, 1958.

Rubinstein, S. Leonard, and Robert G. Weaver. *The Plain Rhetoric*. Allyn and Bacon, Boston, 1964.

Shaw, Harry. *Errors in English and Ways to Correct Them,* 2nd ed. Barnes and Noble, New York, 1970.

Skeat, Walter W. *A Concise Etymological Dictionary of the English Language*. Capricorn Books, New York, 1963. First ed., 1882.

Strunk, William Jr., and E.B. White. *The Elements of Style*. 3rd ed. Macmillan Publishing Company, New York, 1979.

U.S. Government Printing Office Style Manual, Rev. ed. U.S. Government Printing Office, Washington, D.C., 1973.

Zinsser, William. *On Writing Well,* 2nd ed. Harper and Row, New York, 1980.

Index

Language Skills for Journalists
Second Edition

To the student:

One of the best ways for us to plan future editions of *Language Skills for Journalists* is to get reactions and suggestions from you, the student. When you have used this book for a complete course, please take a few moments to answer the questions below. Then tear out this page and mail it to

R. Thomas Berner
% Marketing Services
College Division
Houghton Mifflin Company
One Beacon Street
Boston, MA 02108

1. Is the writing style of the book clear?   Yes _____   No _____
   Are there specific sections that could be made clearer?

2. Circle the number of the chapters you found most helpful.
   1. Writing
   2. Sentences and Paragraphs
   3. Functional Grammar
   4. Conventional Grammar
   5. Modification
   6. Punctuation
   7. Meaning

What was most helpful about these chapters?

3. Which chapters did you find least helpful?

   1   2   3   4   5   6   7

   How can we make these chapters more helpful to you?

4. Were the examples throughout the book clear?   Yes _____
   No _____
   Were there enough examples?   Yes _____   No _____

5. Did you find the exercises throughout the book useful?
   Yes _____   No _____
   Were there enough exercises?   Yes _____   No _____

6. Did you find the self-diagnostic tests throughout the book useful?
   Yes _____   No _____
   Were there enough self-diagnostic tests?   Yes _____   No _____

7. Did you find the Language Usage Test and review exercises at the end of the book useful?   Yes _____   No _____

8. Please feel free to make any additional comments.